Pillars of the Nation

Pillars of the Nation

Child Citizens and Ugandan
National Development

KRISTEN E. CHENEY

The University of Chicago Press   Chicago and London

KRISTEN E. CHENEY was educated at Albion College and at the University of California, Santa Cruz. She is professor of anthropology at the University of Dayton and is the author of five published journal articles.

The University of Chicago Press, Chicago 60637
The University of Chicago Press, Ltd., London
© 2007 by The University of Chicago
All rights reserved. Published 2007
Printed in the United States of America

16 15 14 13 12 11 10 09 08 07   1 2 3 4 5

ISBN-13: 978-0-226-10247-4 (cloth)
ISBN-13: 978-0-226-10248-1 (paper)
ISBN-10: 0-226-10247-5 (cloth)
ISBN-10: 0-226-10248-3 (paper)

Library of Congress Cataloging-in-Publication Data

Cheney, Kristen E.
 Pillars of the nation : child citizens and Ugandan national
 development / Kristen E. Cheney.
     p. cm.
 Includes bibliographical references and index.
 ISBN-13: 978-0-226-10247-4 (cloth : alk. paper)
 ISBN-10: 0-226-10247-5 (cloth : alk. paper)
 ISBN-13: 978-0-226-10248-1 (pbk. : alk. paper)
 ISBN-10: 0-226-10248-3 (pbk. : alk. paper) 1. Children's rights—
Uganda. 2. Children—Uganda—Social conditions. 3. Children and
war—Uganda. I. Title.
 HQ792.U3.C47 2007
 305.23096761'090511—dc22

                                                      2006039082

♾ The paper used in this publication meets the minimum
requirements of the American National Standard for Information
Sciences—Permanence of Paper for Printed Library Materials,
ANSI Z39.48-1992.

DEDICATED TO THE CHILDREN OF AFRICA:

"Africa's flowers are now growing."

Contents

Acknowledgments

My friends in Uganda may have sealed my fate as an anthropologist, a writer, and a teacher when they dubbed me *Nakalanzi*, one who announces or shares what she knows. I am grateful to the people whose friendship and support throughout the years have fostered my love of Africa and its people, most especially Martin Geria, Israel Katongole, Justine Wasswa, and the Damulira family. These dear friends and their families are *my* family in Uganda, and their welcoming arms are why I will always come home.

I cannot express enough gratitude for the openness, enthusiasm, and cooperation of all the children and their families whom I describe in this book. They have made it possible, and I only hope the influence of my research will in some small way return the favor. Special thanks to my research assistants Paul Bangirana and Moses Mayanja, who did much of the grunt work of transcription and translation. I would like to thank the staff of World Vision Gulu Children of War Rehabilitation Center—namely, Florence, Dennis, Martin, and directors Mark Avola and Charles Watmon—for being so helpful and accommodating of my work while doing such invaluable work of their own.

The late Dr. Kasalina Matovu was a champion of African children's rights. "Mama Matovu" was deputy director of the Makerere University Institute of Languages and principle researcher and national coordinator of the Minds Across Africa School Clubs program. She helped me with everything from my preliminary research and invaluable networking to teaching me Luganda. She will be missed.

Funding for this research was generously provided by the National Science Foundation and the Wenner-Gren Foundation for Anthropological Research, Inc. Previous versions of the work contained here have appeared as articles in *African Identities* 1, no. 1 (2003); *African Studies Review* 47, no. 3 (2004); *Children's Geographies* 3, no. 1 (2005); and *Image and Narrative* 11, no. 2 (2005). Materials are reprinted here with their express permission. I have also presented this work at many different conferences and symposia. I appreciate the valuable feedback I received from my colleagues at these meetings.

At the University of California, Santa Cruz, my sincere appreciation goes to my adviser, Carolyn Martin Shaw, for her careful readings, detailed advice, and emotional support throughout my graduate career. She claims she does not know what she does to mentor students. It apparently comes naturally; her accessibility, wisdom, and high academic standards have left a lasting impression on all her students. I only hope I have proven a worthy apprentice. I also appreciate the thoughtful feedback and encouragement I received from my qualifying exam and dissertation committee members, Donald Brenneis, Daniel Linger, and Triloki Pandey. Members of my writing group, Gillian Goslinga, Heather Waldroup, and Riet Delsing, provided much-needed intellectual stimulation that challenged my assumptions, sharpened my arguments, and opened up new directions. But our meetings also provided great company and therapeutic commiseration on those days when it seemed like we would never get through it. Lindsay Kelley also read many presentation drafts and provided technical assistance.

I am grateful to my parents, Robert and Sharon Cheney, who have let me be me—whatever the consequences. I am also thankful to have had Scott Crawford's support and encouragement. Special thanks to Dr. Philip Kilbride for providing encouraging and detailed feedback on earlier drafts of this manuscript. Thanks also to the editorial staff at the University of Chicago Press for investing in this project. I must also acknowledge the support of my grandmother, Mabel Rocamora, who never misses an opportunity to express her pride in my achievements. Though she has never been to Uganda, she has become a tireless advocate for Ugandan children, almost single-handedly procuring the funding to build a primary school for orphans and vulnerable children near Kampala. I'm proud of you, too, Grandma!

Introduction

The Role of Ugandan Child Citizens in the
Struggle for National Development

Uganda has risen from the dark night of postcolonial civil conflict to become a shining star among nation-states in Africa, a continent so beset by political dysfunction that many Westerners have come to see it as inimical to social stability. Uganda began to chip away at that stereotype when Yoweri Museveni took power in a coup in 1986 and established the National Resistance Movement government. He ended nearly twenty years of civil war and government abuse of the populace by ensuring human rights and courting international development agencies. The wars, however, had decimated the infrastructure and left hundreds of thousands of soldiers and civilians dead. Twenty-five years after independence from Britain, Uganda was a nation still in its infancy.

When I first visited Uganda in 1993, I lived on the compound of a girl's boarding school outside the capital city, Kampala. Given the tremendous losses of life and property during the wars, and the brutal onslaught of AIDS that had already killed the most productive young adults in some communities, I had anticipated that I would encounter abundant despair. Once I arrived, however, I found a different story. I came across people who again and again chose to look toward the future rather than dwell on their difficult pasts. People I met did not refuse to talk about the war; they just were not particularly interested. The past certainly

1

lingered into the present, though: at the school where I lived, I met many girls in their late teens named Peace. By inscribing the fervent hope of their parents' era each time they wrote or spoke their names, they also recalled the troubled times in which they had been born. I was impressed by how much hope people held for the future. They believed for the first time in years that their children's futures would be free of the violence and uncertainty that had characterized their own lives. I could do nothing but humbly join them in that fervent hope.

Because of this violent past, Ugandan childhood is constructed in everyday discourse as a primary space in which national prosperity will either be made or broken. This book is about the ways that childhood and children are being co-opted as discursive objects in relation to the nation. Though in many ways this discourse is constructed from the top down, I talked to ordinary citizens—children and adults, from varied backgrounds and positions—who repeated this same rhetoric. People drew on metaphorical similarities to show how, since the nation is still young and developing, it is like a child that requires special care and nurturing. They encouraged their children to identify as Ugandan–sometimes to the detriment of more particular ethnic identities—reasoning that if children are brought up to feel like proud Ugandans, they will raise the nation to prosperity and a new level of international legitimacy. This was no easy task, given the way the infamously brutal ignorance of former leaders such as Idi Amin had made Uganda a tragic figure on the world stage. But I came to see that on the dual fronts of unity and development, Ugandans were conceptualizing childhood in this transitional period as a particularly promising space for reimagining the nation, while they also reimagined children's roles within it: if people could raise their children to feel like Ugandans, then children could raise the nation out of underdevelopment.

I therefore became interested in exploring how emergent ideas of nationhood and childhood were informing and mutually constituting each other. Which people and/or institutions were leading such reformulations, and for what purposes? I was concerned with how power is structured and deployed through childhood and nationhood as social, sentimental categories, and how children accept, appropriate, or challenge those categories. Recent social paradigms in the study of children and childhood emphasize children's agency and contributions to their communities (James and Prout 1997; Mayall 1994; Schwartzman 2001). How, then, do Ugandan children respond to adults' notions of childhood, and how do they construct and operationalize their own identities as citizens? I saw that children were entering into nation-building projects not only as objects but as respondents and participants.

This participation is in part encouraged and fostered by a widespread children's rights campaign launched in the mid-nineties by the National Resistance Movement (NRM) government, in the wake of having ratified the United Nations Convention on the Rights of the Child. In addition, Ugandan children are often thrust into the forefront of certain struggles shaping the character of the nation, such as the AIDS epidemic and war. Though most people are slow to change their cultural attitudes toward children's roles in society, policymakers are starting to pay homage to the notion that, as James and Prout argue, children are "active in the construction and determination of their own social lives, the lives of those around them and of the societies in which they live" (1997, 8). This fact has been theoretically reinforced, but how is it enacted in policy? In Uganda, international organizations and a progressive new constitution acknowledge the key roles that young people will play in the country's future: the national youth anthem even refers to them as "the pillars of tomorrow's Uganda."

Ugandan children are therefore becoming—at least discursively—primary vehicles for social change. Yet children's abilities to participate in the activities of citizenship are still constrained by often-contradictory adult notions of childhood, both local and international (James 1993, 72). Despite all the rhetoric about children's rights, it seemed to me that many children felt rather powerless over their circumstances. My observations of children I met over the course of my research revealed deep, personal commitments to national development but also the paradox of powerlessness that many children experience on a daily basis. Not only are they subjected to the authoritarianism of the family and the educational system, but they are disempowered by poverty, political insecurity, and the AIDS epidemic. Children must therefore negotiate their places in Ugandan society among competing notions of what children should and should not be and do to enable themselves to participate actively in the country's development.

Uganda's postcolonial path to nationhood—still unfolding—provides a unique context in which to examine how contestations over concepts of childhood and nationhood crucially intersect. Further, anthropological approaches are ideal for understanding how these two come into contact with each other. A qualititative methodology that accounts for both a global political-economic perspective and indigenous perspectives of childhood's multiple meanings and children's experiences yields what Alma Gottlieb calls in her ethnography of infant culture in West Africa "a productive balance between the global and the local, the political and the cultural, and the social and the individual" (Gottlieb 2004, 42).

Rather than try to convince the reader of a certain configuration of "the child," I aim to reveal the contradictions inherent in emergent local notions of childhood by showing what discourses circulate to form the Ugandan trope of the child. This demonstrates the ambivalence of the social category of childhood, which affects children's qualitative experience of childhood in a contemporary, developing African country. Ethnographic information helps us to see how this trope plays out in actual social life. Not the least of my goals is to show how children are inventively dealing with these contradictions.

In order to do this, I first explain the historical factors that make this moment in Uganda's history a crucial one for reconfiguring the meaning of children and childhood to the nation. I then lay out the main theoretical issues that frame my research.

Uganda: A Nation in Its Infancy

To understand the importance of this present historical juncture in Uganda, one must understand Uganda's past. At a time when nationalism is supposedly fading under the onslaught of globalizing forces, it still matters very much to Ugandans, perhaps because, since independence, Ugandans have never had the luxury of being able to take the cohesion of the nation for granted. In such "new" nations, this lack of cohesion is often attributed to colonial legacy. Many Africanist scholars place the solidification of African nationalities and ethnic identities at the point when Africans came into direct contact with European colonial rulers and were subjected to their territorial borders (Coleman 1994). Further, they tend to trace the paradoxes and impasses of postcolonial public life to colonial origins. In Uganda, the Buganda kingdom—a very stratified and complex society—welcomed colonial administrators as allies and trade partners. The Bantu-speaking Baganda struck the British as having a highly developed society in relation to their neighbors, so they accepted Bagandan hospitality.[1] They placed the colony's administrative center in Buganda and favored the Baganda in native education, vocational training, and other skills-training programs necessary to function in British colonial society. Nilotic northerners, on the other hand, were regarded as less sophisticated and were hired as laborers and soldiers by the colonial administration. As in many other colonized territories, the division of local people was therefore based on colonists' essentialized notions of ethnic groups. This developed into a significant split in the post-independence era (Ofcansky 1996, 153).[2]

Ugandans today suffer from the double legacy of colonial rule and the despotic rule of post-independence leaders. Scholars have long claimed that challenges to nationalism persist because the African state is formed from the indigenous reformation of colonial institutions (Bayart 1993). A cohesive nation, let alone a legitimate, independent state, was never able to form and prosper because of persistent civil war.[3] Since the time that peace finally came in the 1980s, as Martin Doornbos writes, "the 'national question' has been acquiring a different and more complex content, concerned less with the how of national integration, but with what basis there is for it" (Doornbos 1988, 260). Uganda's independence day in 1962 was the only peaceful transfer of political power in the country's history. The British appointed Milton Obote as the first prime minister, and several ethnic kingdoms, including the powerful Baganda, received federal status. Perhaps Obote's biggest challenge was to integrate the Baganda with national government. He failed miserably, instead attempting to alienate and disenfranchise them. In 1966, Obote abrogated the constitution and created his own, which granted him sole executive powers and banned the federal statuses of all kingdoms within Uganda, precipitating massive violence between northern and southern ethnic groups. He sent his army commander, Idi Amin, to the Buganda palace at Mengo to "collect" the king, Muteesa II. Muteesa fled to avoid being killed, but historian A. B. K. Kasozi argues that "the victory over Muteesa II institutionalized violence as the main instrument of political control" (1994, 88). Obote sanctioned Amin's brutality, which eventually turned on him in 1971. The next six changes of government from 1966–86 all involved hostile coups, largely driven by ethnic divisions (Kasozi 1994, 59). Obote left for a conference in Singapore in January with an ultimatum for Amin to explain misuse of funds in the army. Instead, Amin led a coup and replaced Obote.

Amin's economic policies ruined rural agriculture, authorized excessive government spending, alienated professionals, and contributed to the gradual disintegration of peace. His decision to expel all ethnic Indians in 1972, many of whom were descended from colonial immigrants and had known no other home, created a dearth of managers that led to an effective breakdown of both industry and agriculture due to the sudden scarcity of essential commodities and agricultural equipment (Kasozi 1994, 117). Amin's undisciplined army also terrorized civilians as several rebel movements formed to oust him, including one led by Obote to regain power. After a brief takeover in 1979, Obote's political party, the Uganda People's Congress (UPC), called for elections, which they rigged by military intimidation of the populace. Obote won and resumed leadership, exacting revenge on all those who had supported Amin. The year 1981 ushered in the most bloody period in postcolonial history: Obote's soldiers started rounding up civilians, mostly young Baganda males, and killing them on the slightest suspicion of disloyalty (Kasozi 1994, 146). During the Amin/Obote era, an estimated one million people were killed, one million were exiled, and another one million were internally displaced (Mushanga 2001, 161).

Yoweri Museveni was forming his National Resistance Army (NRA) in the run-up to the rigged 1980 elections. This politically motivated army gained support from the civilian population by ensuring basic human rights and encouraging participation in political decision making.[4] The NRM and other rebel forces sapped Obote's resources until his own soldiers, blaming him for their defeats, removed him themselves (Kasozi 1994). For a second time, Obote was overthrown by his own army, and General Tito Okello was sworn in as president in 1985. Museveni's NRA pressed on and took Kampala in January 1986. The new National Resistance Movement government set about restoring the rule of law in order to begin rebuilding the "tarnished Pearl of Africa" (Ofcansky 1996).[5]

Nationalism for Development, Development for Nationhood

In many developing countries, the concepts of development and nation maintain a reciprocal relationship. People often want to promote one in order to perpetuate the other. On my first trip to Uganda, I frequently heard people conceptualize their collective priority as "cleaning up" the mess left by Obote and Amin. "The wars have underdeveloped us," one man explained to me. "Now we need to catch up." Catch up with what or whom, I wondered? Part of the stakes in Uganda's assertion of its nationhood was proving its legitimacy in relation to other nations. The route to nationhood, most agreed, was through development models, and they are what continue to drive Ugandan nationalism today.

Given the inept leadership that had pervaded all of independence, many Ugandans had grown tired of war and, despite their wariness of military leaders, were eager to trust Museveni. Post–civil war Uganda (see fig. 1) was anxious to demonstrate security and stability in order to be seen as a legitimate nation-state that could join the global community of nations. To mixed reactions, Museveni instigated a ten-point program to restore order that addressed corruption, security, and democracy. The NRM encouraged self-governance through local Resistance Councils and the formation of a new constitutional assembly based on the principle of

1   Political map of Uganda.

participatory democracy.[6] Ugandans started to trust that a comprehensive peace would indeed be restored. As one Ugandan friend remembers,

Museveni allowed participation, allowed freedom of speech. He allowed the newspaper to talk. There was a return of the rule of law. . . . Then he started teaching people politics. Because we used to have seminars, and he would send teachers and they would tell us, "Well, look, this is your country. It's you who are going to build it or to let it down.". . . All the seminars were so educational because they used to show us how the government works. Before, people didn't know how the government worked. And the rule of law—that was very, very good about Museveni.

Museveni earned widespread support with this participatory approach, unfamiliar to most Ugandans. This helped him battle the persistent sectarianism, both ethnic and religious, that had pervaded colonial and post-independence conflict. Museveni viewed such beliefs as antidevelopment, stating that "those who emphasise ethnicity are messengers of perpetual backwardness" (Museveni 1997, 189).

According to Museveni, however, the greatest challenges were economic. The infrastructure was practically nonexistent after two decades of civil war. Industrialization had also severely regressed to the point where peasants constituted 92 percent of the remaining population (Museveni 1997, 188). Underdevelopment and ethnic conflict are the two problems around which Museveni has built his government's vision of national development: "In Uganda, and in Africa as a whole, a large proportion of the population is deficient in enterprise, deficient in savings, possesses no special skills and has nothing to exchange. The effect is to produce countries with a very small tax base. This is no small matter, but a major structural problem. The situation has very serious implications for the continent and it must be addressed and reversed" (188).

Despite the apparent lack of Western democratic institutions in the NRM, the international development community was eager to work with Museveni because he could "speak the language" of international development fluently. To gain access to the resources of the development industry, one must be familiar with its parlance, from jargon to extensive acronyms. "The globalization of the language of development," Alberto Arce writes, "legitimizes abstract normative and accepted social order representations of values and beliefs" (Arce 2000, 38). Some criticized Museveni's banning of political parties as part of his mission to overcome sectarianism, but Museveni has been quite savvy in his defense of a "no-party democracy." The driving force behind this idea has been the basic assumption that political parties will inevitably divide along sectarian lines, and only stable nations can gain access to the vast resources of the development industry. Ugandans and international development agencies alike accepted this argument, at least temporarily: a referendum to repeal the ban on political parties overwhelmingly passed in 1995, with Museveni's support.[7] In any case, Africans who push for democracy are not always so much concerned with creating a cohesive nation as with creating a state that can facilitate economic development (Eyoh 1998, 283). This is coupled with a widespread skepticism over the feasibility of multiparty democracy in the African context, which Museveni claims is not possible until a more cohesive class system based on a cash economy can form in place of sectarianism (Museveni 1997, 187). In this sense, democracy and development become issues of sovereignty: the strength of the nation is thus made evident through its development practices.

The Development of Civil Society

The term *civil society* is often used to describe local organizations that take up the international imperatives of development. Civil society is described as "those birthplaces where the ambitions of social groups created the means of generating additional freedom and justice" (Monga 1996, 148). Theories of civil society usually conceive of such groups as struggling against the state (Comaroff and Comaroff 1999, 21). However, this concept fails to account for the situation of common development participation in Uganda, where civil society more frequently cooperates with government than opposes it (Tripp 1998, 85). Many presume that civil interest groups form in order to influence government to reflect their values, but Nelson Kasfir argues that, in the African context, "The policies government officials put forward may stimulate interest groups to form and to respond rather than the other way around" (1998, 32).

Social theorists also see civil society as being formed along ethnic and class lines. While I would agree with Tripp that this limits the examination of popular political participation,[8] there are other concerns with the concept. Mikhael Karlstrom argues that "if ethnicity-based solidarities and associations are likely to remain a central element of the organizational sector that articulates state and society in Africa, then the analytical task will be to try and understand the conditions under which they can perform this mediating role constructively and the circumstances under which they become divisive and destructive" (1999, 110). A reconceptualization of ethnicity in relation to the Ugandan nation is helping overcome persistent divisions for the purpose of developing the nation. Ethnicity is coming to be understood as a strength: unity comes through diversity, and unity brings prosperity. Museveni even allowed restoration of tribal monarchies (banned by Obote) for ceremonial purposes, though federal status has not been restored. This idea of unity is pervasive in the citizenship education of Ugandan children, whom many hope will overcome the violent sectarianism of the past.

To be successful, development efforts must "nurture people's opportunities to create a manageable way of living" (Adindu and Romm 2001, 53). I argue that Ugandans are doing this through their children. This is especially significant because of the historical moment I describe in this chapter. The proliferation of rights discourses encouraging the protection of children is one example, but we cannot discuss this without also examining the sociopolitical climate in which certain development discourses thrive. Part of what makes children most precious to the nation is their lack of social memory regarding ethnic and religious division. Fostering a climate of national tolerance for difference may help today's children to steer the nation away from such deadly tendencies in the future.

Theorizing Children, Citizenship, and Nationhood: Beyond Dichotomies

With the rise of nationalism in the nineteenth century [children] began to represent the future of nations, which meant that policies had to be devised for ensuring a nation's survival through its children;...we often hear the catch-phrase "children are our future." That is the way many societies view the next generation, as belonging not to itself and a new society, but to the adult present as a means of conserving the values of the status quo.

JUDITH ENNEW AND BRIAN MILNE, *THE NEXT GENERATION*

In the preceding epigraph, Judith Ennew and Brian Milne (1990, 3) highlight the basic associations of children's connections to the nation that both empower them as agents of social change and point out their subservience to adult ideals about both childhood and nationhood. Ugandan postwar nationalism has arisen in the context of global debates about the promises and failures of international development. If we remember that development discourses "produce rather than reflect their objects of intervention" (Arce 2000, 37), then this makes Africans all the more frustrated with the neocolonial paternalism of international development programs, particularly the structural adjustment programs (SAPs) that have only left them more impoverished. Despite this, Ugandans continue to express a fervent hope for the development of new nations. Aside from basic material and infrastructural needs, one thing that Ugandans seemed to need the most at the time of my fieldwork was a definitive break with their recent past and the sectarianism that had led to bloodshed. In this case it was easy to accept the notion of children as symbolic embodiments of the future. While children represent the future, childhood also references an idyllic past in the minds of many adults. As Karen Fog Olwig and Eva Gulløv note, "Adults associate childhood with stability and rootedness as a reflection of their wish to root themselves in the temporally and spatially distant place of innocent and peaceful childhood" (2003, 2). Biographers thus often frame childhood as a nostalgic social space for the present-day adult, lacking children's subjectivity. This theoretical marginalization of children has produced a model that limits children's participation in present day adult worlds. A child's greatest significance is her future: the adult whom the child will become. In this configuration, "the child" becomes a homogenous social category unqualified by other markers of identity such as class, gender, and ethnicity (James 1993, 90).

The political insecurity of their own childhoods kept adult Ugandans from experiencing this supposedly peaceful childhood. The category of "child" therefore bears a heavy burden for a struggling young nation that has seldom known peace or stability. Children thus become a central trope in the discourse of national development, both as an empty signifier and as a potential social agent of its success.

This focus on children is not just about sentiments for a peaceful and prosperous future; it is also about the centrality of children in hegemonic international rights discourse. Arce argues that "linguistic representations from international institutions can become a political instrument which contributes to the maintenance of an international political order and establishment, within a well defined administrative sphere of agency influences" (2000, 34). These affect developing countries' attitudes through controlling access to funds from international development donors. Early in its conception, the United Nations International Children's Emergency Fund (UNICEF) offered assistance to those governments willing to consider children as major factors in human resource development (Iskander 1987, 26). However, as I discuss in chapter 1, children's rights do not always translate neatly across the political arena or the social landscape. Nonetheless, Ugandan civil society has invested children's rights with surprising salience, both in their lives and in that of the nation. The task then becomes to track the articulation of local and global development "languages" that advocate certain conceptions of children and their worth. Where did they originate, and what are their effects? The answer lies not so much with children themselves as it does in children's discursive relationship to nationhood, and in Ugandans' desires to "grow" that sense of nationalism by reeducating their children to identify with it. Development of the child thus complements development of the country.

Conceptualizing Childhood

In 1962, historian Phillipe Aries wrote what is arguably the seminal text of modern childhood studies. *Centuries of Childhood* challenged the static notion of the "child" by arguing that the social category of "childhood" with which we are familiar today came about in eighteenth-century Europe, when the concept of children as miniature adults was debunked (Aries 1962). Adults began to consider children to be at a different level of being and established institutional separations of child and adult worlds, such as different types of schools, children's apparel, games, and so on. Though children and childhood gained new sentimental meaning, Aries claimed that the institutionalization of childhood had the effect of hindering children's relative freedoms by placing them in specialized and supervised settings like day care and schools that separated them from adult public arenas.

It is important to note that modern discourses of childhood and citizenship emerged simultaneously from Western European Enlightenment rationality (Wallace 1995, 291). Neil Postman attributes the rise of the concept of childhood to the invention of the printing press (Postman 1982), just as Benedict Anderson credits print media with the creation of "imagined communities" and the rise of the nation-state (Anderson 1991).[9] The stability of one depends on the other, and both are negotiable. The anthropomorphizing of the nation takes root in "the health, welfare, and rearing of children" (Rose 1989, 121). Further, childhood memories become symbolically linked to nationalism, in which individual life narratives become metaphors for the national narrative (Eriksen 1997). In these ways, the nation's destiny is linked to children's welfare, which becomes the responsibility of the state (James, Jenks, and Prout 1998, 7).

Though childhood and nationhood share some intriguing conceptual links in terms of the types of care, respect, and protection that citizens are supposed to provide to both children and their nation, children's subjectivities within nation-building projects have not received much attention in scholarly literature. In fact, children and nations are often shown to be dichotomous categories. Carolyn Sargent and Nancy Scheper-Hughes (1998), for example, describe Brazilian street children as liminal because they do not fit the mold of normative childhood, yet they are not entitled to the citizenship rights of adults; "children" and "citizens" appear in their work as oppositional categories. This is not atypical, yet it is seldom criticized. This fact in itself represents a crisis of representation of the child-national subject. Adults tend to view children as a largely apolitical social group occupying the apolitical space of childhood, yet the exclusion of children from discussions of politics and nationalism belies this assumption.

For Sharon Stephens (1995, 9), the proliferation of writings about disappearing, lost, or stolen childhoods, coupled with the simultaneous spread of the "universal child" model through international organizations such as UNICEF, present a crisis in the study of childhood that calls for a redefinition of the child in light of growing attention to the threat of invasion or pollution of childhood domains by adult worlds. These same phenomena, however, can act as sources of empowerment for children (Jenkins 1998; Spigel 1998). Postman assumes that if children gain access to "adult" knowledge, they cease to be children. But if, as Jenkins posits, "the myth of childhood innocence...'empties' the child of its own political agency" (Jenkins 1998, 1), the defeat of innocence likewise signals the loss of childhood through the recovery of agency. It is necessary to debunk this myth of dichotomies in order to expose unequal adult-child power relations. Robert Coles's book *The Political Life of Children* (1986) powerfully argues that national politics deeply affect children in terms of their senses of morality, consciousness, security, and worldview. Yet we continue to think of childhood as an apolitical social space, while those classified as "youth"—another ambiguous category usually referring to teenagers—are merely seen as social problems. Deborah Durham (2000) notes the prevalent "cross-cutting images of youth as victims of circumstance and the manipulations of older people in power, and also images of youth as unruly, destructive, and dangerous forces needing containment. Traversing these notions, youth enter political space as saboteurs." (113). These assumptions are especially persistent in Africa, where young people have acted both as liberators, as in South Africa (Ndebele 1995; Reynolds 1995), and as oppressors, as in Sierra Leone (Rosen 2005). Despite acknowledgement of the structural violence that precipitates many youth problems, youth are cast as disruptive and violent.

The Role of Children's Rights: Deferred Citizenship

Children's rights discourses tend to reify constructions of apolitical childhood in such a way that the systematic exclusion of children from the full rights of citizenship receives little notice. Laws passed to protect children often serve to further entrench discrimination and the denial of rights to children, increasing adult intervention in their lives (Franklin 1986, 3). In this configuration, the category of "the child" could refer more to a delineation of power than of individual, biological chronology. The argument for the political rights of children rests on a distinction between legal and moral rights, and we tend to advocate the latter for children while denying them the former. Judith Ennew writes,

Children suffer from a double disadvantage precisely because they are children. The situation of children in society has actually changed little since the eighteenth century,

13

when they were legally compared with the dead. It isn't pushing the comparison too far to say that just like a corpse, which lacks the ability to act because it has no biological life, a child lacks the ability to act because it has no legal life. (Ennew and Milne 1990, 14)

In most analyses, the adult-child relationship is thus revealed as nothing other than a hegemonic one. Conceptualizations of childhood have been directed by adults' ideas about the child's role in society's future (James 1993; James and Prout 1997; Jenks 1982). The category of childhood serves as a repository for the projection of all kinds of adult hopes, desires, and fears, from nostalgia to social stability and the feeling of powerlessness in the face of modernity (Jenks 1996; Wallace 1995). The control of these emotions is couched in terms of the protection and even surveillance of children. What is categorically meant to be "in a child's best interest" is really what adults deem to be best for maintaining social cohesion through the constructed boundaries of childhood as a particular stage of inno-cence and dependency. The concept of childhood ultimately becomes a mechanism for control and maintenance of the social environment (Katz 2003). The category of "the child" becomes tied to the family, and societal concern for the welfare of children translates into the extension of governmentality into households.

Schools are where children are most inculcated with nationalist ide-ologies, through textbooks (Anderson 1989; Nganda 1996; Pigg 1992), community studies, and even music festivals (Ness 1998). As I discuss in chapters 2 and 3, schools are likewise the main conduits through which emergent Ugandan national identity is transmitted. Ugandan school-children learn about Uganda's history, national symbols and boundaries, and definitions of citizenship. Most researchers see this as a top-down type of socialization, but my own research indicates a much more com-plicated process. While children are learning about citizenship, they are also forming their own, at times resistant, ideas regarding the content and meaning of the category as it pertains to them, negotiating their identities as individuals and as social selves (Cohen 1994; Harris 1989).

Again, we can attribute the gap between "child" and "citizen" to the fact that children are socialized within an adult perception of childhood as an apprenticeship for *future* adulthood and citizenship (James 1993; James and Prout 1997). This might occur through the attainment of what Pierre Bourdieu (1993) calls cultural capital, and what Anthony Giddens refers to as "the discovery of 'moral meaning'" (1991, 41). We may also view the gap as an attribute of the masked protectionism of the privileged position of adulthood. Sargent and Scheper-Hughes provide a prime example of this: in their introduction to *Small Wars: The Cultural Politics of Childhood*, they claim that "there is something wrong with the rights discourse when it is applied to young children. Suddenly, they are transformed into socially competent adult actors" (1998, 13). They suggest that extending civil rights to children makes them too much like Aries's premodern "miniature adults." Though I do not claim that children are as socially competent as adults, I do believe that they need to be taken seriously as social actors with some levels of competence (usually more than adults give them credit for). Further, they often achieve certain social competences earlier than laws and mores recognize (Archard 1993, 62–63). Indeed, in African societies, children are commonly expected to assume duties central to the maintenance of the household, such as water-gathering or cattle-herding, from ages as "tender" as three.[10] Yet the Convention on the Rights of the Child arbitrarily defines a child as any person under eighteen years of age. It thus does nothing to distinguish between the very divergent abilities of infants and teenagers, for example (Ennew 2002, 341).

The social sciences have just begun to contribute to different cultural understandings of childhood, as evidenced by the gross underrepresentation of children, especially in anthropology. Lawrence Hirschfeld argues, "[Children] are located in the transition to cultural competence rather than as having genuine mastery of it. As a consequence, discussion of children is typically transformed into talk about *adults* and the ways they organize the environment in which children develop so as to facilitate the acquisition of the cultural competence appropriate to the society in which they live" (2002, 614). In this way, social scientists contribute to the effacement of children's agency.

As social scientists, we might reflexively question the probable consequences of preserving the category of "adult" and all its attendant privileges for child advocacy purposes; not only does it potentially do a drastic disservice to children by placing childhood in opposition to social competence, but it risks misinterpretation of the arguments of most child rights activists; advocates are not trying to impose an adult-centeredness or complete erasure of childhood as a protective category for young people, but a broader and more democratically based notion of young people's agency.

All this is to say that *the social sciences have yet to treat age as a social variable equivalent to others such as gender, class, and ethnicity.* By conducting research on children's actual competencies and paying attention to children's lived experiences, we can see childhood through the phenomenological lens of child subjectivity and thus dissolve the myth of dichotomous child and adult spheres. Such research also draws the debate back to its center: children themselves. On the basis of my observations as an anthropologist and development worker, I do not see childhood, in Uganda or elsewhere, as endangered; rather, I see that children themselves are endangered—and that they often feel endangered by both the discourses that circulate around them and their daily experiences, which subjugate them to subadult or subhuman status. For this reason, I argue that childhood can and should be analyzed as a productive social category integral to—rather than separate from—broader social relations. This must become an essential aspect of child research if it is to address the power differentials undergirding the discursive practices that define childhood.

Toward an Anthropology of Childhood

Pioneers of De-Essentialization

The few anthropologists who have concerned themselves with children have mainly been interested in the category as a de-essentialized social construction. Culture and personality studies such as that by Margaret Mead and Martha Wolfenstein (1954) have demonstrated the cross-cultural nature of childhood, thus pushing theory toward a multiple conceptualization of childhood. Mead was criticized, however, for following a simplistic model of children's culture and personality that ignored all influences on children outside the domestic sphere (LaFontaine 1986, 12).

The goal of John and Beatrice Whiting's Six Culture Study in the 1960s and 1970s was to assess the validity of both universal and culture-specific models of child development through cross-cultural comparison of children's behavior patterns at different stages of childhood (Whiting and Edwards 1988; Whiting and Whiting 1975). Their findings indicate that both models have some validity, but mainly in combination. While their studies are quite methodical in their assessment of children's lives and do not employ much in the way of detailed or extensive ethnography, they are useful for seeing how certain children's character traits have been linked to various cultural environments. For example, children reared in extended-family households and engaged in subsistence farming or pastoral activities tend to learn responsibility and obedience earlier in life. They are given more duties and chores from an early age. Beatrice

Whiting's later work with Carolyn Pope Edwards pays more attention to agency in changing, modern contexts, most notably in Kenya (Edwards and Whiting 2004).

Beyond Ethnocentrism

Other social scientists have made important contributions to childhood studies by pointing out that Western conceptions of the "correct" childhood have been imposed far and wide through the media, aid agencies, and public discourse alike (Boyden 1997). This ethnocentrism is criticized for ignoring the particulars of children's various social environments and actually contributing to their stigmatization. James (1993) claims that "whilst the concept of 'childhood' may give to individual children an identity as 'child,' the experiential process of 'being a child' is not so easily categorized; . . . the Western ideology of childhood as a period of happiness and innocence works to exclude those for whom it is not" (28). This was certainly the case in Uganda, where children excluded from schooling due to poverty, or those caught up in war, only felt more marginalized by knowing their "universal" rights. The challenge, then, is to map some of these variations in particular circumstances to see how they share similarities or differ cross-culturally. Several ethnographies have been written with this aim, though some do not engage the question of childhood in particular so much as various cultural conceptions of personhood in their respective field sites. Still, their work can enlighten us about cultural notions of childhood and their effects on children.[11]

African Ethnographies: The Importance of Demography

Anthropological research on children in Africa often centers on "traditional" models of African social relationships.[12] As with those mentioned above, ethnographies that concern themselves at all with children in Africa often focus on societal models of personhood rather than specifically on children's subjectivities. In light of the immense social and political upheavals on the African continent in the past few decades, it seems logical to assume that conceptions of childhood have also changed and varied dramatically. The need for a better cross-cultural understanding of childhood is evident in demographic shifts alone: in contrast to Europe, for example—whose population is getting older, with octogenarians quickly outnumbering teenagers in some Scandinavian nations—the population of Africa is growing dramatically younger due to the onslaught of AIDS as well as war and increased poverty. Life expectancy for

Africans is now around the mid-thirties in many countries. Africa is thus an area where ethnographic work can contribute to our understanding not only of how notions of childhood are changing in specific ethnographic contexts but also of how certain material conditions are affecting the experience of childhood. A number of anthropologists have recently begun working toward that end, with promising results. They often fall short, however, of examining children's realities from a child-centered point of view. My inclusion of children's life histories in this book is intended to highlight children's views of their own social worlds, rather than focusing solely on adult interpretations of children's needs.

Childhood in Uganda: Statistical Realities

Today as never before, children are being discursively co-opted as objects in relation to the Ugandan nation, especially in terms of national development. My investigation was concerned with exactly how this process worked and with its consequences for children. In chapter 1, I detail how international childhood discourses like those promoted by UNICEF and the Convention on the Rights of the Child conveniently accommodate the Ugandan government's neoliberal approach to development. While this process certainly seems to work from the top down, these ideas are eventually interpellated, localized, and actualized in very specific ways, especially in Ugandan classrooms. For me, learning about the lives of individual children drove home the realization that while children are learning about their rights, they must struggle to actualize them against the structural violence imposed on children born in lesser-developed nations. These dual aspects of structure and agency thus guide my analysis of the political economy of Ugandan childhood.

About 12 million children under the age of eighteen live in Uganda today, 4.3 million of them less than five years old. In a total of 25 million people, children make up nearly half the population. Following Uganda's participation in the 1990 World Summit for Children and ratification of the 1989 Convention on the Rights of the Child (CRC),[13] the Ugandan National Programme of Action for Children (UNPAC) was subsequently designed, according to President Museveni, "to identify policies and actions that would improve the survival, development and protection of children" (Evans 2001, 8). The Children's Statute of 1996 detailed some of these policies, but their implementation is hampered by lack of resources and overwhelming social, economic, and health problems, most especially HIV/AIDS and malaria.

Health Statistics (UNICEF 2001)

	% of total child population
Fertility	7.0
Infant mortality	8.3
Under-5 mortality	13.1
Stunted growth	38.0
Underweight	26.0
Fully vaccinated	38.0
Access to safe drinking water	47.0
Illnesses attributable to poor water/sanitation	50.0

Health

Uganda ranks thirty-second globally in its mortality rate for children less than five, with 131 deaths per 1,000 live births (table 1). Eighty-three of these are children who die before they reach their first birthdays (Evans 2001, 62). Many of these deaths are attributable to lack of safe drinking water and poor sanitation. According to UNICEF, "Malaria remains the biggest killer of children" in Uganda (Evans 2001, 62). In addition, only 38 percent of children are fully vaccinated, down from 81 percent in 1990. The government finances only 8 percent of vaccinations. There have been some health gains, though: In 1992, Uganda had the second-largest number of Guinea worm (a debilitating waterborne parasite) cases in the world: 130,000 (Evans 2001, 40). Today, this parasite is practically eradicated thanks to cooperative health education campaigns. Polio, endemic to Uganda in the 1960s, is also nearly eradicated, with 55 percent vaccinated against the disease.

Malnutrition has also adversely affected the child population. Thirty eight percent of children less than five show signs of stunted growth (Evans 2001, 62). Many are chronically malnourished. In rural areas especially, children become deficient in certain essential vitamins because their diets lack adequate variety. In addition, many children go hungry for lack of resources. These numbers tend to be highest among displaced populations such as those in northern Uganda, where an astronomical number of children suffer from kwashiorkor.

The AIDS pandemic is by far the biggest health crisis, effectively rolling back life expectancies across Africa to those of precolonial times (table 2).

AIDS in Uganda (2001)

HIV prevalence nationwide	8%
HIV prevalence in pregnant women aged 15–24	10%
Total AIDS fatalities	838,000
Child AIDS fatalities	83,000
Life expectancy in 1970	46
Life expectancy in 1990	42
AIDS orphans	1.9 million

Kampala's HIV prevalence among pregnant women reached 30 percent a decade ago and now stands around 10 percent. Uganda is one of two countries in Africa (the other being Senegal) where the HIV-prevalence rate is steadily dropping. The U.S. Agency for International Development (USAID) attributes this to a strong yet decentralized government response, emphasis on prevention, and behavioral change (Hogle 2002, 3–4).[14] As a result, Uganda has become a model for other African countries battling AIDS. Despite Uganda's success, however, 838,000 people have died of AIDS, 10 percent of them children. AIDS is among the leading causes of death for children less than five, and 1.5 million Ugandans were still HIV-positive in 2000 (Evans 2001, 26).

The most direct effect of AIDS on most children is orphanhood. As of 2005, about two million—or 16 percent—of Uganda's children have become AIDS orphans.[15] That number is expected to double within several years as more HIV-positive parents develop AIDS and die, putting an unmanageable strain on Uganda's already overburdened extended families, who have traditionally provided for orphans. Paternal aunts and uncles are traditionally expected to care for their deceased brother's children, but with the decreasing involvement of fathers, any extended family can be called upon to assume responsibility for orphaned children. The extent of the AIDS pandemic, however, means that aunts and uncles are also dying young, thus leaving holes in the social safety net that are endangering children's well-being, both physical and emotional. Further, the stigma around AIDS infection adversely affects the orphaned children of AIDS victims, who are also presumed to be HIV-positive (Lusk and O'Gara 2002). In actuality, few contract the disease from their parents, but society often forces these survivors to bear the shame for their parents.

There are currently no comprehensive government social programs for orphans, so UNICEF is working with government to devise a national policy to assist orphans. Because research has shown that orphanages disadvantage children—and can even "generate" more orphans in the community by offering services unavailable to other vulnerable children—assistance efforts focus on strengthening the capacity of families to care for orphaned children. I met one seventy-year-old grandfather who was caring for ten grandchildren after two of his children had died. "What can I do?" he asked. "I am too old to work for money, or even in my own garden. I can barely feed these children, let alone clothe and educate them."

Today, Ugandan children are inundated with AIDS-prevention messages and are better educated about the disease than their parents' generation. Ten-year-olds told me that people got AIDS from "playing sex," and that one should abstain, be faithful, or use condoms—reciting the lauded ABC approach to AIDS prevention.

Education

Generally speaking, Ugandans have always placed a high value on getting an education, even if it was often out of reach of the general population. Chapter 2 details the stakes of educational attainment for children and their families, which is closely linked both to citizenship and to class mobility.

Civil wars left the educational system decimated, and it became the NRM's aim to address both the quality of education and the quantity of children in school. When the government introduced Universal Primary Education (UPE) in January 1997, enrollment skyrocketed from 2.9 to 5.4 million in just two months (Evans 2001, 14). It put a huge strain on teachers and exacerbated the acute shortage of educational materials (USAID and The World Bank 1999). Classrooms with no desks were filled with 150 or more pupils, and many schools were teaching classes outdoors under trees.

After UPE was introduced in 1997, Kubili Primary School, where I conducted fieldwork in Kampala, had as many as 2,100 children housed in ten classrooms. During that time, teachers told me, they also had to partition the main hall to use as classroom space. Still, teachers had more than 100 students in their classes. By the time I arrived, their enrolment was set at about 1,600, the main hall had been reclaimed for extracurricular functions, and the average class size was about 65 students—which was still quite crowded.

In response, the government doubled its educational spending to 30 percent of the total national budget. By 2001, the number of pupils had risen to more than seven million. Most of these new students were girls, who made up 48 percent of primary school enrolments in 2000. Women's literacy thus began to rise much more sharply than men's. Between 1980 and 1999, literacy for men rose from 60 percent to 74 percent, while for women, it rose from 31 percent to 50 percent. Yet girls are dropping out at a rate twice that of boys because of negative parental attitudes and the inadequacies of school facilities and teaching methods for meeting girls' needs.[16] Though the number of universities grew from one in 1986 to thirteen in 2001 (Evans 2001, 8), only 15 percent of boys and 9 percent of girls even go on from primary to secondary school, let alone university (UNICEF 2001, 93).[17]

Economic Growth and Persistent Poverty

Despite the incredible gains that Museveni's government has achieved since 1986, half the country still lives in absolute poverty (Evans 2001, 63). As one parent put it to me, "Poverty is almost like another war." More than one-third of Ugandans live on less than $1 per day, and, despite an impressive growth rate, the 1999 gross national product still stood at US$320 per person—less than $1 per day (UNICEF 2001). Children comprise 62 percent of the poor, and their experiences of poverty tend to be more emotional and personal (Witter and Bukokhe 2004). Because adults perceive children as dependent and lacking skills or knowledge, they have little opportunity to participate in independent, income-earning activities for themselves. The children whom I met while they were street vending or performing menial tasks usually did so at the insistence of their parents to help contribute to family income, but many were discouraged from seeking employment for personal income.

As a nation, Uganda is still striving for economic self-sufficiency. In 1998, Uganda received $471 million in official development assistance, and though it qualified for World Bank debt reduction and cancellation, aid still comprises over 50 percent of the national budget. Nevertheless, the country is registering steady growth rates.

Security Issues

Refugee crises are the legacy of prolonged regional unrest. Uganda hosts a hundred and ninety thousand refugees from conflicts in neighboring Rwanda, Sudan, and the Democratic Republic of the Congo (Evans 2001, 54). Ugandan rebel groups have threatened the country's periphery over the past decade, causing widespread insecurity for families and children.

In addition, 1.2 million internally displaced people live in protected camps, resulting in food crises and educational disruption. This is most apparent and persistent in northern Uganda, where Joseph Kony's Lord's Resistance Army has terrorized the population for two decades, forcibly abducting children into their ranks. In response, the national army has herded civilians into protected camps, leaving hundreds of thousands of children and families destitute and reliant on international aid. A 1998 report stated that as a result, "Children have lost confidence in their parents. The parents no longer symbolize protection and support" (Barton, Mutiti, and the Assessment Team for Psycho-Social Programmes in Northern Uganda 1998, 25). Chapter 5 details some of the challenges for children living with prolonged war in that region, many of whom relief agencies now call "night commuters"—tens of thousands of children who, with the recent resurgence of rebel attacks, trek each evening from rural villages to town centers to avoid abduction.

Statistics such as these frame children in Uganda as embattled and beleaguered, but we know little about the process by which they come to internalize these perceptions and react to them. This book supplements these statistics with qualitative research to highlight the process of children's interpellation in development discourse, as well as their agency in navigating adverse circumstances.

Fieldwork: Critical Ethnographic Methods

Because I came to anthropology through a sense of social justice, my main aim here is to analyze not only the political-economic status of children during a critical historical juncture at my field site, but also to critique children's status in the discipline of anthropology. The lack of contemporary anthropological attention to children's social and cultural experiences betrays anthropology's activist origins, particularly with regard to African area studies (Schumaker 2001); anthropologists hired to facilitate colonization often ended up defending the rights of the colonized instead.

Just as anthropology found its disciplinary feet in an era of colonial destabilization, the current era of cultural and economic globalization challenges anthropologists to contribute their knowledge to socially responsible policy creation and reform. In Uganda, attempts at nation-building amidst unprecedented poverty, persistent war, and the AIDS pandemic— all facilitated (and even fueled) by globalization—encouraged me to write this ethnography in such a way that it might contribute to policy reforms that will improve conditions for African children. This research was therefore driven by a dual concern for children's representation within processes of nation-building as well as the production of anthropological knowledge.

This book is based mainly on fieldwork conducted from August 2000 to December 2001. Though my research entailed attention to various social institutions that promote ideological concepts of nationhood and childhood, including the Ministry of Education, UNICEF, and nongovernmental children's rights organizations, my research design prioritized children's voices to augment the steadily growing discussion of childhood in anthropology.

The chair of Uganda's Education Policy Review Commission, W. Setunda Kajubi, wrote in 1991, "The importance that the government and people of Uganda attach to education as a means of national development cannot be overstressed" (323). The Ministry of Education, UNICEF, and civil society organizations all affirm this belief. With the 1997 introduction of Universal Primary Education, the education system is many children's most direct link to national development. In Kampala, Uganda's capital, I interacted with children and teachers at two local primary schools to see how schools disseminate notions of childhood and nationhood. To get a sense of how these ideals mapped onto children's lives, I asked children to write essays and journals, and also recorded five children's life histories.

When I told people that I was going to do life histories of children as part of my fieldwork, I got a lot of sideways looks and perplexed furrowing of brows. This at first glance seemed to some to be an odd choice of methodology to use with children because of the brevity of children's lives, but it is ideal for child-centered ethnography. Part of my motivation in using life history was, admittedly, political; the assumption that children do not have life histories to speak of only exacerbates the anthropological neglect of children as cultural actors. When we see the depth and richness of even the shortest lives, we cannot avoid the conclusion that children's life histories are important access points to larger cultural indicators.

The life-history approach is a long-standing methodology of anthropological fieldwork. Anthropologists have used it as a humanistic research tool that not only establishes an intimate bond between ethnographer and informant, but also helps organize information in a way that relates individual lives, developmentally and psychosocially, to broader social customs and institutions. Through life histories, we start to see how cultural practice and social discourse come to bear on individual lives of varying status. But as Stanley Brandes notes, life histories also act as "excellent indicators of socio-cultural change" (Brandes 1979, 12). Given that my objective was to understand how children perceived, experienced, negotiated, and were constrained by contemporary social changes in Uganda, this methodology was especially appropriate (Runyan 1986, 183).

A further benefit of collecting children's life histories was that doing so served to convince child informants that they had something important to say (Langness and Geyla 1981, 35). Contrary to skeptics' presumptions, the life-history methodology proved to be ideal for my purposes because providing such accounts of themselves fostered a greater sense of agency for the children with whom I worked. Engaging with children in this way drew them directly into the collaborative project of knowledge production that is ethnography. Eliciting life histories may thus yield new forms of self-fashioning, especially for young people.

Ultimately, life histories, as Michael M. J. Fischer states, "need to be played interrogatively so as to open up the aporias, critical debates, contradictory pressures, and changes in which they participate" (1991, 26). This is precisely the spirit in which I employed life histories in my fieldwork and in the creation of this ethnography. With these children as my primary guides, I observed them in interactions with teachers and fellow students in classrooms and on playgrounds, followed them and other children through daily routines, and interviewed their families and teachers. Thus, their life histories aptly convey the major themes that emerged from my overall research and therefore frame much of the book's theoretical discussion.

Field Sites

Given the potential breadth of the topic and logistical concerns, I focused on a few main "sites" of ethnographic inquiry, chosen for their engagement of children in national development. These are selected Kampala schools; the National Primary School Music, Dance, and Drama Festival; and the World Vision Gulu Children of War Rehabilitation Center.

Kampala Schools

The schools where I worked were located near a large housing development for children of national law enforcement officers. Students therefore came from all over the country. The barracks sandwiched by the schools were originally built in the early twentieth century to house local civil servants. Some original housing structures remain, including row houses, apartment complexes, and administrative buildings. Now there are also conical huts made of galvanized metal, which must resemble solar ovens inside during the afternoon hours. Lines of laundry stretch between them, and children run throughout them playing and performing small chores for their mothers. At a bustling trading center in the middle of the barracks, one can do everything from get a haircut to have film developed.

Approximately twenty thousand people inhabit the barracks, and overcrowding makes sanitation poor. During my walk through the barracks between the two schools, I passed several garbage dumpsters overflowing onto the road. I often saw domestic animals feeding from the rubbish piles, and the sickly sweet smell of rotting pineapple permeated the air. Nevertheless, there were also several impressive communal gardens, a church, and a small nursery/primary school. My presence in the barracks always elicited excited cries of *"Mzungu!"* (white person) from the children, most of whom were not yet old enough for school. They rarely left the barracks and so rarely saw white people. Their mothers would often point me out to them when they saw me coming, so that by the time I reached them, the children were lined up along the rutted dirt road as if for a parade. They shouted at me, and I replied by telling them my name and asking them theirs, so that after a while, I was greeted equally with shouts of "Christine!" It was close enough. Some of the students from the schools also knew me and would greet me as "Teacher Christine."

Kubili Primary School lies in a valley between several main roads leading out to Kampala's suburbs. It was founded in the 1930s by the colonial government as a school for civil servants' children. The school was part of the UPE program. Kubili is a typical urban primary school comprising five main blocks housing one or two different grade levels each. The blocks are made of cement with corrugated iron roofs. Each has ample windows on each side, but the glass is gone in all classroom blocks, so only wire mesh separates them from the elements. The walls show the remnants of paint applied long ago and of hundreds of handmade posters that have been glued to the walls to decorate and educate over the years. The classrooms have wooden-bench desks with cubbyholes underneath for books. Three to four students usually sat at a desk, even in the upper classes. The desks were usually arranged so that up to eight students could work together in a group. A large table at the front of the room served as a desk for the two class teachers and others who came to teach their subjects. The classrooms lacked electricity, though it was available in the administrative block and the main hall. The kitchen at the back of the compound used logs to cook beans and *posho*, stiff maize-meal porridge, for the entire student body.

The river that separates the school from the barracks receives run-off and open sewage that flows down from the barracks in one direction and from the local trading center in the other. The trading center is very crowded, and open gutters run down the main road from the top of a hill where a dumpster is often overflowing. The sewage blocks the gutters at the bottom of the hill, right by the school gates, causing flooding (and potential disease) during heavy rains. Children were often sick as a result.

With all the children playing on it, very little grass remained on the compound, so that it was either dusty in the dry-season sun or muddy in the rainy season. Despite this, the teachers often brought their classes out with slashers and brooms to keep the compound neat. The environmental club got active in the second term and planted some saplings, which were quickly trampled by the other children. So they replanted and built protective barriers around them out of split wood and twisted polythene bags (*buveera*).

Several teachers live in houses on the upper edge of the compound, but many commute from the local area or live in the teachers' quarters located just inside the barracks off the main road. When I first arrived there, the teachers had no lounge and so either stayed in their classrooms or pulled a few desks and chairs out of the P7 block to sit under the two giant mango trees near the administration block. This was where I got to know a few of them and gained entry to their classes. There was a timetable, but no one was too particular about following it, so it was difficult to know what would be taught when I went to a particular classroom, even if I consulted the teacher ahead of time.

St. Michael's Primary School is on another main road running along the opposite side of the barracks. Its association with the Catholic Church gave it access to church financial resources. Its students were therefore slightly better off than those at Kubili. The recently refurbished school blocks were painted in the school colors, and the landscaping was strictly protected with low, barbed-wire fencing. There was an adjacent secondary school and a nearby hospital. The primary school took both day and boarding students, a few of whom came from neighboring countries like Kenya and Tanzania.

I lived at the other end of the local trading center, which comprised various restaurants and bottle stores, butcheries, and movie houses: run-down lean-to's where ultraviolent movies such as *Rambo* and martial arts films are shown on videotape, while a translator stands in the back, dubiously translating the show into vernacular Luganda. Tickets are typically one thousand shillings (sixty cents), and parents discourage or prohibit their children from going there because the movie houses are generally seen as central to the degradation of morals. Children, particularly boys, therefore clandestinely go every chance they get.

World Vision Gulu Children of War Rehabilitation Center

The children I met in Kampala schools were fulfilling a normative conception of child citizenship through their engagement with school. But what about children embroiled in war to a point where such "normal" childhood activities as schooling were frequently interrupted by insecurity? How did the involvement of children in armed conflict present a crisis of agency, threatening childhood and nationhood? In chapter 6, I describe how the dire situation for children in northern Uganda poses critical questions for the normative concepts of childhood expounded by international children's rights advocates.

Though President Yoweri Museveni established Uganda's first stable post-independence government in 1986, peripheral rebel groups have continued to threaten the country's fragile peace. The Lord's Resistance Army (LRA) is the most prevalent and enduring of these groups. The LRA is an outgrowth of years of post-independence civil war and ethnic discrimination in Uganda. Its charismatic leader, Joseph Kony, seeks to overthrow the current government and run the country according to the Ten Commandments. Ironically, the LRA's main tactic has been to abduct more than twenty thousand children from their own impoverished northern region, brutally disciplining them into soldiers, servants, or (in the case of many girls) sex partners. Children are then ordered to ambush their own communities to loot food, abduct more children, and terrorize people. If they refuse, they die. If they submit, they kill. Many thousands have died, and an entire generation that has never known peace remains in danger of annihilation.

Many children have managed to escape, however. After debriefing by the army, escaped LRA abductees are sent to the World Vision Gulu Children of War Rehabilitation Center and similar local nongovernmental organizations (NGOs) to receive medical treatment, psychological counseling, family tracing aid, and community reintegration skills. With the assistance of World Vision's gracious staff, I interviewed a number of LRA escapees and sat in on their group counseling sessions. I followed the progress of two children throughout their rehabilitation and reintegration, recording their life histories and talking with their guardians and counselors. This technique provided a good sense of the temporal aspects of the rehabilitation process as experienced by many ex-abductees. I also visited several of the area's protected camps, to see how the war has affected even children and families (especially single-mother households) who have not been abducted by the LRA but whose lives have been severely disrupted nonetheless by displacement, uncertain food supplies, and lack of education. Nearly two million Ugandans internally displaced by the war live in the camps, serviced (inadequately) by the World Food Programme and the United Nations High Commission for Refugees (UNHCR).

Despite incredible hardships and extreme marginalization, however, children in northern Uganda are learning to cope by harnessing international children's rights discourses to gain crucial entitlements and facilitate reintegration with their communities. Chapter 6 details the complexities of the situation that confronts northern Ugandan children each day.

National Music Festivals

Music and dance are cultural forms accessible to a broad range of Ugandans. National music festivals were created as a way to preserve (and even revive) cultural forms in which Ugandans feel pride. But the National Primary School Music, Dance, and Drama Festival has also become a means for spreading development messages through schools and communities, so that children may become the stewards of national unity and development.

Aside from being an energetic environment for fieldwork, the festival provided an excellent and detailed opportunity to examine children's active involvement in processes of cultural production. I extensively observed a school choir as they prepared for and competed in the national primary school music festival—a key event in the dissemination of national development messages through children's performances. Chapter 7 describes my observations of the formulation of different songs, dances, speeches, and plays relating to the theme of "The 1995 Constitution and National Development." I accompanied the students on trips to zonal, divisional, district, and national festivals, where I was able to witness other schools' entries in the festival. At the national festival, I interviewed children and choir trainers from all over the country on children, schooling, culture, and unity. I found that while children are recruited as messengers for the state's development agenda, they also creatively utilize the festival stage to launch cultural critiques that point out just how far they have to go to claim their rights as children.

Reflections on Fieldwork with Children

Anthropological work with children presents particular challenges to the ethnographer. When I decided to do an ethnography of childhood, many of my models were outside the field of anthropology. Though it seemed a ripe opportunity for that reason, it was also a lonely road. My experience has been that, as Hirschfeld states, anthropologists have neglected child-centered research because of " an impoverished view of cultural learning that overestimates the role adults play and underestimates the contribution that children make to cultural reproduction" (Hirschfeld 2002, 611). On the other hand, observing children's actions is the most direct way "to witness children learning what it is to be a child, in the social and political contexts they operate in" (Mayall 1999,16). But children do this against a backdrop of social messages telling them what it means to be children in their society, revealing tensions between ideals and realities, potentials and situated possibilities. For children, childhood is more than a concept; it is the social mode through which they experience the world, and thus more a practice than a state of being. How can we utilize this knowledge of various concepts of childhood to build a more useful tool for understanding the actual lived experiences of children and their relations to other aspects of society? More than a few child researchers have argued that ethnographic methods are especially appropriate for getting at these questions (Christensen and James 2000; Holloway and Valentine 2000; James 1993).

I have focused here on children's voices because I suspected that I might reduce the estranging effects of child studies by considering how children's lives share similarities and intersect with adult social worlds rather than where differences lie between adults and children. To achieve this, some researchers have advocated an approach from within children's peer culture (Berentzen 1989; James and Prout 1997), but this approach is often inadequate for linking children to the larger social structures that define the parameters of their childhood (Laerke 1998). The most important lesson most child ethnographers note is that we do not need to accomplish the impossible task of becoming children in order to move within their social circles. Though Clifford Geertz may argue that anthropologists "claim some unique form of psychological closeness, a sort of transcultural identification with their subjects" (Geertz 1983, 56), James argues that anthropologists, whether working with children or adults, do not necessarily have to view the world exactly as their informants do in order to identify with them (James 1993, 8). Concerning fieldwork with children, it has not been useful or productive for researchers to hark back to their own childhood memories during fieldwork. It is hard enough to be mindful of how our own histories and personalities affect our field-work without trying to apply the dimension of past experience to the field data (James 1993; Laerke 1998). Most important, both researchers and subjects must develop a transparent and mutually understood rela-tionship through "concrete experience and communicative interaction" (Fabian 1983). In other words, the self-reflexivity involved in doing field-work with children does not differ that much from the self-reflexivity involved in working with adults.

However, privileging children's voices proved methodologically chal-lenging when children themselves, following adult cues, often devalued their own outlooks and opinions. It was also challenging to get chil-dren to trust me and communicate openly. Ugandan children are not commonly encouraged to express themselves openly and emphatically to adults. Children commonly define adults as people with power over them, which points to the importance of becoming an atypical, less pow-erful adult within children's social groups (Corsaro and Molinari 2000, 180). Children in Uganda are taught, above all, to be obedient and sub-servient to adult authority through a deeply stratified social hierarchy, both in families and without, especially among the southern Bantu (Kil-bride and Kilbride 1990, 88–89). I wanted to follow Laerke's suggestion that in doing ethnographic work with children, one should try as much as possible to enter their social worlds (Laerke 1998, 5), but this proved more difficult than I initially thought, partly because Ugandan children found it so strange. I was initially met by bewildered looks and nervous whispers when I sat down with them in their classes and took notes in my exercise book. The second obstacle to entering children's social worlds was that their adult interlocutors would not accept it. When I was first introduced to the students of Kubili Primary School, the head-master instructed everyone to call me Teacher Kristen, thrusting me into a particular kind of relationship with the students that I would find very difficult to undo. Children were led to think that I would actually start teaching their classes on a regular basis, while my intention was to sit in on their classes as a student to learn what I could about their perspectives on the material being taught.

Teachers often inadvertently reinforced and maintained my adult sep-aration from the children on my behalf. Without intending to, the ways in which school staff and faculty extended their hospitality undermined my attempts to get the children to identify with me and open up. If I approached teachers to talk with them, they would often send children to get a chair or a snack for me, just as they would send a child on such errands for themselves. I would try to go to the tuck shop to buy snacks for myself so children would get to know me, but the vendors would also show respect for my age by shooing away all the children as I approached and insisting that I hop the line despite my mild protests. It probably also did not help that I gave them assignments as the teachers did; I asked them to write short essays for me on certain topics of interest to my research, such as identity formation and political consciousness (chapters 3 and 4). Though it was not ideal, it was a good starting point under the circumstances; this approach gave children an acceptable way to initiate interaction with me that did not upset their own established hierarchies.

Another thing that worked was simply to jump in and get involved with children wherever it was possible outside the gaze of adult supervision. I once joined a playground game of "Round," where girls drew four large circles in the dirt in a square pattern, something like a small baseball field with very large bases. The players had to run around the bases, while two girls with a makeshift ball (usually a bunch of old plastic bags densely wadded up together) tried to hit them below the neck with it. They counted their bases as they ran them, and whoever ran the most before being tagged by the ball was the winner. At first, all the girls (boys were off playing their own games, like soccer and kung fu) gathered around to see the *mzungu* play. It was quite a novelty, especially since I spent the first few minutes running the bases without knowing why. But eventually they taught me the game's goals and rules, they warmed up to my participation, and they were less shy about approaching me afterwards. William Corsaro posits that this occurs because an adult's incompetence, especially in something at which children are quite good, effectively levels the playing field between adult and child, helping children accept an adult like me not as a child, but as an adult who is different from most of those they know, in that I do not know everything. Foreign ethnographers often appear as less threatening or authoritative adults to young people because children see them as lacking certain social and cultural skills, basic cultural knowledge, or linguistic ability (Corsaro and Molinari 2000, 183). Indeed, anthropologists conducting research outside their native cultures are often seen as "childlike" by local people (Powdermaker 1966). Thus, in my case, children saw themselves as more socially adept than an adult, a feeling that brought them confidence and a rare sense of social control in an adult world.

Another issue that distanced me from the children was being white. Ugandans regard whiteness with a deference that I honestly found alternately humbling, disconcerting, and advantageous. Mainly on the basis of encounters with missionaries and aid workers, they tend to perceive individual white people—especially Americans—as friendly, rich, and generous. The first assumption facilitates relationships with people; the last two complicates them. Each week, children, teachers, or parents, some of whom I did not know at all, accosted me to ask whether I could assist them with school fees. Students often wrote me letters requesting sponsorship. Since I was a student myself, I had little ability to help others financially, and I did not want the possibility of financial help to be the motivation for my informants to volunteer their time. The children with whom I did become close did not directly ask me for money, but their friends thought they were benefiting greatly from my friendship and constructed elaborate rumors about me adopting them. When I did pay all my informants' school fees for one term, I asked them to keep it quiet lest it send a flood of letters and consultations.

I also had to be mindful of the gatekeepers who can control access to children and young people's social groups, mainly parents and teachers. Appearing to be socially inept as an adult may have its advantages with children, but it may also make the researcher more threatening to the adults around her, who may develop suspicions about the researcher's motives. Here is where transparency is particularly important, especially with a heightened sense of "stranger danger" around the world. Ugandan teachers and parents were always very gracious and welcoming toward me, but my presence tended to alter the social dynamics of the classroom or household significantly; teachers tended to choose lesson topics based on my known interests, sometimes teaching a lesson over again to the same class just for my benefit. Parents also tended to receive me as they would any honored guest, and this disrupted the regular flow of daily household life. Mr. and Mrs. Obonyo, the parents of Jill, one of my lifehistory children, would chat with me for hours in their sitting room, and, like most Ugandan parents, they thought it bad etiquette even to allow children in the sitting room when a guest was present, so it was very difficult for me to interact with parents and children together in their homes. Where children were allowed to stay, they had been taught to be silent, so their answers to questions were usually timid and truncated. For this reason, I often encouraged children to write instead. I did not change informants' actual language except where comprehension was jeopardized; these changes are indicated with brackets.

Ugandan children are taught to listen rather than to talk; to speak quietly and briefly in the presence of adults. Even so, schools are very loud places, and when I tried to take children to an empty room to talk with them, their voices were usually barely audible above the clamor of children playing outside (and trying to peek in the windows to steal a look at me, the white lady). They initially had trouble answering questions that required something besides a yes or no, so I often felt like I was asking leading questions to get information. Further, they often seemed to think that each question that I asked had a right answer. Getting children comfortable enough to share stories about themselves therefore took time, more with some than with others. As a result, many of the extended quotations in this book are actually composites constructed from multiple conversations with children. I found that through socializing with children on the terms by which they accepted me, I was gradually able to gain an understanding of which differences between adults and children (or individuals in general) made the most difference to the children around me. In short, I took my cues from them.

Organization of this Book

In this book, I emphasize the discursive construction of childhood and its consequences for children. I embrace a conceptual framework that focuses on the discursive categories that bind children to the nation, and on the political economy of childhood at local and global levels—always linked to a theory of children's agency. The first chapter presents a discursive analysis that sets up several major ethnographic arenas for the intersection of childhood and nationalist discourse. These include education, identity formation, and political consciousness, each discussed in its own chapter in part 1. Children's life histories in this part ground my theoretical considerations in ethnographic material as they contextualize national development, education, and identity discourses to show that they influence children in paradoxical ways that prevent them from claiming full citizenship. Part 2 provides detailed case studies for the arguments put forward in the introduction and part 1. They locate childhood and nationhood discourses in children's everyday experiences in order to underscore the contradictions children encounter when they attempt to actualize the ideals of those very discourses. A concluding epilogue provides an update for each of the children in the text as well as for Uganda as a whole. Their circumstances continue to illustrate how national political problems directly impinge on children's abilities to advance the ideals set forth in citizenship discourses. At the same time, as young people struggle to make their way toward development goals, they are necessarily reconfiguring children's and adults' "proper places" in society.

Life-History Narratives: The Children

One means for developing a child-centered approach to my research was to take the life histories of several children with whom I worked closely. These children became my guides into the larger issues of the political economy of Ugandan childhood. Relating their experiences not only gave them voices, but it revealed the rich and complex ways in which children exercise considerable agency in order to maneuver through incredible structural and personal obstacles. They are introduced throughout the book in relation to certain themes upon which their lives touch.

I start here by introducing Malik, whose life so far represents the experience of many contemporary Ugandan children. He is an orphan who has suffered severe disruption and abuses, but who takes it all in stride, relying on the generosity of relatives and benefactors to see him through, one day at a time. His story provides a sense of the structural challenges to children's agency in a developing African nation, as well as the personal resources that children marshal to meet these challenges.

Malik: Overcoming Adversity with the Aid of a Strong Agogo

Malik was one of the talented musicians I got to know during choir practice at St. Michael's. He played the drums, and he usually smiled his chip-toothed grin as he did so. Malik was a rough-and-tumble twelve-year-old boy whose knees and elbows were usually banged up. In fact, he and his friends Kizza and Emmanuel all had chipped front teeth, and when I asked how they each came about, I was met first with giggles, then with stories of football mishaps and rough-housing in the dorms. Malik's abundant smiles belied the fact that at twelve years old, he had already endured quite a few hardships, most at the hands of his own family members. His experience signifies the considerable shift in extended family responsibility brought on by AIDS and economic crises. Malik was a double orphan, a child who has lost both his parents. He was one of the increasing number of orphaned Ugandan children who was being raised by a grandparent. But I was to learn how his family had adjusted and was trying to make the best of what they had to work with, including kind people whom they could ask for help.

"My mother was the firstborn of her family," Malik explained. "She met my father while working at the airport. He was a Muganda Muslim and had twenty-four children, four by my mother. He had a number of co-wives who didn't get along." Having stayed with stepmothers for most of his early childhood, Malik had become convinced that it was not a good idea to have more than one wife. "Some wives cannot live together," he said, "because you can be there when they hate one another or from this one's home you sleep at another's home one time and that makes them annoyed. And when you buy food....One family you buy for them much food and when you go to another's family, you buy for them small food, that one also makes them annoyed."

As a child, Malik bore the brunt of his father's co-wives' hatred for his mother. The stepmother who often cared for him when his mother was away at work was abusive. "When I have made a small mistake she just gets my hands and beats them," he told me as he laid his hand flat on the table and showed how she would hit him across the knuckles with a piece of wood. He had faint scars across both hands. "They are not paining me now," he added. "They are becoming okay."

After his father died when Malik was nine years old, presumably of AIDS, his family refused to provide for his children.[18] Initially, his father's firstborn son was supposed to look after Malik, so he stayed with him for a while in Mubende, northwest of Kampala. He started school there and progressed quickly. "I was doing well in P1, [so] they told me, "Go to P2." When I was going to do the exams going to P1, they just told me go and do the exams of P2 and you go in P3." When the exam results were released, Malik had the third-highest overall score. He also learned to play the drums in Mubende and participated in most school functions as a musician. He enjoyed school in Mubende, but they sent him away to his mother's family when the stepbrother who was responsible for him also died. His uncle contacted Malik's mother's family and told them to take the children away and care for them themselves. By this time, his mother had become so ill that she could not care for her children.

His mother had come from western Uganda. They were Banyankole and spoke a different language from his father's people. His mother's family, resentful that they had to take care of the boy when it should have been the father's family's responsibility, were rather cruel to Malik. "They [were] telling me something when I could not understand. They say, 'That boy doesn't know Runyankole!'"

Malik changed hands among different relatives six times after his father died. His mother spent the little money she had on her own health care and on helping other relatives, so she left virtually nothing once she passed away, only ten months after the death of his father. But she had bought a plot of land for her mother before she died and told her that she should build a house for her children there. So in 2000, Malik came to live with his *agogo* (grandmother) in Najjanankumbi, a southern urban section of Kampala I had often heard described as "a den of thieves." Because the airport lay further down the road, cars were often ambushed and drivers robbed there. Malik concurred that there was a lot of crime, but he had done a good job of staying out of harm's way. He had two older siblings and a younger brother, and his grandmother provided for all four of them, plus her own two youngest sons.

Malik's grandmother knew it would be difficult for her to make ends meet, but she had heard that there was a teacher at St. Michael's named Mr. Kisakye who recruited musically talented children for his cultural dance troupe, the Folklore Ambassadors. They performed at weddings and other functions, and the money earned often went toward school fees. So they took Malik to see Mr. Kisakye, who thought him promising and decided to help him. Malik would be able to go to school, though it was several hours' walk to and from his grandmother's house. He was enrolled in P4 and enlisted by Mr. Kisakye for the Folklore Ambassadors. Mr. Kisakye was a bachelor and had a small room on the school compound that he often opened to members of his dance troupe after late rehearsals or before early performances, so that children like Malik did not have to make the long walk to and from their homes every day.

Though the dance troupe was fun and Malik was learning a lot, the money they made was not enough to cover every member's school fees, and Mr. Kisakye had understood that Malik's family was still expected to pay his fees. One of Malik's older half-sisters said she would take on the responsibility for a while, but she defaulted. Malik asked a few times to borrow my cell phone to call her, and even traipsed across town in search of her residence to ask for his fees, but to no avail. As a result, Malik was often sent home from school for weeks at a time until he could collect the fees, and his marks suffered as a result.

Mr. Kisakye and I were both very concerned about what was happening, so we went with Malik to his home and met with his family. Malik had warned me that his grandmother might ask us some tough questions; grandmothers and grandsons typically have special bonds cemented through joking relationships between alternate generations (Epstein 1978). "She is always teasing me," Malik admitted, but I could tell by how he spoke of his grandmother that he also knew that she loved him very much. Malik's grandmother was able to fill in a lot of the blanks for me and Mr. Kisakye, and we were both actually relieved to see that though the family's resources were severely stretched, they were very loving and were striving to care for Malik.

The day we were to go to Malik's house, we all met at St. Michael's, where Malik was limping because his leg had suddenly started to ache.

He showed me what looked like a small bite on his calf, and the tissue around it was swollen and tight. He said he did not think that anything had bitten him and that the sore had just come on by itself, but he could barely walk on that leg. In the taxi, we looked at it again, and though it looked like it needed medical attention, Malik assured us in his typically carefree and self-effacing manner that he was attending to it himself. Health care is one area where African children often exercise agency, through extensive knowledge of medicines and self-treatment practices (Geissler et al. 2001, 362).[19] Malik was used to attending to his own minor ailments.

It took us quite some time to get from St. Michael's to Najjanankumbi, even by taxi. "It is very far from St. Michael's!" Mr. Kisakye exclaimed incredulously as the kilometers rolled by. Only a minute or two from the main road, school would have been easier to get to if Malik had had money for transportation, but he rarely did. His house was one of several small, unpainted cement structures with a corrugated tin roof on a crowded compound with no wall or fence—just some shrubs to close it off. We followed Malik into the sitting room and were greeted by two young men and a spunky old woman in a customary *gomesi* dress. These were Malik's youngest, maternal uncles and his grandmother. A grandaunt, Malik's younger brother, and a housegirl were also living there at the time. They had cooked lunch, so they served us huge yellow chunks of boiled *matooke*, the staple plantain, with purple groundnut sauce and sodas.

The sitting room itself was a typical Ugandan scene, with a simple set of chairs and a couch, faux linoleum on the floor, and calendars printed for companies like Nice Pens and Brushes dating back to 1997 that adorned the smudged yellow walls. There was also a framed picture of Jesus entitled "The Prince of Peace" and a framed picture next to it of the *kabaka*, the king of the Baganda, at his coronation in 1993. A defunct clock with a dead battery and a picture of a young woman in a *gomesi* hung on the wall. This was Malik's mother. There was a small table in the opposite corner with an old portable stereo on it, covered by a doily. They had about a dozen *emikeeka*, colorful woven straw mats for sitting on, rolled up in the corner near the door. In the kitchen, they had a big table at which Malik, his younger brother Isaac, and his cousin Mary sat, eavesdropping on the adults' conversation—which they were warned not to interrupt.

Malik's grandmother was a lively lady: tough and hardworking. Her twenty-year-old son Alex came in and sat in the corner opposite me. His mother explained that he was doing a correspondence course in accounting from London and would soon be finished. Before Malik's mother died, she had asked him to look after her children like a father, and the young man said he intended to do just that as soon as he was employed.

Mr. Kisakye asked about the circumstances that had delayed Malik's fees, and his grandmother launched into the family history. She pulled out a bunch of photo albums to illustrate the people to whom she was referring. She showed us pictures of Malik's mother. We laughed at pictures of Malik as a baby because he looked like a bald old man with bright eyes. That was the one time Malik abruptly stuck his head in the room to see what we were looking at. He blushed and immediately retreated to the kitchen.

Malik's grandmother complained that she had received Malik and his siblings at a time when she was still trying to help her own two sons through school. She explained that Malik's mother was not "officially" married to his father because he had not paid brideprice for her. So Malik's father's family believed that he only had the name of his father but no other claim on them. The stepsister who was supposed to pay his fees provided for Malik initially for religious reasons; in the Muslim faith, his grandmother explained, "you get a few points with Allah for doing something to help an orphan." So his stepsister did not feel obliged to continue after she had paid for a short while, even though Malik is her half-brother. Malik's grandmother had a plot at her family's ancestral home in Mityana, which she farmed to help provide food and income for the household. She left workers there and occasionally went there herself to harvest and bring the crops to town. This was how she was providing for all of them. She proudly pointed out that the food she had served us was all grown on her farm.

Mr. Kisakye was satisfied with the information and suggested that now that he knew a little more, he would see about taking Malik's fees completely out of the dance troupe's profits. He might someday take Malik in, too, since it seemed that he lived too far from the school. His grandmother and brother seemed to react somewhat favorably to that. Malik had come into the sitting room to sit in the other chair, and I asked him what he thought of that. He was repressing a smile, but he said it would be okay with him. "All sides will try to bring him up as a man that this country would be happy to have," Mr. Kisakye said. Malik's grandmother and uncle agreed and thanked him profusely.

Malik's experiences share some significant similarities with many Ugandan and African children's lives, most notably orphanhood, particularly due to AIDS. Though intertribal and interfaith marriages are quite common these days, Malik's case illustrates some of the challenges that arise for the children of these unions, especially with extended family, once parents have passed on. Malik had trouble with language difference and securing financial and emotional support. Being in a polygamous family might at one time have been advantageous to children reared in a family compound (Kilbride and Kilbride 1990), but Malik pointed out how this family structure ended up with less resources to share in a cash economy. As a result, he suffered resentment and abuse from his mother's co-wives. In this instance, his grandmother had come to his rescue. Anthropologists have long noted the significance of alternate-generation relationships across cultures, in which children and their grandparents form special bonds. As I discuss in chapter 5, AIDS orphans are increasing grandparents' responsibilities when they are well past their economically productive prime. Yet living with their grandparents is proving to be a more stable experience for many children than living with other kin, who, like Malik's relatives, often reluctantly and only temporarily take them in. Many children in this situation carefully strategize ways to navigate these obstacles to growing up by utilizing their mobility through social and family networks and drawing on their own marketable talents— in Malik's case, music. Even so, a strong social network is crucial to gaining access to resources that will ensure survival.

Malik's leg was still painfully swollen as Mr. Kisakye and I made our exit from Malik's home, so I asked whether we could take Malik to a doctor to look at his leg. His uncle Alex assured me he would attend to it. Malik later told me that his uncle took it upon himself to lance the wound and drain pus from it. After that, it felt just fine, and Malik had barely a scab to show for it. He was back to playing soccer with his friends in the schoolyard the next day.

Malik's grandmother walked us out and showed us the dogs that Malik had rescued. They were two spunky, flea-bitten, yellow puppies he kept in a wire mesh and wood cage. Dogs are usually not so much pets as scavengers in Uganda, so I was surprised to see such well-fed dogs. "They are very fat!" I noted. His grandmother told us that Malik loved them so much that he would go to the restaurant across the street every evening to ask for scraps to feed them. As she "gave us a push" (accompanied us) to the road, she joked that I should take her to the United States. She had never been there, but she suspected life as a grandmother with several grandchildren to raise would be much easier there.

Despite all that he had endured, Malik was a playful and kind boy with a good heart. But he also had big dreams. He loved playing the drums and was anxious to learn to do many traditional dances as well. Since he had heard that, before he joined, the dance troupe had traveled to Italy for an international folk dance competition (and had won), he looked forward to developing his talents so that he too might use them to see the world. He already saw Mr. Kisakye as a father figure, so he was investing many of his hopes in this good Samaritan. But he also had great respect for his grandmother. She took good care of him, and she also made him laugh. He was glad that Mr. Kisakye and I had come to his house to meet her, because it had put her suspicion to rest. She had been teasing him a lot lately: "You are lying!" she would playfully accuse him. "You say you are going to choir practice, but I think you are really out getting into trouble after school. . . . And you don't really have a *mzungu* asking you questions, do you!?"

ONE

Global Rights Discourses, National Developments, and Local Childhoods

The last decade has seen nothing less than a revolution in the way in which we approach the challenge of responding to children and youth in Africa. That is the revolution in the rights of the child.

URBAN JONSSON, UNICEF REGIONAL DIRECTOR OF EASTERN AND SOUTHERN AFRICA

On the fortieth anniversary of Uganda's independence in 2002, *New Vision*, the national newspaper, printed the following editorial, accompanied by a picture of children studying under a tree in rural Uganda.

A YOUNG NATION

As independent Uganda turns 40 today, millions are reflecting on what has been and what could have been, and are also focusing on what can still be.

In the human life, 40 is a relatively mature age—independent from parental care, raising a family, educating children, and having the best things of life.

Many times, we expect our country to develop at the same rate as we individuals. We want the country to go through the cycle of life at the very same pace as our parents, our peers, our children. We also expect the country's progress to be smooth all the way.

These expectations are illusory. *Just like an individual's life is full of ups and downs—birthday parties, illness, qualification to the next class, bereavement, loss of job, promotion, marriage, quarrels with the neighbour—so too is the country's.*

But in this time, we have also recorded economic growth, empowered millions politically and socially, and *established ourselves as a real nation*. Relative to others like Egypt, Great Britain, China, or Brazil, whose histories and civilisations go back hundreds of years, we are still a young nation who can only hope that the ups outweigh the downs as we continue our growth through history. (*New Vision* 2002a; my emphasis)

Childhood and nationhood are inextricably linked by the analogy of development. The editorial suggests that the nation has a life cycle, in which Uganda is, compared to other nations, still a "child." Such anthropomorphizing of the nation is not unusual: Thomas Hylland Eriksen points out that, "like a person, the nation is endowed with a biography by its imaginers, and it is presumed to have gone through phases of self-development. Its past, like that of the individual, is being fashioned so as to make sense of the present and, like the ideal bourgeois individual, it is being symbolically represented as sovereign, integrated, and inhabited with a soul" (Eriksen 1997, 103). In Uganda, the soul of the nation was deeply bruised before it had a chance to develop. Ugandans' belief that early behavior is crucial to the later development of the person or the nation is signified in the Luganda proverb, *Akakyama amamera: tekagololekeka*: "'That which is bent at the outset of its growth is almost impossible to straighten at a later age'" (Kilbride and Kilbride 1990, 89). Uganda's political independence got off to a crooked start, and now Ugandans are turning to young people to straighten out a young nation. This chapter examines how, through international development discourse, the Ugandan government has come to subscribe to the idea that children's welfare is crucial to the growth of the nation as well as the security of the state.

If increasing people's capacity to make choices about their own lives and creating choices for individuals constitute development (Sen 1999), then rights protection is important in assuring *national* growth and development as much as personal growth and development. Because of its metaphorical connection to national growth, the discourse of children's rights has become a crucial aspect of the construction of the child citizen. The notion of childhood in many countries is thus being reconceptualized in relation to the nation in order to accommodate development goals. In turn, local definitions of children and childhood are being transformed by the influence of international organizations and their guiding philosophies about the "universal" child, but childhood is also a culturally specific idea. Though local definitions may be accepted for the purpose of facilitating national development, it is important to understand how these global discourses of children's rights translate into local praxis.

We can easily view the language of "rights" as a global discourse imposed by those with more power and resources. International development organizations sometimes presume that when the traits attributed to the "universal child," which are typically informed by Western values, are absorbed by local value systems in developing countries, they free children from the negative constraints of their own traditional cultures, often seen as negative and dichotomously "antimodern." While many of the tenets of ideal childhood propounded by organizations such as UNICEF do help raise the role of children in Ugandan society, they do not always neatly translate across the social and cultural landscape in ways that foster development goals. In some respects, universalized notions of children's rights set children apart from local society where they might otherwise be integrated in vital ways—in the labor force, for example. Thus, because of the ways in which the language and practice of children's rights has spread from Western ideology to public policy in developing countries like Uganda, the emergent trope of "the ideal child" comes to embody contradictions that prevent children from becoming fully functional in local praxis. This fact challenges the common motto, "Develop the child; develop the nation."

Despite how they conflict with local culture, international children's rights discourses have so permeated Uganda that even children—often more than their parents and guardians—emphasize attaining their rights as essential to full citizenship. Further, Ugandan children doubtless represent the experiences of children in other developing countries. This chapter maps the way this powerful influence in Uganda has affected local discourses of childhood and national development, as well as the lived experiences of children themselves.

In my fieldwork, I met many children who were striving to embody social ideals not only for personal but for national gain. Sumayiya is a determined child who demonstrates how far some children will go in order to claim—and enact—their rights.

Sumayiya: Adversity and Fortitude

Having been orphaned at an early age, Sumayiya at thirteen had already confronted serious challenges to her rights. Her desire for education motivated her to make tough choices and to take her future into her own hands by escaping abuse and claiming her right to education. The global rights discourse provided Sumayiya with a language in which to articulate her desire for education and to defend the difficult actions she took in her own best interests.

I first met Sumayiya as a member of the choir at St. Michael's Primary School. She was a bit bigger than most of the other girls in fifth grade: bright and energetic, yet always neat and polite. She was not at all shy about coming to talk to me, whether it was about children's issues or television shows, and we became good friends. When I suggested coming to visit her in the following term to hear more about her life, she was very excited.

Upon my return, I quickly discovered the reason for her eagerness. We sat in the school's tiny library, and I started by asking her to share some basic information, such as when she was born and what her family was like. She eyed the librarian cautiously, and once he left the room, her demeanor grew solemn. "I haven't revealed the true story to anyone at the school," she whispered, "but I feel I can tell you about it." She then launched into a detailed and unexpectedly bold story about her life.

Sumayiya was born in 1987. She was the fourth child and the first girl in her family. Her parents divorced when she was two, and her father took her to live with him. He was not a rich man, but he was the head of a Baganda clan. He occasionally worked as an adviser for the *kabaka* (king). When Sumayiya was about six years old, her father died under suspicious circumstances. She believes that *juju*, or witchcraft, was involved "because sometimes when he was sick, he was crying that something was crushing him. But even if you touched him, he would whine, 'I am not feeling anything.' They took him in hospital, but they could say nothing [about his condition]. So they brought him back to the village, and he stayed there." She had heard speculation that he died of AIDS, but because the hospital never diagnosed him, she was not sure what to believe. She herself was shocked at first because she did not think she could lose a parent when she was that young. "My mama came and took me away from him just before he died. So sometimes when I hear that he died, I say, 'I can't believe it' because I didn't see him." Since her father had been paying her school fees, Sumayiya stopped schooling shortly after he died. Her mother did not work regularly, relying instead on boyfriends for support. After her father's death, Sumayiya's mother had two more children, each by different men.

One day, Sumayiya's paternal uncle came for her. As is customary, he had promised his brother before he died that he would look after his brother's children, so he wanted to take Sumayiya away. Her mother did not want to give Sumayiya up to her ex-husband's brother, so she ran away with Sumayiya and the younger children to her home village in Rukungiri, in far western Uganda.[1] Sumayiya believes she spent about a month there, but it may have been longer. "We were all just sitting, not going to school," she recalled.

Her mother also kept her out of school when she moved back to Kampala and settled in Katwe, a poor and crowded enclave of metalworkers on the south side of town. Though her mother's new lover had a job at the bus park, he would not pay Sumayiya's school fees and would not allow her mother to work for them. He was also abusive to the children.

While she was not able to go to school, Sumayiya would do housework, listen to music, watch television, and try to read some books to keep up with other children who were still being educated. Mindful of her growing disadvantage, however, she wanted to return to school. "In Uganda, it is too difficult to have a good life if one is not educated," she explained. Her older brother did not finish school, and he was "just working in the taxi park." She believed that going to school would increase her chances to do something more with her own life.

When she was eleven, Sumayiya heard that her uncle would be willing to send her to school. Five years after her father's death, she decided to run away from her mother to find her uncle and go back to school. When her mother left for the market one day, Sumayiya packed her clothes and left a note. "I said, 'Mum, I never wanted to leave you, but I wanted to study. Your husband, he was so bad to me.'" She walked to her grandparents' home in Kabowa, where her uncle eventually came for her.

Sumayiya went to stay with her aunt and uncle in another part of the city near St. Michael's. Her uncle worked as an adviser to the *kabaka*, and her Aunt Mary was a doctor at the local hospital who had traveled to various countries for AIDS conferences and workshops. Since they were relatively well off, they housed several relatives' children, aside from their own. Sumayiya shared a room with four of her female cousins.

Though it is fairly common for children not to live with their biological parents in Uganda, Sumayiya worried about bearing the stigma of being an orphan or a runaway. When she came to live with her aunt and uncle, she immediately started calling them "Mummy and Daddy." Mary said she was actually impressed at how quickly Sumayiya adjusted to the family. Sumayiya was grateful to her aunt and uncle, but despite her quick adjustment, she admitted to me that she still felt like an outsider. She observed that sometimes her aunt and uncle did not provide the same things for her that they did for her cousin Jackie, who went to an expensive private school across town. Sometimes, Jackie treated her badly; she was threatened by Sumayiya's presence in the house, and it hurt her feelings. "She likes to quarrel too much," Sumayiya sighed. Jackie was always bossing her around, yet she had no regular chores at home. "I think she behaves this way because she goes to a fancier school. She is a biological child to our parents, so she thinks she is better than others." This subservient position as a more distant relative often silenced Sumayiya. When some cousins came to visit one Sunday, Jackie came in several times while Sumayiya was sitting quietly on her bed and yelled at her to start fixing food. Sumayiya finally told her that she did not appreciate her behavior, but Jackie threatened to report her to their parents. "I usually just stay quiet when Jackie quarrels, but I feel bad all the same." It strained Sumayiya to the point where she preferred to stay at school for as long as she could before going home. She tried to keep a low profile rather than stir things up. Her basic needs were fulfilled, though: school fees, school supplies, shelter, clothing, and food. Her "mother" especially responded when she needed things. "My mum is very nice. She even gives me money for snacks at school," she once told me proudly; she got enough money to share snacks with her friends, which made her very popular. More important, it made her feel more like a "normal" child.

Sumayiya came to St. Michael's in 2000, when she was twelve. She sat for an interview, and they told her to go back to third grade, which she had already completed before she stopped schooling. Her uncle argued that they should let her try fourth grade and just give her a little help to catch up. They let her reenter in fourth grade, and she ended up being eleventh out of eighty-eight students that year. Even with the years she had missed, she was not the oldest in her new class. By the time I met her, she was steadily improving in fifth grade, and she was positive that she would continue to improve with hard work and coaching.

I was surprised by this modest and gracious girl's assertiveness, and I commented on it once she had finished her story. "It was hard to leave my mother," Sumayiya responded, "but I am glad that I did so that I can go to school. I made the best decision for myself." Her mother had not come to find her, and she had not talked to her since she left home. She was not even sure where her mother lived anymore. All her friends at St. Michael's thought that her aunt and uncle were her real father and mother. "Even the teachers and some relatives who come at home, they think that they are my real mother and father. And I can't tell anyone because if I say it now, they will want to take sides." Sometimes she found children who had similar stories, and she confided in them, but she was cautious and slow to make friends because of her past; she did not trust people at school not to gossip. I assured her I would keep her secret from them.

Sumayiya's desire for education when she ran away was based more on her knowledge of the social consequences of remaining uneducated than on a clear understanding of global children's rights. She never specifically mentioned her rights as a major motivator for her bold actions, but they certainly provided justification as she learned more about them through social studies classes and choir performances. She became more comfortable with her own decisions and gained confidence that she had done the right thing. Education was the right she valued above all, and being back in school made her feel more like she belonged. She was very proud that she was a student again because she saw education as the key to a good life. "When I finish school, I want to work in an office or travel outside the country," she said. "I would like to be a lawyer, or maybe a flight attendant." According to Sumayiya, the risks she had taken to make this possible had paid off because she was "now living as children should be."

The Global Influence of Children's Rights Discourse

Stories like Sumayiya's encourage consideration of the ways international rights discourses influence national development campaigns to reach children like Sumayiya, and how children translate those messages into social practice. Many of the current notions of children's rights circulating most publicly in Uganda filter through UNICEF. The organization has had a long history of promoting consideration of children as an integral part of national development schemes throughout Africa and the developing world, offering assistance to governments willing to consider children as major factors in human resource development in order to eradicate poverty. However, Maggie Black contextualizes this by stating that "at a strategic level, the new enthusiasm for 'aid' was a reaction to the arrival of many newly independent countries—especially in Africa— onto the world stage and fear in the West of their assimilation into the Soviet camp" (Black 1996, 9–10).

At the UNICEF office in Kampala, a large plaque with the organization's mission statement hangs on the wall. One UNICEF goal is "to establish children's rights as enduring ethical principles and international standards of behavior towards children." The next part of the mission statement says "UNICEF insists that the survival, protection and development of children are universal development imperatives that are integral to human progress."[2] This explained much of what I had been hearing and seeing in the media pertaining to children around Uganda. The complete mission statement reads as follows:

UNICEF is mandated by the United Nations General Assembly to advocate for the protection of children's rights, to help meet their basic needs and to expand their opportunities to reach their full potential.

UNICEF is guided by the Convention on the Rights of the Child and strives to establish children's rights as enduring ethical principles and international standards of behaviour towards children.

UNICEF insists that the survival, protection and development of children are universal development imperatives that are integral to human progress.

UNICEF mobilizes political will and material resources to help countries, particularly developing countries, ensure a "first call for children" and to build their capacity to form appropriate policies and deliver services for children and their families.

UNICEF is committed to ensuring special protection for the most disadvantaged children—victims of war, disasters, extreme poverty, all forms of violence and exploitation and those with disabilities.

UNICEF responds in emergencies to protect the rights of children. In coordination with United Nations partners and humanitarian agencies, UNICEF makes its unique facilities for rapid response available to its partners to relieve the suffering of children and those who provide their care.

UNICEF is non-partisan, and its cooperation is free of discrimination. In everything it does, the most disadvantaged children and the countries in greatest need have priority.

UNICEF aims, through its country programmes, to promote the equal rights of women and girls and to support their full participation in the political, social and economic development of their communities.

UNICEF works with all its partners towards the attainment of the sustainable human development goals adopted by the world community and the realization of the vision of peace and social progress enshrined in the Charter of the United Nations.

Ugandan Priorities

In the context of international development goals, UNICEF has been very successful in Uganda at mobilizing political will on behalf of children (see fig. 2). Yet much of it was still limited to rhetoric in 2000. To turn rhetoric into action, UNICEF launched the new Global Movement for Children campaign. It was designed to raise awareness and hold nations accountable for the pledges they had made to protect children when they signed the Convention on the Rights of the Child (CRC). A shiny poster hung in the UNICEF lobby with a box of pledge cards.

2   A children's rights billboard in downtown Kampala. Photo by the author ca. 2000.

The card stated, "Where I live, the three most important issues are... "
Voters chose three of the ten items listed as top priorities:

1. Include all children.
2. Put children first.
3. Care for every child.
4. Fight HIV/AIDS.
5. Stop child abuse.
6. Listen to every child.
7. Educate every child.
8. Protect children from war.
9. Protect the environment for children.
10. Fight poverty by investing in children.

The voter was asked to sign below the following statement: "I believe that all children should be free and should grow up in a healthy, peaceful, and dignified environment." How could one disagree with such a statement, I wondered? The campaign asked people to pledge their ideological commitment, but UNICEF needed to give it salience. They first went to the president and first lady with the voter-card campaign. Their framed voter cards hung on the wall next to the campaign poster, highlighting the children's issues they found most pressing. They voted for basic education for all children, protection of children from war, and the elimination of poverty and HIV/AIDS. They both wrote brief explanations of their reasons for choosing those particular issues as the most urgent in relation to Ugandan children. In the comments section, President Museveni wrote, "By educating every child, we are investing in our children. By investing in children, we are empowering our people. By empowering our people, we shall fight and eradicate HIV/AIDS and Poverty."

First Lady Janet Museveni chose "Put children first," "Educate every child," and "Protect children from war" as her highest priorities. She commented, "By putting children first in everything we do, we shall provide them with quality education. By protecting children from war, we shall ensure a world fit and safe for children."

The comments of the president and first lady on the Global Movement for Children pledge form clearly linked putting children first with rapid development of the country, in line with the UNICEF mission statement. Their concerns, not surprisingly, represented the policies of the governing National Resistance Movement (NRM) in Uganda: they both chose number seven, "Educate every child." Considering the Museveni administration's policy of Universal Primary Education (UPE), they had already taken a step toward achieving that item, so they could claim it as a triumph in the Global Movement's progressive agenda. As Sumayiya's story shows, however, this priority was also common among the general population, including children themselves, who were working to secure it.

A View from UNICEF

Despite the Global Movement for Children's solicitation of pledges, the local UNICEF office carefully separates its mission from those of the Ugandan people and government to avoid accusations of cultural imperialism. To understand how and why it operated this way, I talked to Mads Oyen, the UNICEF external relations officer, about the organization's role in Uganda and how it was shaping concepts of childhood. As a key representative of the organization, Oyen provided a clearer picture of UNICEF Uganda's operating philosophies and perceived obstacles.

A lanky, young, Scandinavian man, Oyen led me to his office, which offered a partial view of the town past the lush tropical vegetation swaying in the breeze. I asked him how UNICEF views childhood in its mandate. He said unapologetically, "The CRC is absolutely a universal model of childhood, deriving from the Universal Declaration of Human Rights. UNICEF is the government partner in implementing the CRC, to which

Uganda is a signatory." UNICEF supports the government in that effort, using technical advice and funding to help create internal programs at the district level.

Oyen explained that UNICEF operates within Uganda primarily from a CRC perspective rather than dealing with cultural specificities. This is partly because UNICEF's mandate changed during its history from its original mission, which was to help children who were medically disadvantaged by World War II. Their purpose became rather unclear after wartime emergency needs were met, but the organization felt a need to perpetuate itself by diversifying its response to children's needs. UNICEF therefore reformulated its approach from charity-based to rights-based work.

Oyen reasoned that this approach, which claims that children's rights are primary rather than secondary to other development concerns, is better for achieving certain victories over structural violence in society. For instance, he had just finished a child-soldier rehabilitation program for about 170 teenage boys who had been airlifted out of the fighting in the neighboring Democratic Republic of Congo. Oyen described the kinds of opposition he encountered while trying to demobilize soldiers under eighteen years of age. Ugandans thought that UNICEF workers were naive to consider these soldiers, aged fourteen to eighteen, children, because we assume that children are innocent. Oyen recalled, "'How can you call these innocent children!?' they would say to me. Rather than get into debates about cultural relativism with people, I just point out that I'm only helping enforce what their government committed themselves to."

UNICEF remains righteous in its mission to promote universal ideals, and is pleased by the Ugandan government's compliance. "The Uganda government [has] one of the most progressive constitutions in Africa," Oyen pointed out. "The problem is not on that level; the problem is, 'Does it filter through?' And my answer is yes it does, but it takes time to reach everywhere." He cited daily violations of children's rights that happen right outside his window, such as corporal punishment in schools and the existence of street children. "The main problem is poverty, but there is also attitude. The primary duty there is not UNICEF's; it is not the government's; it is the parents. . . . That has to filter through to the general population, and there has to be a change of attitude."

"The Constitution is in compliance with all the Conventions," he continued, "but the law system is not. Uganda's laws are a mess!" He believed that Parliament was not passing and changing the right laws, and that the police did not follow the law. Oyen cited the example of child delinquents being arrested; children are not supposed to be put in prison, "but people want that: the popular concept [is] that if you have a problem with children, you put them in prison when they are young, and that will teach them a lesson. But that is illegal. If that is the intention, you should not use [imprisonment] as intentional punishment." Yet it is regularly used for that purpose in Ugandan police stations. "The Constitution does not evolve from that [local] moral framework."

The members of the Constitutional Assembly were an educated elite, many of whom came out of exile to write it. So though it was supposedly made "by the people, for the people," it does not necessarily reflect the moral framework of the majority of Ugandans, some of whom would be outraged to know that it includes provisions that go against traditional cultural norms such as the settlement of disputes by patriarchal privilege. "The duties and obligations are clear," insisted Oyen. "How exactly that will be achieved—how those rights will be realized—is *not* clear at the moment." The social factors responsible for the failure to implement children's rights are numerous and daunting, but Oyen was aware that the international development industry bore some of the blame for the situation. "You can blame the government, but at the moment, Ugandans are very frustrated at a higher level because they feel that they have done all the things the World Bank and other lending institutions told them to do." Yet the economy has not improved as much as expected. Even though Uganda qualified for debt relief thanks to the UN Millennium Development Goals of 2000, donor dependence is only increasing, and donor support to the budget exceeded the 51-percent aim to account for more than it should.

Oyen believes that development programs fail "because the World Bank economists assume a Western cultural economic model that isn't always viable in developing countries." It apparently had not occurred to him, however, that applying universal principles of childhood could also be problematic on the same grounds. As long as UNICEF continues to operate on the assumption that declarations meant to protect children's interests are universally applicable, they eschew local economic and social realities in favor of hegemonic ideology. Where international actions have not been culturally sensitive and have ignored factors that adversely affect children's welfare, they have failed in their ultimate goal. For instance, Western social programs incorporate family models based on an estimated two children, though the ideal family size in East Africa is about four, and actual family size reaches eight or more (Kilbride 2000, 147). When a two-child model is applied to African development schemes, it leads to a perpetual shortfall of development goals and only increases personal poverty and national indebtedness.

A Commitment to Rights for International Legitimacy

If the average Ugandan is slow to embrace international children's rights, the president and the Constitutional Assembly have demonstrated their definitive commitment to them. UNICEF Uganda writes, "In the Convention on the Rights of the Child we have the framework against which we can assess legislation, policies and resource allocations to ensure they are child-friendly" (Evans 2001, 63). Oyen claims that one of the motivations for such support is raising Uganda's image as a "normal country" among other progressive nations. His theory is backed by Alex de Waal, who recognizes this trend throughout Africa. "African states rushed to sign and ratify the CRC—Ghana was the first country in the world to do so, and more than half of the early signatories were African—but it took more than ten years for just fifteen African states to accede to the African Charter, even though its provisions are little different" (de Waal and Argenti 2002, 4). De Waal suggests that perhaps African governments, more concerned with their global than continental reputations, may have signed the CRC largely as a symbolic gesture to achieve status or access to funds, without expressly intending to deliver on their commitments. Uganda, however, seems to be an atypical case, in which government is genuinely trying to address the interweaving of rights with goals and strategies synonymous with national development aims and indicators— education and health care, for example (de Waal and Argenti 2002, 5).

Identifying childhood as a crucial moment for participation in Uganda's national development did not come automatically to Museveni's government. Indeed, Museveni has recently written,

The government of Uganda has been influenced by the language of the Global Movement, with the new emphasis on the basic rights of all children rather than their needs. . . . Investing in our children today provides us with a practical way of addressing some of the core concerns and problems of our times. Children's rights must be seen as being the cutting edge of human rights. Ensuring they are respected would do more to solve society's long-term problems and to prevent crises and conflicts arising than anything else we could possibly try to do. (quoted in Evans 2001, 8)

That belief is now firmly ensconced in various state apparatuses as well as in state ideology. It started early in Museveni's administration with the Ugandan National Programme of Action for Children (UNPAC) to identify the needs of young people. Its greatest achievement to date has been the drafting and promulgation of the 1996 Children's Statute, "the essential legal framework for dealing with the concerns and rights of children" (Evans 2001, 12). The Children's Statute serves to clarify the duties and obligations of the state to children, which include providing support to children in armed conflict, the implementation of Universal Primary Education, and—perhaps the most difficult to enforce effectively— paying greater attention to children's voices.

Local Concepts of Childhood

UNICEF's ten-year Uganda program report says of the 1996 Children's Statute, "Districts were responsible for translating the national goals that were in turn derived from the global goals" (Evans 2001, 12), suggesting a neat translation. They started by taking a census to get accurate break- downs of age, including "youths aged 14 to 18 who had not previously been thought of as children" (21). The sudden shift in designations of who children are signifies international influence; the CRC declares that children are any people under the age of eighteen. While these discrep- ancies point to the arbitrariness of legal categorizations of young people, they are also much more rigid than local definitions of children. Many Africans continue to reject legal definitions of children because of so- cial factors that make the definition locally situational, such as labor and marriage. For example, "girls would usually be married shortly after achieving sexual maturity, and consolidate that adult status when they became mothers, while boys would achieve 'adult' status by degrees, through initiation, eligibility to fight, marriage, acquisition of land, and elevation to the position of elder" (de Waal and Argenti 2002, 14). In Uganda, status typically increases gradually with age and varies accord- ing to achievement of certain milestones, including having children one- self; hence a legally fixed age of majority is both arbitrary and rigid in comparison.

The language of achievement is instructive here: in Africa, the social status of adults is *achieved*, much more so than in Western culture, where the age of majority is reinforced by law. When the Women's Commis- sion on Refugee Women and Children (WCRWC) interviewed children in northern Uganda about their own definitions of these categories, their ambivalence showed awareness of both legal definitions and cultural ob- servances of age-based identity; they told the commission that adoles- cents were people aged 10–18, but that girls become women once they began to menstruate or got married. They considered youth to be people aged 15–30, their main difference from adolescents being that they were sexually active.[3] For these children, the most striking distinction between child and adult had not to do with turning eighteen, but with getting married. Marriage (and having children) makes an adult. Yet many people in their area were getting married younger, especially girls in camps for internally displaced persons, who were often forced to marry soldiers or others with resources to both unburden and bring wealth to their own resource-strapped families. Under international scrutiny, traditional notions of social responsibility become antithetical to children's rights, while at the same time, austere economic conditions demand "adult" responsibility of children, such as their participation in commercial activity for the survival of the household. Postcolonial economic decline only entrenches persistent African cultural notions that children are essential family resources, not individuals endowed with rights and freedoms independent of family and community. Such local factors create pressure to lower the age of majority to sixteen (Uganda Child Rights NGO Network 1997, 5).

There is also the issue of age-based authority: when children's rights are defined and promoted by the state, they often meet resistance from older generations fearful of having elder authority overturned. Over a bowl of steaming *matooke* at her home one day, Malik's grandmother told me how she felt that children's rights were destructive of adult-child relations generally. Her grandchildren all sat quietly eavesdropping in the other room and, appropriately, did not interrupt. "The freedoms that children have nowadays aren't good because the children are becoming just like adults," she complained. She said that teachers are partly to blame because they have become timid about disciplining children in schools, fearing that police will intervene.[4] "My neighbors appreciate the fact that I am raising my children strictly," she boasted. "Other children are always running around doing immoral things like going to discos."

Further, many Ugandans believe that UNICEF interprets greater responsibility for children negatively: children cannot be children when they are caretakers, cattle tenders, or water carriers, particularly if these activities are seen to interfere with education, health, or mental development.[5] Yet these tasks help children learn to be nurturing and responsible toward their communities, a hallmark of achieved personhood in African societies (Whiting and Whiting 1975, 103). Contrary to Western opinions, the introduction of children's rights and laws promulgated in "the best interest of the child" threaten "the survival of the old safeguards intended to prevent the abuse of children" in local cultures (Rwezaura 1998, 253). For example, the Kilbrides' research has shown that in Kenya, discouragement of polygyny has actually lessened children's overall welfare. Polygyny has not gone away; it has only become informal and clandestine in response to religious sanction and "modern" law. Adultery relieves fathers of responsibilities toward their children, overburdening mothers while still limiting their means of income through gendered labor discrimination (Kilbride 2000, 147). Reinstatement of traditionally sanctioned but socially reinvented polygyny might therefore better serve children's needs, but it goes against hegemonic global gender sensitivities.

Navigating the Cultural Contradictions: Children as "Persons"

Mixed messages of powerful possibilities and cultural deference form a dichotomy on the spectrum of public discourse about appropriate childhoods and legitimate nations, which both children and the Ugandan state are trying to navigate successfully. On a macro-structural level, developing countries like Uganda are commonly infantilized by policies of international assistance. Reputation is not the least of things at stake; monetary assistance rides on a government's ability to jump through the ideological hoops set out by the World Bank, the International Monetary Fund, various United Nations organizations, and donor countries— hoops set out in developing countries' "best interests." This trend has been well-documented in development literature (Cooper 1997; Fairhead 2000; Ferguson 1994; Long and Arce 2000; Pigg 1992). However, its actual effect on children's lives has not been adequately scrutinized by policymakers and influential international organizations like UNICEF (Boyden 1997; Kilbride 2000).

Local activists are working to reconcile the ideology of children's rights with practice by educating children and the public at large, but this lack of compatibility creates a structural vulnerability where an inherent one is presumed. As Lansdown puts it, "There is a tendency to rely too heavily on a presumption of children's biological and psychological vulnerability in developing our law, policy and practice, and insufficient focus on the extent [to] which their lack of civil status creates that vulnerability" (Lansdown 1999, 35). While a stronger children's rights discourse may prevent adults from falling back on culture to justify acts of abuse or neglect, the law's portrayal of children as developmentally unable to protect themselves puts the power of protection in the hands of the very people from whom the law says children need protection: adults.

Cultural conflicts around rights talk are nothing new: during the drafting of the Convention on the Rights of the Child, members of many developing nations complained that the definition of *child* was too narrowly delineated according to Western standards that did not aptly categorize children in their own countries. Many developing countries did not even participate in drafting the CRC because of the dominance of Western values in determining normative childhood, and partly because state intervention is seen as threatening to family sovereignty (Boyden 1997, 204). Traditional family customs that involved children, such as communal harvesting, became a potential violation of children's rights under the drafted UN charter (Comaroff and Comaroff 1987). In response, the Organization for African Unity (OAU) adopted its own African Charter on the Rights and Welfare of the Children to reflect African values in its construction of children's rights and obligations to society. The OAU's charter emphasizes responsibility and community belonging.

On the streets of Kampala, "development speak" is ubiquitous, mirroring the extent of development discourses' influence in Uganda. Many nongovernmental organizations (NGOs) operating in Uganda reinforce and perpetuate UNICEF's convictions that raising the status of children in society will raise national development levels more generally. In the process, the figure of the child becomes central to national development rhetoric. This notion may be compatible with local understandings of the roles of children in the community. Hansen and Twaddle point out that "from the local point of view ... development is a continuous and creative interaction between the universalist, the individualist, and the familial, e.g., developing a family through having children" (Hansen and Twaddle 1998, 232). Further, persons and families are subsumed in the larger group identity. The Kilbrides explain that among the Baganda, "The collectivity: family, clan, lineage, or ethnic group, takes precedence over the individual. The ideal typical person is one who is firmly rooted in the group with a commensurate orientation to social responsibilities. The parent, therefore, literally has children for the social group. Children are raised as social persons who will be properly oriented to the group, its ancestors, and the needs of their own parents" (Kilbride and Kilbride 1990, 84–85).

Geertz would call these children "consociates" who grow into "successors" (Geertz 1973, 367). Yet the sense of children as individuals, or persons with social agency, is less commensurate with development goals than the child as object of community growth. In her ethnography of the Taita of Kenya, Grace Harris notes that "a child was treated socially and religiously as an extension of the parents' social personhood" (Harris 1978, 79). If we agree with Harris that we should separate often-conflated theoretical concepts of "individual as member of the human kind, self as locus of experience, and person as agent-in-society" (Harris 1989, 599), then the kinds of persons that children are in contemporary Uganda becomes more clouded and complex as global rights discourses, to which Ugandans increasingly subscribe in order to spur national development, encounter local notions of children as persons. As Susan Reynolds and Michael A. Whyte point out in their work with the Bunyole, "In one sense individual achievement is consonant with family growth and prosperity. In another sense, the amity of kinship, or the 'economy of affection,' is antithetical to individual achievement" (Reynolds and Whyte 1998, 237). For example, whenever young people find gainful employment, they are expected to help members of both their nuclear and extended families financially to such an extent that they themselves are often left with no money. This appears to be one way of both mediating and perpetuating the contradictions between individual and communal obligation.

Global rights discourse constructs children as sovereign individuals (itself problematic in many African cultures where community takes precedence over individuals) and not as persons, while African cultures tend to see children as "potential" persons, possessing limited competencies that gradually increase throughout the life cycle, with the ultimate goal of achieving full personhood (Morris 1994). Again, this cultural fact might seem to make children ideal stewards of development. But the process by which this is accomplished also follows strict moral codes that hold children accountable to the community. This is exemplified by the local concept of *mpisa*, a code of conduct that applies specifically to children: "*Mpisa* [custom, habit, conduct] includes such things as being obedient to authority figures; not interfering in adult conversation; not eating while walking on the road; greeting people properly; and many other social expectations. The content of *mpisa* constitutes a code of social etiquette on how to relate to other people. Specifically, having *mpisa* requires one to become socially involved with others in the proper way" (Kilbride and Kilbride 1990, 89).

In some ways, *mpisa* is effectively co-opted by development messages as a cultural device through which to encourage development; if local cultural conceptions continue to hold that children are, at least potentially, full social persons, then they have capacities for action that are authored by cultural norms such as *mpisa*, to which, according to the freedoms granted by their rights, they must choose to conform. *Mpisa* thus exemplifies the complex interrelationship between children as persons and children as individuals within a larger community.

In sum, through the interpellation of global children's rights discourses with local notions of child personhood, Ugandan children are becoming persons more and more central to the society's social, material, and moral development, not as mere objects of parental obligations to community, but as particular kinds of social (and socializing) agents in their own right. This process is such a contested negotiation, however, that to become the ideal child *citizen* of the state requires very different competencies that those of traditional social norms of African child personhood. Subsequent chapters examine these expectations—and children's innovative negotiations of them—in more detail.

Translation: A Key Cultural Issue

Part of the local negative interpretation of children's rights can be explained as a literal problem of translation. The development industry's formalized language lacks the situated knowledge that would make it semantically meaningful when grounded in the diverse local contexts of daily life (Arce 2000, 44). In the absence of an internal development language, local people work to give terms like *rights* their own productive, locally applicable content and meaning. When I visited the Uganda Child Rights NGO Network (UCRNN) office in a bustling Kampala suburb one rainy day, I found them struggling with this issue. "Most local languages do not have a word that means *rights*," Virginia Ochwo, a senior trainer, pointed out. "In Luganda, the closest word that we use is *ddembe*, and this means something like, 'You are free to do what you want.' So when you go to parents and you tell them that their children have *ddembe*, they are not pleased," Ochwo said, with typical Ugandan understatement. If not explained carefully, the idea of children having *ddembe* makes parents and elders resent what they come to see as foreign impositions that overturn traditional social hierarchy in destructive ways: when children have *ddembe*, they start to disobey their elders, and the social order of *mpisa* breaks down. One solution is to balance children's rights with their responsibilities. The UCRNN produces posters with two columns: one lists children's rights, such as education, and the other lists their corresponding obligations, such as "to respect and obey your parents and teachers" (fig. 3). This format was commonly replicated on homemade posters in Ugandan classrooms.

As mentioned in the introduction, the particular distinction between children's rights and other human rights is that they are more narrowly

CHILDREN'S RIGHTS IN UGANDA

Who is a child? A child in Uganda is defined as a person under the age of 18 years.

1
A child in Uganda, has the same rights irrespective of sex, religion, custom, rural or urban background, nationality, tribe, race, marital status of parents or opinion.

2
The right to grow up in a peaceful, caring and secure environment, and to have the basic necessities of life, including food, health care clothing and shelter.

3
The right to a name and a nationality.

4
The right to know who are his or her parents and to enjoy family life with them and/or their extended family or is unable to live with them, he or she has the right to be given the best substitute care available.

5
The right to have his or her best interests given priority in any decision made concerning the child.

6
The right to express an opinion and to be listened to, and to be consulted in accordance with his or her understanding in decisions which affect his or her well being.

7
The right to have his or her health protected through immunisation and appropriate health care, and to be taught how to defend himself/herself against illness. When ill, a child has the right to receive proper medical care.

8
A child with disability has the right to be treated with the same dignity as other children and to be given special care, education and training where necessary so as to develop his or her potential and self-reliance.

9
The right to refuse to be subjected to harmful initiation rites and other harmful social and customary practices, and to be protected from those customary practices which are prejudicial to a child's health.

10
The right to be treated fairly and humanely within the legal system.

11
The right to be protected from all forms of abuse and exploitation.

12
The right to Basic Education.

13
The right to leisure which is not morally harmful, to play and to participate in sports and positive cultural and artistic activities.

14
The right not to be employed or engage in activities that harm his her health, education, mental, physical or moral development.

15
A child, if a victim of armed conflict, a refugee, or in a situation of danger or extreme vulnerability, has the right to be among the first to receive help and protection.

The responsibilities of the Child in Uganda

A child in Uganda has responsibilities towards his or her Family, Society, Country and then the International Community. A child according to his or her age, ability and rights has the duty to:-

- work for the cohesion of the family, to respect his or her parents, elders and other children and to assist them.
- use his or her abilities for the benefit of the community;
- preserve and strengthen cultural values in his or for relations with other members of the society, in the spirit of tolerance, dialogue and consultation, and to contribute to the moral well being of the society;
- preserve and strengthen the independence, National Unity and the Integrity of his/her Country.

REDD BARNA

National Council for Children
P. O Box 21456, Kampala.
Tel: .236519 Fax: 232311

NCC

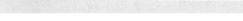

3 Children's rights poster from the Uganda Child Rights NGO Network.

defined as obligations and prohibitions, both for parents and children. Children's freedom of choice is usurped by an adult conception of "best interest" (Archard 1993). Laws passed to protect children can often therefore serve to further entrench discrimination and the denial of rights like those accorded by adults to children (Franklin 1986, 3). There are also specific ways in which the notion of *ddembe*, when applied to children in national development contexts, exacerbates social inequities—a fact not lost on NGOs attempting to help children independently of their families. I discussed the ironies of children's rights debates one day with Geoffrey Denye of the international NGO World Vision. "The issue of child labor is a contentious one," he said. "Is it helping or hurting a child who, for example, is an orphan and needs to support himself but who supposedly isn't supposed to work? Sometimes the will of children is set against their rights."

Expanding Definitions of Abuse

Another crucial example of cultural incongruity is the definition of abuse. Not long after I finished my fieldwork, an article in the national *New Vision* newspaper reported that more than 50 percent of Ugandan children less than ten years old had been sexually abused. This truly alarming figure, however, was based on a definition of abuse that derived from international concepts much broader than what most Ugandans consider abusive. Indeed, it seemed that part of the very purpose of raising the figure in the media was to educate people about the definition. Quoting the chairman of the UCRNN, the article explained, "Child sexual abuse is not only about sexual intercourse. Exposing young children to pornographic material or looking at adults having sex are also forms of sexual abuse" (Ntabadde 2002).

Police inspector Nakhanda, speaking on children's rights at a St. Michael's assembly, asked for definitions of *defilement* and then said herself, "It's if any male forces you to have sexual intercourse, with consent or without consent." Ironically, some of the highest incidents of defilement and domestic violence happen in the various city police barracks. They recorded 2,400 defilement cases and 1,300 child-neglect cases in 2001 alone (Candia 2002). Given that such offenses are typically underreported, these numbers are astronomical. Inspector Nakhanda pointed out that slums and living conditions like those in the barracks contribute to incidents of both the expanded definition of abuse and defilement cases because of overpopulation. Neighbors and relatives living close together endanger girls in particular. Lack of privacy is also the reason for increased sexual abuse in the form of witnessing adult sexual acts. Public opinion is hard to sway, however, if the law itself, which accounts only for the more extreme instances like rape and molestation, does not also reflect these definitions. If possible, the inspector said, parents should give boys and girls separate bedrooms. "Even uncles and fathers can do it, so don't allow them to touch you. 'Leave me alone,'" Inspector Nakhanda advised them to say, "'I have rights on my own body. You don't have any rights on my body.' Men go after young girls because they think they are free of AIDS," she told them. "He might offer nice things, but that's all shit. Grow up, have a relationship, and marry a man of your choice." The inspector's surprising use of an expletive indicates how contentious and emotional an issue this has become in Uganda, but her use of rights talk was meant to empower children to combat such abuses.

Most of the reported forms of sexual abuse involve intercourse with a child. *Defilement* is the legal term Ugandans use to refer to the rape of a girl-child by any male. In 1990, women and children's rights activists lobbied to raise the age of consent from fourteen to eighteen and to pass the defilement law (Parikh 2004, 82). When I talked to Oyen, he reminded me that Ugandan law states that the punishment for defilement is hanging, but "defilement is so common that either they get away with it or there is [monetary] settlement." Many still feel that customary law, under which payment is sometimes accepted by the victim's father as punishment (or an assailant is required to marry the victim), is preferable to punishment under constitutional law. However, according to an October 2002 *New Vision* article, "Defilement accounts for 65% of the criminal cases in the High Court" (*New Vision* 2002b), indicating that Ugandans are starting to feel that such injustices against children deserve punishment. Though passage of the defilement law has had the unintended consequence of aiding adults in their efforts to regulate young peoples' relationships rather than challenging male patriarchal privilege that allows older men to take advantage of girls (Parikh 2004), the marked increase in prosecution indicates that the problem is so widespread that incarceration is not a realistic option, partly because of the ways the law is utilized and also because the state lacks resources. And hanging so many people did not seem like the best solution, either. Oyen expressed morbid but development-minded skepticism: "If they hung every defiler in Uganda, at least it would create a lot of jobs for women making ropes. You would need a lot of rope and a lot of trees."

Sensitization: A Positive Step?

Local NGOs and civil society are working on various strategies to mediate these contradictions, but their main strategy is "sensitization." This word is commonly used in development programs, especially those targeting attitudinal and behavioral change. Such campaigns assume that local people are not aware of the benefits of progressive approaches to local issues. If they can be "sensitized" to the need for something and its benefits, then they will follow better practices and reap the rewards. For example, if parents are sensitized to the benefits of children's education, they will be willing to invest in it. Again, a type of paternalism prevails in discourses of sensitization, which often overlook local realities in favor of ideology. The reason that children are not in school usually has more to do with the parents' or guardians' lack of funds than with a negative attitude toward schooling, but stereotypes of poor people's ignorance and apathy prevail.

Even where they succeed in raising awareness of children's rights, NGO programs espousing children's rights may have unintended negative outcomes for particularly vulnerable children in both their families and communities. I once sat in on a children's rights lesson given at the World Vision Gulu Children of War Rehabilitation Center for children who had been abducted and had subsequently escaped from the rebel Lord's Resistance Army (see chapter 6). The counselor, Charles, started out saying that rural children are not taught "things they should know as kids," whether the parents are aware of them or not. Charles urged them to know their rights and to take them home to teach others. They will be the "future pillars of this nation," he reminded them, "so it is imperative."

Charles started by saying that parents cannot abuse their freedoms. He mentioned orphans who had been enslaved in Gulu; the case of Sempanga, a boy who was severely neglected in Kampala; and a lady in Rakai who killed four of her children.

"Why are your rights abused?" he asked.

No one was really attentive or eager to answer at first, but then a girl stood and suggested, "Parents think that young ones can't make decisions."

Another girl reiterated that parents are ignorant of rights themselves, and a second counselor suggested that parents sometimes mistreat children out of frustration over persistent poverty and insecurity. "So who has been abused at home?" he asked them to confess.

None responded until they were prodded gently. Then an older boy stood, and before he could start, the counselors told him resolutely, "You are a victim." Other hands shot up, as if the label somehow appealed to them.

The first boy gave testimony. His parents had died, so his uncle put him in an orphanage where the owner would take their things and sell them for profit. Counselor Violet asked which children stayed with guardians, and most raised their hands. One girl told her story of how she stayed with her grandparents because her mother had gone mad. They gave her less of everything than the other grandchildren, and she received no other assistance. Violet kept encouraging stories like this that she knew the children had hidden, and they picked up momentum. The children usually cried as they aired their grievances—a very rare occurrence, as it was typically discouraged in Acholi culture. A boy with a broken arm said that his uncle, with whom he stayed, would divert funds sent by his mother to his own children, leaving him unable to go to school. He was made to cultivate the fields instead. "After a while," he admitted, "I hated my uncle so much that I actually hoped the LRA would come abduct me." Violet told a story of a girl she had met whose father did not allow her or her siblings to see their real mother, claiming that she wanted to kill them. The girl was raped by her stepmother's sons. "The girl should have spoken out instead of living with the hurt for so long," Violet suggested, "because then someone would have been able to help her."

While this type of exercise both educated children and sanctioned their expression of suffering, it also had the potential to add to the strain of intergenerational relationships and daily realities. Counselors had already mentioned to me how the war in the north was straining the family structure, so what would this do to it, I wondered, and had World Vision had far-reaching discussions about the consequences? Charles and the other counselors seemed to warn children most against their own families, and it made me wonder what would happen if the children were to try to claim their rights at home. Under the circumstances, it seemed it could do more harm than good. Like other types of international aid and assistance, psychosocial support potentially worsens the crisis it purports to relieve. The following article from *New Vision* highlights the dangers of intervention in the lives of marginalized children.

Non-governmental organizations (NGOs) might need to rethink their strategy in supporting child-headed homes.

New findings have shown that careless interventions by NGOs have destroyed the community social support systems of orphans and actually contributed to the proliferation of child-headed families.

Frederick Luzze, a former programme officer with the World Vision in Uganda said NGO interventions have at times made the orphans more vulnerable.

"When NGOs move in, they improve the affluence of these child-headed families and the communities start perceiving them as favoured groups rather than very vulnerable members of society," Luzze told the on-going Early Childhood Development (ECD) conference in the Eritrean capital—Asmara.

While hailing World Vision for its interventions in Rakai, Luzze said child-headed homes have tended to emerge more where NGOs supporting them operate.

The conference was organised by Eritrea in conjunction with the World Bank. (Eremu 2002)

At the same time, the proliferation of children's rights discourse in the context of daily poverty makes "sensitized" parents feel like failures. Many Ugandan parents were well aware of the problems their children faced and were sympathetic to them, but often they could do little to improve the situation. A parent once told me,

These children of mine sometimes they don't perform well [in school]. But when you realize the condition they pass through, they walk a lonely path. Sometimes they have not taken tea with milk for two days; they have taken dry tea [tea made with water]. . . . [My daughter] tells me she is feeling pain, stomach pain somehow, because we have not taken food yet. . . . Now when she does a test and she gets lower marks, sometimes the father tries to say, 'Why have you performed very badly?" But I say we should not only do that but we should know other conditions which contribute to this child's performance. Maybe there are factors which we don't see. Because there are so many things: physically your body may be weak or sick.

This mother knew that she sometimes failed to provide adequately for her children when it came to things like medicine or nutritious food, and that these deficiencies could contribute to children's ability to achieve. "But it doesn't help that in Africa," she said, "children are not supposed to complain of lack of energy or illness. You must use your powers to force him to work . . . since we always need free labor from children and you have authority over them, you don't want hear that the [child] is sick, so we force and sometimes you find that it is . . . deteriorating their day-to-day life, or whatever they do."

Paradoxes of Sensitization: Inspector Nakhanda

If parents saw the difficulties of implementing children's rights in their daily lives, so certainly did the children. They were most often direct targets of rights talk, despite their limited ability to enforce or defend their rights. Rather than freeing children, normative discourses of childhood based on international rights were often used to constrain children by suggesting to them how they should be, what they should have, and how they should behave. When Inspector Nakhanda came to the schools to talk to students about rights and safety, all the children filed into the St. Michael's hall and sat close together on the floor. The inspector's introduction was interrupted by the arrival of two different television camera crews, one from UTV and one from WBS. This excited the students, and the teacher paused to remind the children that since they would be filmed, they should act "naturally": "Smile and laugh when necessary, but do not laugh for too long." To me, this sounded like a command to literally act like children. She then went back to introducing the inspector, who also hosts an educational television show. "She wants to see children grow to be important people in the country," the teacher explained.

Inspector Nakhanda first allowed the choir to lead the school in the national anthem and the school anthem as well a song and dance about children's rights that choir director Felix Kisakye (see chapter 7) had composed:

The Ugandan child and the children all
Are precious things we must protect.
Let us all join our hands.
Together their rights we must defend!

The inspector started by pointing out that she is also a parent of three and therefore has to give discipline, love, and care to her children. Her agenda for the talk focused on children's rights but also included safety information on bombs, traffic, and abduction—all perceived threats to local children's lives.

After talking at length about how to identify bombs for the sake of avoiding them, Nakhanda asked children to list some children's rights they knew about and those she called on mentioned things like education, security, medical care, basic needs like food, shelter, and clothing, the right to live with parents, and protection from violence. This last one she responded to by saying that girls especially should not tolerate anyone touching them. They had to protect themselves from men who tried to approach them sexually. She warned against teenage pregnancies and sugar daddies. "Boys telling you now that they will marry you are lying. They will not marry you. They will make you pregnant; they are only giving you AIDS." She gave girls the specific example of teachers going after students, which was apparently quite common, even at the primary school level. The late Dr. Kasalina Matovu of Makerere University, founder of the Minds Across Africa School Clubs program, told me that when she encouraged children to express themselves, girls commonly confessed that male teachers had made sexual advances toward them. "It seems to be even more common in sixth grade than in seventh grade, perhaps because most girls are just developing womanly features at that time," she suspected. Inspector Nakhanda said they should report such acts to another teacher or the headmaster or to parents. Children might complain that a teacher does not give them good marks because they have refused the teacher. "That teacher of yours who is disturbing you here now is not going to be the one who is marking you in UNEB," the Uganda National Examination Board that administers the primary certificate exams. "Leave men alone until you go to university," she implored them. "Then you can find a husband. Now, you are too young. We don't expect you to be mothers," she said. "And you the boys, we don't expect you to be fathers."

Inspector Nakhanda's attention to girls' problems in particular indicates how sensitive Ugandans are becoming to the problems of "the girl child"—a positive outcome of international development discourse. Uganda has a Ministry of State for Gender and Cultural Affairs as well as a Ministry of Gender, Labour, and Social Development to redress issues of gender discrimination. However, this attention often comes with contradictory statements about how girls are culpable in others' behavior toward them. After warning girls of men's foul intents, the inspector recited a long checklist of things girls and women should do to repel sexual abuse: "no overdrinking, no moving at odd hours, no sexy dressing or provocative walking (which she mimicked to the children's delight), no going to bars, receiving gifts from any man, accepting lifts, or lying, i.e., no means no and yes means yes." A teacher even took over the microphone to reiterate the main point: "We have children; we don't have women." However, she gave no specific advice to boys regarding avoiding assault—or becoming assaulters, for that matter.

To return to the point of children's responsibilities more generally, and to tie children's rights to *mpisa*, Inspector Nakhanda then talked about honoring parents "to live longer on earth." Quoting the Bible, she said, "Your mother and father are the *what*? The God you have on earth. You hear that?"

"Yes," the children replied. She asked them to repeat her words loudly and often. "We want a God-fearing country," she said. "So children must respect their parents."

She pointed out that children should not be subjected to hard labor or other abuse by adults such as stepparents.[6] If they are being abused, children should go to the police to report those who violate their rights.

They have to behave, though. If the children go for videos instead of going to school, the police will punish them instead of the parents.

The inspector ended with advice for academic success: "We want you to get smart friends," she said. "Those smart kids can help you. If you hang out with truants, you will be no good. Those ones want to become useless to the nation." In fact, she said, those people should be reported to the police. "I want children to respect adults, not to live in fear. We want you to develop to be the *what*? The future of Uganda. You are the flowers of Uganda. You are the *what*?"

"The flowers of Uganda," the children repeated.

"The nation's flowers of Uganda are now growing."

Children's Agency and the Reception of Rights Messages

Assemblies like Inspector Nakhanda's indicate how local authorities are trying to reconcile the principles of *mpisa* with international children's rights discourses not only for the sake of the family, clan, or ethnic group, but also for the betterment of the nation. This sensitization can create a sense of hope, but more often it creates anxiety, especially amongst children: when the media increasingly cover the most shocking cases of abuse and neglect, children as a population become more sensitive to their own vulnerability. While children around the country are being educated about their rights, they are also realizing that they suffer from rights abuses. Their marginalization from normative global childhood ideals create the stigmatizing trope of the African child. This is the child whose gaunt, fly-covered face acts as the international symbol of misery and preventable human tragedy (Ennew and Milne 1990, 9). This child, usually severely malnourished and diseased, stripped of agency and personality, acts as the poster child leading the cry for international assistance.

This image has become so prevalent that African children buy into it themselves. At an affluent Kampala private school, children put on a variety show in which at least three different classes, from first grade to sixth grade, took up this trope. One class of first-grade children with white gloves and dazed faces recited a poem entitled "The African Child":

The African Child, the African Child.
We are the children of this continent.
We are the children of this nation.
Why should we be mistreated,
As if we are born from another land?

Stop mistreating us!
We are human beings, the leaders of tomorrow.
As [babies], some of us are thrown in pit latrines and dust bins.[7]
During growth, some of us are insulted and mistreated.
Not enough [food] is given to us.
They slaughter us as animal sacrifice.
Do not forget us, teachers of this nation!
Do not forget us, government of Uganda!
Enough is enough!
Stop child abuse!

The students recited this poem complete with hand gestures of hunger and slit throats. The angry tone in which they spoke was startling and powerful, especially considering the children's tender ages. As this poem solidifies a common child identity that demands recognition of their rights, it reminds parents in the audience that the state of some children in the nation is indeed abysmal and deserves action and protection, in accordance with the CRC. This is not possible without somehow categorizing children as embattled and marginalized. Another class sang a song of the same name that lamented, "Little children suffering, little children crying." These particular children were all well-fed, well-schooled, and did not fit the stereotype they were promoting. Yet their performances simultaneously condemned and reproduced the image of the singular African child who is impoverished, dejected, and robbed of her potential, even as they drew attention to her plight.

Where children do have legitimate claims of rights abuse, they feel they have little or no recourse. Sumayiya often told me about instances of her peers being abused, physically or sexually, by relatives or adult strangers. One day she repeated that a girl was found at school, possibly raped by an older man. The girl was in obvious physical pain. After she was raped, her aunt chased her out of the house, putting the blame on her for her own defilement. Sumayiya said she worried about such things happening to her, too. She tried to protect herself, but she expressed some skepticism about her own and others' abilities to do that. She told other children about her problems, but she did not tell many adults because she felt that they would not help. "Kids don't feel like even teachers or local council members are very helpful," Sumayiya said. "I suffered a lot with my uncle in Mbarara, but I just stayed quiet." Talking might only have threatened her already precarious situation, so she suffered in silence. Despite—and perhaps because of—her heightened awareness of her rights, she felt powerless. "I even wished to die

4   A child's drawing of abuse, created for a pamphlet published by the Uganda Child
     Rights NGO Network.

when times got tough. Even if you tell someone, he will not help you at
school," she said. "Maybe he will talk over you. So the best thing to do
is to keep quiet, about each and every thing."

The same thing had happened in the case of Sumayiya's friend, who
was being physically abused by her father and stepmother. She was coming to school with bruises and burn marks from having had scalding-hot
water poured on her arm. The local chairman was notified and talked to
the father. "She told me the chairman told her father, 'If you beat that
child again, I will arrest you.'" The father then turned around and threatened the girl for talking about it publicly. Sumayiya worried that her
friend would end up going to the streets if things did not change for her.
"She used to tell me, 'For me I will go away from home because my father
hates me.'" The girl had followed all the procedures the inspector had
taught them about: do not stand for abuse, talk to an adult, report your
situation to the authorities. But it only served to increase the tension at
home between the abusive parent and the child seeking protection. The
end result of such situations is that, despite all the rhetoric about children's rights, children see what little intervention occurs on their behalf

as feeble at best. Such a position is indeed the direct result of the inherent paradox of children's rights discourse (Ennew and Milne 1990).

Sumayiya and her friends repeatedly showed me that it was common for children to feel powerless (fig. 4). They were well aware of the gulf between the children's rights ideals they were being taught and the reality for most children. For all their knowledge, children lacked the power and resources to enforce their rights. "Adults just have more power," Sumayiya sighed. For all their knowledge of their rights, children remained disempowered and did not have much hope for change in the immediate future. However, their increasing awareness of children's rights enabled them to believe they could battle injustices toward children of the next generation: "When I am a lawyer," Sumayiya told me resolutely, "I want to make laws to protect children."

Crucial Components of Child Citizenship

The chapters in part 1 work together to portray children's understandings of crucial elements that constitute their citizen identities as "the pillars of tomorrow's Uganda," as well as the formative events that shape those perceptions of children's subjectivity as being parallel to that of the nation. Through life histories, my central analytical concern in these chapters is to present as well the paradoxes that face children as they struggle to claim citizenship and establish their roles in the Ugandan nation-building project. I argue that while children are encouraged to be educated, to know something of their ethnic identities, and to develop their political consciousnesses, they also receive various cultural cues that inhibit them from considering themselves as fully integrated persons, or as "agents-in-society" (Harris 1989, 600). Global rights discourses that treat children as individuals endowed with protective rights clash with local cultural notions of children as social persons and agents-in-training. But material and structural obstacles also arise, as evidenced in chapter 2. The importance of educational attainment is well understood and agreed upon in Uganda, but becoming educated is harder to achieve under current circumstances, which jeopardizes the potential growth and development of individual children, their families, communities, and the nation.

Chapter 3 reveals the process by which children's identity formation becomes tied to national conceptions of social belonging. Children's malleable understandings of their identities in the national context incorporate complex layers of community that intertwine to form a strong, if marginalized, sense of identity. I tease apart these strands to see how they are constructed through children's lived experiences, including contact with ethnic "others," language use, cultural practice, and interpellation into nationalism through school lessons.

Because these issues are fundamentally political, chapter 4 specifically examines children's formation of political consciousness, challenging commonly held beliefs about intergenerational transmission of political values. Drawing on fieldwork done during the 2001 presidential elections, I argue that children's abilities to decipher political issues are denied to the extent that children themselves deny their own potential contributions, thus confirming their political disenfranchisement.

TWO

"Education for All"

The Dilemma of Children's Educational Attainment, National Development, and Class Mobility

During my observations with Jill Obonyo in her sixth-grade classroom, a disheveled boy in tattered clothing and an old army hat often came to the windows of the class and peered in. "He was in our class last year," the teacher explained to me when I inquired about him, "but his mother recently passed away, and he became mentally disturbed. Now no one is paying his school fees." This unfortunately had become a fairly common story in Uganda. The boy was a regular fixture, staring with wide eyes through the open windows with his fingers clutching the iron grates. Jill and the other students talked to him and sometimes offered him food. "They like him so much," the teacher sighed. He even loitered by the window of the school office, where the secretaries would greet him. No one tried to chase him away as they might other trespassers, but they did not invite him in, either—and he never attempted to enter any of the buildings himself. That right was now reserved for the other children. Though they took pity on him, they knew it—and so did he.

This chapter details the past and present stakes of education in Uganda, both for national development and individual class mobility. Just as the nation hopes that widespread educational attainment will lead to greater global parity for the nation, Uganda's poor hope that education will lead to greater socioeconomic mobility for them and their families. Jill, whose life history is highlighted in this chapter, is one example. Despite the Ugandan government's efforts to educate the majority of its citizens through such strategies as universal primary education (UPE), educational attainment remains greatly limited, and thus usually contributes to rather than diminishes class stratification in Ugandan society. In the context of the country's prevalent "education for national development" mission, children are often caught in a double bind: while they are told that schooling is essential to their own future and that of the country, the challenges of quality and access keep them back from reaching those goals. James's life history later in the chapter shows us how poor children are often put in the difficult position of acquiring education for themselves, how much stress it causes them and their families, and how resourceful they can be in their strategies to maintain or improve their educational status, hoping thereby to raise their family's social status as well as the country's.

Education and Status

In the last chapter, I established that if you ask any Ugandan primary school student if she has heard of children's rights, she is likely to say that she has. Most will be able to tell you quite a few of their rights. Further, if you ask students where they learned their rights, most of them will say that they learned them in school. And when you ask them which right they value most, they commonly say, "Education."

One afternoon, several seventh-grade students struck up a conversation with me about children's rights. All named education as the most important right they had. They agreed that education was essential to getting jobs, and these primary school students were well aware that well-paying jobs were essential to escaping endemic poverty. "You can't be a secretary without speaking and writing English," one girl pointed out. Uneducated people end up as unproductive citizens, stealing or in prison.

Ideologies of schooling in the nineteenth and twentieth centuries have consistently been about either establishing or transmuting class hierarchies (Willis 1981). Desires for education have to do with development through individual, family, and class mobility. Thus, educational attainment is a major indicator of the type of person a child becomes. Class mobility through educational attainment is an ideology that has been long in the making but has been thwarted by Africa's post-independence national development crises. Uganda is a prime example of a country whose development has been frustrated by social and political violence, economic austerity programs, and crises of education. The relative economic stability of the twenty-first century, however, coupled with human rights discourses like those discussed in the previous chapter, is providing educated citizens, especially children, with a language to articulate development aspirations, even if economic and educational trends still mean that little help is available to the majority of children for realizing those aspirations. Given the limited availability and quality of schooling, access remains limited. Despite the recent establishment of universal primary education, the boy at the window is a stark example of how lack of access to education becomes a significant source of anxiety—for a nation trying to build and assert its self-sufficiency, and for children and their families who are striving to do the same. This dilemma originated in a colonial history of subservience, dependency, and perceived underdevelopment.

A Brief History of Education in Uganda

Precolonial Educational Strategies

As in most African countries, education in Uganda has always been linked in some way to cultural citizenship. In precolonial times, children were taught the rules and etiquette of their society so that they would become useful members of it. They also had to have some knowledge of their society's structure and history. Historian J. C. Ssekamwa, who has written several books on the history and development of education in Uganda, writes,

If somebody tried to challenge [Ugandans] that they did not belong to the particular clans and tribes, they could defend themselves through knowledge of the history and organization of their clans and tribes . . .

In fact during those old days, the knowledge of the history of the clans, tribes, and of the customs and beliefs of the tribes, assured a person of his/her citizenship and it acted as the Passport of today. (Ssekamwa 1997, 9)

Much of precolonial education consisted of *production learning*: children were taught by doing, and by doing, they performed services or produced goods and materials that were immediately useful to society. Learning was done around the homestead, and any number of neighbors or family members could act as teachers. Because there was no formal education, British colonists arriving in Africa often ignorantly presumed that children were simply not being taught anything. The knowledge that the British offered took a totally different form (literacy), taught by a specially train-ed person (a "professional" teacher), and took place in a particular loca-tion (the school). The definition of education thus became formalized through a narrowing of the concept. As a result, even Africans came to believe that whites "brought" education to Africa (Ssekamwa 1997).

The "Arrival" of Education

Formal education came to Uganda at the invitation of Kabaka Muteesa I. Missionaries were already making inroads in Africa, spreading the Christian gospel through schools they had established throughout the colonies. Muslim traders had begun teaching people about their faith before Christian European missionaries arrived in Uganda in the nine-teenth century, but in 1877 Muteesa sent a letter (drafted by the explorer Henry Morton Stanley) to England inviting the British to send teachers because he thought they might teach his people skills and create diplo-matic relations with Western powers that would help defend against a possible invasion by Egypt. The Protestant Church Missionary Society (CMS) responded by sending teachers in 1877, followed by the Roman Catholic White Fathers Society in 1879.

Muteesa I soon came to regret his decision to invite the teachers. Buganda is a highly stratified society, with thirteen clans established by the god Kintu and ruled over by the *kabaka*. The missionaries, directly or indirectly, persuaded Muteesa's followers—many of whom were Baganda elite—to disrespect his political and religious authority. Ssekamwa writes,

[His subjects] always told Muteesa I that they did not want to annoy God because the British, the French and the Arab teachers had taught them so. However, at that time it was quite difficult for any person to refuse to do what the Kabaka told him/her to do. If such a person refused to obey the Kabaka, he/she would be easily executed on the orders of the Kabaka for his/her disobedience. Therefore, the early students of the Christian and Muslim teachers must have been very courageous. They "fell in love" at once with what the new teachers were teaching them. (Ssekamwa 1997, 30)

Ssekamwa's account of colonial contact through missionary education suggests a ready acceptance of missionaries and their foreign educational system in Uganda, at least on the part of the common people to whom educational opportunities eventually opened up, allowing them to chal-lenge and even defy traditional authority. The only one who seemed to have a problem with the missionaries, according to Ssekamwa, was the very person who had invited them: Kabaka Muteesa. Yet British colonists and missionaries formalized Western education in Uganda according to their own needs and the perceived needs of native Ugandans (Paige 2000, 20); missionaries needed to save souls, and, since Uganda was not a settler colony, colonists needed labor and civil servants.

To make matters worse, the British and French teachers refused to help convince their own governments to help Muteesa defend his kingdom or teach his people how to make guns. As the threat of an Egyptian invasion lessened, Muteesa I saw no further use for the missionaries. But their popularity had already taken hold: when Muteesa I's son Mwanga burned more than thirty Christians and Muslims to death at Namuwongo in 1886, he only ended up martyring them, as he was driven into exile. National Martyr's Day memorializes this event in Ugandan history.

Energized by their triumph over the despot king, the missionaries and their followers set up boarding schools to bring peasant children into the fold. Their hope was that these children would come to identify themselves not only as Christians, but as *Ugandans* rather than members of the different tribes within the Protectorate (Evans 1971, 124). "They would then be different from those who did not attend those boarding schools and so they would help create a new order in Uganda since on completion of their studies, they would return to society, and the rest of the members of society would copy their behaviour" (Ssekamwa 1997, 44). Further, the boarding schools, modeled on the British public school system, attempted to produce civil servants for the colonial government and create British subjects who reflected bourgeois European values (45). The content of this education was necessarily cultural—foreign in most ways to the children who were transported to boarding schools to be educated. Yet they purportedly embraced this new knowledge, sometimes becoming too enthusiastic for the British colonial administration; educated Africans came to believe that education would help them to obtain the same standard of living and access to commodities that British colonials and missionaries had. Until the 1920s, the colonial government was happy to let the missionaries handle native education, but at that time they decided they too needed to have a hand in education in order to control both the goals of education and the educated themselves. Children of the elite who were reaching the upper limits of education in Uganda were either putting pressure on the colonial administration for suitable civil servant positions or seeking in increasing numbers to extend their education abroad. To deter emigration, Makerere High School was established in 1922 and later became a premier university in East Africa. The seeds of independence movements were planted there and at other universities around the continent.

From 1945 until independence in 1962, educational policy in Uganda was concerned with preparing Ugandans for independence. In the wake of World War II, men who served as Allied soldiers had come to realize that Britain was no longer the most powerful force in the world (Turyahikayo-Rugyema 1982, 219). The newly formed United Nations drafted the Universal Declaration of Human Rights in 1948, which, because it "did not discriminate between sovereign and dependent peoples" (Ibingira 1973, 63), clearly advocated an end to colonial rule. Because the British considered Uganda a "black" protectorate as opposed to a settler colony, such as neighboring Kenya, the British government started preparing Uganda for self-rule (Furley and Watson 1978, 269). Colonial administrators presumed a transition to Western-style national democracy, however, and therefore claimed that the populace had to be educated according to Western standards.

This political change was shrouded in a thin veil of engineered cultural preservation. Colonial Governor Sir John Hall wanted to change the prevailing attitude of Ugandan students. He saw missionary education, which was largely academic, as denigrating manual labor and agricultural work. Missionaries agreed but did not see why it was a problem: the educational system replicated that of the British, meant to produce intellectuals and office workers. CMS teacher T. C. Vincent wrote, "Parents send their children to mission schools with the hope that they will escape from the routine of village life to which they themselves were subject, and not that they may return to it with new knowledge and ideas that would make that life acceptable and of worth to them" (Ssekamwa 1997, 189). Whatever it meant to the British, to Africans schooling meant becoming cosmopolitan, academically educated, and employable in the colonial regime, hence attaining the living standards of colonial administrators. This orientation to educational attainment became the foundation of modern class formation in Uganda.

The New Social Stratification: Preparation for Independence

Given the direction of formal education, this attitude only continued to grow as education expanded. Despite Governor Hall's efforts to reeducate rural people about agricultural techniques and sanitation, Africans had already established a preference for reading, writing, and arithmetic—skills that would land them jobs as civil servants and thus allow them to occupy the cutting edge of an emergent new class system based on wage labor. In response, Hall sought to reduce access to primary education on the basis that it "made the youth of Uganda to hate to participate in

productive work which required physical exertion, 'considering themselves to have automatically joined the ranks of those who ordered others
to work'" (Ssekamwa 1997, 157). The main goals of the colonial education system had been to remake Africans in the image of the British
themselves, but they had been all too successful; many educated Africans
had indeed been prepared for lucrative white-collar jobs and had gone
to work in government offices, but supervisory positions were reserved
for the British alone. Still, why would educated Africans want to go back
to "digging"? In the end, though education had freed many Africans
from the land, it had also created colonial subjects who, as assistants to
British and Asian superiors, would subsequently lack confidence in their
abilities to perform managerial tasks upon independence.

In addition, Uganda lacked a fervent nationalist movement. Grace
Ibingira, himself an acclaimed father of Ugandan independence, writes,
"On first view it may seem strange that a subject people should have felt
and lived in contentment under their foreign rulers from 1893 until the
1950s. Yet this was true of Uganda Africans" (Ibingira 1973, 67). The push
for independence in Africa was typically led by Western-educated elites
who were frustrated by limits on their possible advancement under
colonialism, indicative of the degree of acculturation and white-settler
presence (Coleman 1994, 30). The level of acculturation in Uganda was
relatively low in comparison with that in settler colonies such as neighboring Kenya, yet a vital group of intellectuals spoke out for self-rule. Educational attainment—and with it economic mobility—was therefore a main
motivator of the Ugandan nationalist movement. An independent country would need skilled and educated people (Paige 2000, 30), so the public was eager to participate in programs offered by new technical schools
designed to increase industry (Furley and Watson 1978, 287). Today, this
belief that economic independence requires skilled and educated people
is integrated with national development and educational policy.

Independence in 1962 brought a surge of optimism regarding Ugandan class mobility when many departing foreign colonial administrators
left vacancies. However, government ministries became bloated due to
clientelism, while schools lacked teachers to keep up with the demand.
Uganda had to resort to recruiting teachers from the former colonial powers and the United States, which sent volunteers. This produced many
graduates who were job seekers but few job creators, which limited the
ability to spur the economy (Callaway 1974, 46). This is still the complaint today, perhaps because the government in 1986 had inherited an
even worse economic situation from decades of civil war than the 1962
government had from colonialism. Its legacy is enduring; adults still

cite the lack of job creators as a problem for Ugandan economic development, and children hoped that their schooling would provide them with the tools to run businesses in order to create more jobs.

War: Educational Casualties

When war broke out with Idi Amin's coup against Milton Obote in 1971, many intellectuals became potential targets of political violence. They fled the country in search of safety and better opportunities abroad, precipitating the country's first "brain drain" (Zeleza and Veney 2002).[1] Schools and scholastic materials became casualties as often as did civilians who were caught in the ensuing conflicts. Ssekamwa recalls, "Money became short and many irresponsible people began looting books in libraries and institutions which they sold either to veranda book vendors or to market men and women for wrapping tomatoes, oranges, pan-cakes and the like. Thousands of valuable books, magazines and journals were lost" (Ssekamwa 1997, 185). Various rebel and government troops took over schools throughout the country for use as field camps, burning desks for cooking fires and using books to light them. Despite security breakdowns, however, Ugandan families continued to invest heavily in education. Paige observes, "Between 1969 and 1979 primary enrollments rose from 600,000 to 1.2 million, requiring additional facilities and furnishings for an average of 230 new schools per year during the period" (Paige 2000, 3). One explanation for this is that, as we will see later in this chapter, "Education offers more than a job possibility. It endows the child with a status and prestige that is shared by his or her family" (Paige 2000, 140). Though liberal education stresses the individual rather than the community, African families started to encourage their children to get ahead in the new system so they could raise the family's economic status; children are always reminded of their continuing obligations to their families and communities.[2]

The White Paper: Education for National Development

Education is a right, and the key to promoting development and democracy.... Our priority now must be to ensure that children also have access to good quality education in schools that are not overcrowded, unhealthy and poorly equipped.
—UNICEF

As early as the 1960s, UNICEF started dedicating more research to adapting prevailing educational forms in Africa "to the needs of African children and to the requirements of national development" (Iskander 1987, 29). This effort fell short of making substantive changes, however, because by that time, Africans' educational needs were still being determined by donors with their own interests. Perceived needs remained incongruous with Africans' desires for educational attainment. Graduates in the 1970s had few job prospects or none; having been alienated from the land, they were often forced to enter the informal economy.

But past failures did not keep officials from trying; while wandering the vast halls of the Ministry of Education and Sports (MOE) one day in 2001, I met Mr. Aloysius Chebet. He explained that the person I was looking for in the room across the hall was out for the week, and we started to chat. He asked what my research was about, and I explained briefly.

"Ah," he said, "you might want to look at this." He produced a big, thick wad of paper resembling an unbound phone book. "This government white paper on education is what still guides the national curriculum."

"What about national development?" I asked.

"National development is the Bible of Ugandan education!" He said I could borrow the paper, and that I might also check out the preceding Education Policy Review Commission Report, which the white paper was trying to implement.

When I got home and opened up the white paper, I found innumerable references to national development. In fact, it was the reason for the paper's existence: "A Consultancy Team of Ugandans was set up to review the Primary school curriculum. Among its most important tasks was the definition in more comprehensive and concrete terms of the national goals of development" (Republic of Uganda 1992, 4).

Africans have complained that school does not properly prepare them for life's realities—a major contradiction to their aspirations for and ideologies about schooling. The white paper supports claims that schools fail to reflect indigenous educational values and learning processes, instead reverting to the rigid authoritarianism of rote learning (Callaway 1974, 14, 69). Despite an admission that "the curricula both in primary and secondary schools at present do not cater for the social and economic needs of the country" (Republic of Uganda 1992, 5), school success ultimately depends on exam performance. Not only does this system reinforce knowledge of subjects more relevant to Western cultural systems (Prewitt 1971, 16), but its rigors preclude children at every level from possibilities to continue their education.

The white paper sets forth a critique and calls for change: "Without any provision for the assessment of other objectives of the curriculum, such as promotion of moral values, practical skills and participation in social and cultural activities, the teaching in schools is geared toward the achievement of good marks in examination subjects at the cost of other important educational objectives" (Republic of Uganda 1992, ix). In my own fieldwork, I met quite a number of people—parents, teachers, children, and MOE officials—who agreed. Yet I did not see that this was changing. Over the course of my fieldwork, I saw that Ugandan education continually replicated the British system because, as in colonial times and after independence, the popular belief persisted that it facilitated entrance into well-paying civil service jobs and, for a select few, offered the possibility of attaining higher education. This is not surprising when one considers how "international lending institutions condition their loans to such Third World states upon acceptance of Western schooling models" (Levinson and Holland 1996, 16). But educational attainment has to do not just with economic but with cultural mimesis; parents and children alike see education as their only chance to rise out of endemic poverty, and global connectivity allows for a continuity of aspiration to the same standard of living as those at the metropole.

Universal Primary Education: Education for All?

In 1993, the new NRM government, placing faith in Structural Adjustment Program dictums that broader investment in primary education would fuel economic growth (Meinert 2003, 185–86), diverted money from the military and higher education to primary education, increasing its budget by 55 percent (USAID and The World Bank 1999). Donors also added support. These efforts increased the quality of schooling, but half the country's children still could not afford school fees after the 1993 reforms. Universal Primary Education (UPE) was therefore instituted in 1997. Under UPE, up to four children from each family were entitled to free primary education. Some critics questioned the practicality of such a move, but Acting Director of Education Sam Onek pointed out, "If you look at education as a basic right, you can't leave some people out and say some children will have to be denied an education until we have enough books. We had to start somewhere" (Evans 2001, 16). The program paid particular attention to gender balance (at least two of the children benefiting from UPE in each family had to be girls) and the integration of disabled children into regular schools.

The government white paper of 1992 had laid out a plan in which "school attendance will become compulsory for all children of relevant age, for every class in which free education is introduced. By the year 2001/02 all primary education will be free and compulsory" (Republic of Uganda 1992, 48). It was neither by that time, but some gains were being made. In 2003, Museveni declared that all children were entitled to UPE. UPE schools were free in most rural areas, with minimal tuition in urban areas (fifteen thousand shillings, or US$9). These costs were still prohibitive because students also had to pay school-imposed materials fees to make up for budget shortfalls or top up teacher salaries. Teachers at Kubili Primary School complained that universal primary education was ultimately bad, at least from the teachers' perspective. They made ninety thousand shillings (about US$55) per month, and their workload had skyrocketed with the increase in class size since the introduction of UPE.

Students require uniforms, books, pens, and other school supplies. Kubili Primary School even asked each student to bring two rolls of toilet paper to school each term. This added up to 22,400 shillings per term at Kubili (about US$12.50). If one has several children and no salary, this amount quickly becomes an exorbitant financial burden. In Gulu, where war and displacement had left residents absolutely impoverished, parents could not even afford basic uniforms costing as little as US$4, and materials fees of five thousand shillings were usually not forthcoming, which meant that children were constantly sent home or their reports withheld until their parents paid. Many schools do not serve lunch, either, affecting students' abilities to perform well academically. It is still not viable to make school compulsory for children when costs remain so prohibitive for many parents, and insecurity in some parts of the country makes the operation of schools dangerous. Many children are forced to drop out of primary school, and even if they complete primary schooling, a rigorous exam system and exorbitant fees for secondary school prevent many children from continuing their education.

The first generation of UPE students graduated from primary school in 2004 to a secondary system that has not expanded to accommodate them (*New Vision* 2003). Though the system has usually failed them, this predicament often leaves children feeling like they are the ones who have failed (Serpell 1993). Despite Museveni's 2001 election promise to establish universal secondary education, Ugandan students are still waiting for the cost of secondary schools to drop so that they can attend school.

The transition to education for development thus stems from both international and local traditions that have influenced Uganda's history. This alignment also has to do with desires for individual, family, and national class mobility, evident in the documents circulating through government offices such as the Ministry of Education. In my fieldwork,

Jill's family presented a vivid example of how these attitudes influence a family's educational strategies.

Jill: Building a Bourgeoisie Through Education

Jill was a good student, but she always felt the weight of the structural obstacles that challenged her educational goals. Luckily, Jill's parents valued her education just as much as she did, and so together they were struggling to make it happen.

Jill was ten years old when I met her in 2001 at Kubili Primary School. She was born in August 1990, the second child of Vittore Obonyo,[3] a laid-off railway worker, and his wife Margaret. I quickly got to know Jill's entire family. Her older brother, Michael, was twelve years old and extremely talkative. Jill was in sixth grade, and Michael was in seventh grade. Their younger sister Michelle was five years old and went to nursery school near their home. Since their parents did not have regular work, they often invited me to their house to chat. We talked nonstop for hours, and I learned a great deal about the whole family.

Jill started school at four years old, which she thought was very late because some of her friends began school as early as three.[4]

I had the measles when I was two, and then my father got very sick with tuberculosis. My father was working for the railways. My uncle, my father's brother, told us we should go and stay with him at his home until my father got better.

So I started school at four years old. I went to preschool at St. Michael's for two years. The teachers saw it was too late for me to join top class when six years old, so they decided to send me to P1. I was not prepared. It was hard. When they said that they would take me back to kindergarten, the teachers got interested in me. I was very active, so I passed and went to P2. At P2 I came to Kubili Primary School because my father had been retrenched from the railways, and at St. Michael's they had increased the school fees.

Since then, Jill has been a very good student at Kubili, always placing in the top quarter of her class. In 2001, she placed tenth in her P6 class of eighty-four.

While Vittore was employed, the Obonyos had free housing in the railway quarters, nearer to the school. They used to rent out the house they owned in Namuwongo, a crowded and vibrant trading center several miles from Kubili. But when Vittore was retrenched, they moved into the house in Namuwongo, where Jill's older half-sister and her baby joined them. It took Jill and Michael an hour and a half to walk to school along a busy street and through a bustling trading center The Obonyos ran a small tuck shop attached to their home, where they sold dry goods, matches, and other household supplies. Vittore made ends meet by maintaining a garden plot and some livestock in his northern home-town. Margaret was not employed but was taking a development and money-management workshop sponsored by Christian Children's Fund, which helped pay Michael's school fees through an Australian sponsor.

Jill was a gracious, intelligent, and thoughtful person, and she was very interested in political issues. She was had internalized national de-velopment messages on schooling, and often replicated them in her own speech. She took her national development duties very seriously, often repeating the youth anthem, "We are the pillars of tomorrow's Uganda." She wanted to be a lawyer. She said that she decided this when she was nine, in Sunday school. "The teacher asked us what job we want to do when we are old enough, and I said I wanted to be a lawyer. My heart just decided," she explained. Then she added, "Lawyers are respected. And they also get to wear those wigs." Jill liked to follow lawsuits in the news, especially those dealing with political issues.[5] She once explained to me the details of a high-profile election dispute being argued in the courts at that time. "I want to be a political lawyer," she said upon reflection.

Though Jill could speak her mind fairly articulately, she was some-times upstaged by her brother Michael, who was both loquacious and adventurous. Teachers said he was stubborn and willful, but he always told the truth. The first time Jill introduced me to him, he told me all about his Christian Children's Fund sponsor from Australia, and even when the police helicopter buzzed over us and landed across the street, wildly distracting most of the fifteen hundred students on the com-pound, he kept right on talking through the noise. The next time we talked, I was to learn where he got it from: I sat with him as he was wait-ing for his mother to arrive at the school to register him for the National Primary Leaving Examination, and he chattered on for an hour and a half about mangoes, Museveni, and various regional conflicts. Once his mother approached us, he suddenly and without announcement got up and returned to his classroom, leaving the bench next to me open for her to sit down. It was like a tag team: where Michael left off, Mrs. Obonyo picked up, talking rapidly regarding how she was flattered by the letter I had sent with Jill requesting to meet her. She quickly moved on to other topics like crime and witchcraft, hardly letting me get a word in.

Jill had already learned a lot from her parents about the struggles of their generation. She knew that she was growing up in a very different time from her parents, but she believed that as long as she had her parents, she should not have to work for her school fees. Still, she would be willing to do so if it became necessary—"Any work which there is." Not going to school was out of the question for her. Having already cultivated a schooled identity, she believed her childhood was better because she did not have as much work to do as her mother did when she was a child. Jill washed her school uniform and watched the family tuck shop on Saturdays. I also saw her drawing water and performing other menial tasks when I visited their home. Yet the entire family's unspoken understanding was that Jill was always a student first and foremost.

Jill realized the centrality of education to her reciprocal relationship with her parents: they provide for her now, and she will provide for them later. "They want me to help them when they are in times of need," she said, "like when they are sick you take them to the hospital. It is many of the same things they do for me now." Like many children, Jill mentioned the material things her parents provided for her as evidence of their love. Fear of loss of a parent often equals fear of loss of these things and attendant opportunities, most especially the opportunity to go to school. For that reason, she often cited adults such as her parents and teachers—and even her uncle who took care of her while her father was ill—as the most influential people in her life. A religious person, Jill prayed three times a day to be sure she retained familial support and education. "In the morning," she told me, "I thank God for my family, I pray for safe passage when traveling to and from school, and at night I pray that God keeps me until the morning."

High Expectations: Parental Views of Education

While education in its current state focuses heavily on national development, it still fails to become more accessible due to Ugandans' contradictory desires for both mass education and elite status. "I want my children to be educated up to a high level," Mrs. Obonyo once told me proudly. At times, the Obonyos seemed to suggest that attaining an education was a valuable end in itself. But Mr. Obonyo also expected his children to become exceptional wage earners when they finished school. Mr. Obonyo subscribed to fairly universal parental ideals: he wanted to teach them "the right way." As a parent, he wanted to guide them, especially to warn them about corruption and the ills it causes. But he saw these goals as more difficult to achieve in a place like Uganda, where lack of development limited educational opportunity:

Most of the parents if not all the parents would want to educate the child so that in future the child becomes able to take care of himself, not that you are educating so that he will become unable. You want his future not to be as dark as your own future. We want only to give them a better future. But some of these things, most of these are hampered by development. You want to help your child to do the best, to go to the highest education, but then you are hampered.

To the Obonyos, another part of the problem was the poor quality of public schools. Mrs. Obonyo decried the quality of the education her children were getting when she saw their exercise books:

What do we see in these books of our children? You find some wrong things being marked as right answers! I have even complained in a meeting at the school. One time I went and asked in a meeting, "I now want to ask this question. You prove me wrong or right if this thing is right or wrong." But my child was given a right mark when it was wrong, which means the teachers are misleading. When I talked, the headmaster was ashamed. In fact, he apologized.

Mr. Obonyo blamed the government for the failure of teachers. "People who fail out of other programs go to teacher training colleges as a last resort," he said. "These are the ones who end up teaching our children."

"Most teachers are drunkards," Mr. Obonyo stated matter-of-factly. He acknowledged that parents had a responsibility, but the teachers were the ones to impart knowledge to children. Parents blamed teachers because of the way they have commercialized teaching. They complained that teachers placed too much emphasis on additional instruction, called "coaching." In the evenings and on weekends, teachers charge a nominal fee to coach students on syllabus material that might not have been covered in regular classes. In their day, Mr. and Mrs. Obonyo said, there was no coaching, and the teaching was better. "Teachers today spread themselves thin across several schools in an area to make money," they said. The amount of money teachers get from coaching is sizeable, so the way they teach normal classes makes it necessary for parents to send their children for coaching if they want their children to excel. "Coaching is corrupt," Mr. Obonyo said, "and yet it's necessary." Even Jill and Michael wanted to go because they felt they were falling behind their classmates. They also complained that teachers were often absent, or that they taught certain topics to some classes and not others.

Betty and Violet, two of Jill's teachers at Kubili, explained that they had to coach students for extra money in order to survive. "We are educating other people's children when we can't even afford to send our own children to school!" Violet complained. Though UPE had decreased primary school costs, fees for secondary school remained high, starting at around two hundred thousand shillings (a little more than one hundred US dollars) per term. When most parents are providing for an average of five children, it is almost a given that only a few of them will complete secondary school.

"At least university is free, though," Betty sat back and folded her arms, satisfied.

"Why is that such a good thing?" I asked, surprised.

"At least then some students can get a higher education," Violet replied.

I rebutted, "But then only those rich enough to get their children successfully through primary and secondary school will benefit."

"But those people will help develop this country," Betty argued, "so it is important that they get a university degree."

"Then you end up with a very small and well-educated elite," I replied, "and a large population of semiliterate people who've had to drop out of school early. I think it makes much more sense to me to provide basic education for as many people as possible."

They considered my idea, but both teachers still thought that school should carry fees up until university. They could not convincingly tell me why, though, especially in light of their complaints about the high cost of education.

Teachers, as important transmitters of cultural values, may easily pass on these assumptions about exclusive educational entitlement, frustrating even their own educational goals for their students and children (Kneller 1965, 75). This reinforcement of a culture of educated elite that eliminates so many from basic education indicates the prevalence of the class split created by the inaccessibility of education.

Ever-increasing opportunities for elite children creates the opposite effect for children of poor families, who are becoming "de-schooled" by the lack of commensurate educational experiences (Boyle 1999, 73). This shift indicates a disconnect between social stratification and the state, because elites are managing to subvert the power of the state to set the educational agenda by establishing private schools where high-quality state education does not exist (Boyle 1999). While this is certainly true to some extent in Uganda and other African countries, most urban poor who cannot afford private schooling for their children increasingly look to the state to uphold standards and increase access. The government has made great strides with the implementation of UPE, but in the face of overwhelming demand, the state still fails to fulfill the expectations of potentially middle-class parents and its own national expectations for education: that children will become gainfully employed so that they can help their families—and the nation—out of poverty.

Class Formation: Education and Mobility

The Obonyos and Jill's teachers show how the Ugandan educational system and Ugandans' desires for education help solidify a still-developing national class structure. Further, the specific concepts of development and nationalism now prevalent in education form a language that fosters the articulation of aspirations for class formation and mobility. Schools serve as sites for the inculcation of state ideology that both enable and worsen social inequality—"hence [they are] places where the student-as-subject would become ideologically positioned to assume his or her role in the class structure" (Levinson and Holland 1996, 5).

Discourses of children's rights and citizenship for national development are two means of reinforcing class and education. When children talk about these ideas, they constantly evoke a gradual process of stratification through educational attainment. Jill and her friends often told me that they wanted to stay in school because being educated would grant them access to better jobs as adults, which they were confident would be better than the opportunities available to previous generations. This they would pass on to their own children. As Jill once put it, "When we grow up, we want also to teach our children to go to school, and when we grow up, we shall not have jobs if we have not gone to school and if we didn't have education."

Children still encounter an ideological paradox in which, though older generations encourage participation in class-based educational posturing, children's access to the social and economic tools necessary to fulfill education's promises are limited. This is partly because parents and the state have their own hands tied by economic crises, but also because adults are not willing to relinquish their power over children's lives and choices. In response, children strategize for the future in ways that indigenize imported concepts of nationalist ideology in an effort to make national development goals relevant, not only in the hearts and minds of society at large but to their own environmental realities.

However, class maintenance remains significant in the philosophy of schooling, despite prevailing social limitations. A side effect of the value placed on schooling while many cannot afford it is that parents have few alternatives to schooling for their children, though they may be aware well ahead of time that they will not manage to pay school fees for them. Kubili head teacher Beatrice once told me, "The national goals for schools are broad, but within the school, the goal is to produce people who will be self-reliant in the future using the knowledge gained from school." A main part of this is helping children who cannot continue with schooling to develop skills that will help them earn livings. "We should develop a child completely," she said. She reminded me of the school mission, which says, "To produce children who can work for themselves, and . . . succeed in the work they are doing." Beatrice believes that teachers should serve as substitute parents for children while they are at school. If children are not getting what they need from home, or if duties at home interfere with school, teachers also need to try to counsel the parents about their roles as caregivers. "We need to tell them some of their roles," she said. "Parents expect the school to perform wonders in their children. . . . They want the teachers to bring their children up to be useful citizens. Of course, that is the first reason why they send the children to what? To school." Teachers are always blamed for poor exam results, Beatrice complains, but parents do not realize that poor performance is due to lack of adequate parental support. Paying fees is not enough; children also need books, clothes, and supplies to do well in school.

The Production of the Educated Child: Schooling Pedagogies and Practices

Along with ideologies of schooling come practices, symbols, and languages that reinforce the construction of educated citizens. Throughout my fieldwork, I observed countless incidents in which teachers, subtly or forcefully, tried to mold children into "proper" students, drawing from established norms of both schooled identity and ideal childhood. Further, schools, parents, and children are harnessing nation-building discourses to produce a particular subjectivity in the educated young citizen. This was a subjectivity I saw reinforced in schools and in homes, and I saw children act it out constantly, even before education had been truly attained.

At one of the first Kubili school assemblies I attended, all the students lined up by class on the open ground in front of an elevated block that served as a natural stage. Several of the teachers stood with a small microphone and amplifier. Teacher Beatrice started by reminding students to keep their classrooms tidy. Due to some petty thefts around the school, Beatrice announced that students should only be in their own classrooms and that the doors would be locked at certain times of the day. Then she went on to talk about appropriate hairstyles. "Hairstyles that involve plaiting, beads, or hair that is long enough to grab and pull between two fingers are hairstyles that we don't wear in school," she admonished. Uniforms were to be kept clean and ironed. Everyone should come to school looking "smart."

This double entendre is significant because children were constantly interested in cultivating a schooled identity. School uniforms and short hair that cannot be "worked" into fashionable styles constitute in themselves a "style" that marks one's educational and class status. Though one might argue that going to school and actually being educated are two different things, parents and children alike feel a sense of accomplishment even when children merely take on the appearance and comportment of students. As uniformed schoolchildren make their way along crowded streets to school in the morning or clog the taxi parks on their way to and from boarding schools, they become walking symbols of their families' desired class status. Whenever they knew I had a camera, students pestered me for a photo in their uniforms, with their school supplies and other class markers (fig. 5). These are just some of the visual cues that signal the educated child.

Students are also supposed to be obedient and hardworking. But they are expected to manifest those characteristics on cue and in very specific ways and situations. More broadly, schools strive to produce a concept of ideal child subjectivity. Children are supposed to be happy and carefree. After Beatrice's announcements at the assembly, the children were expected to sing. A second-grade girl with a squeaky voice took the microphone, stood in front of the student body, and confidently led a song called "Everyone Was Once a Child." The teacher with the other microphone encouraged the other children to sing along and clap. "I want you to jump and enjoy!" she exclaimed. "You are children; you are not old like us. Please jump around and sing because you are children." Most of the seventh-graders declined, considering themselves too grown up for such a thing. The teacher pointed accusingly at them, shouting, "There are some there who are not children: they are not enjoying!" After the little girl finished singing, the teacher invited other students to lead a song. "You can sing anything" she said, "except for disco or reggae."

The teacher's sentiments, typical in Ugandan primary schools, illustrate how children are encouraged to enact their childhood identity: by jumping around and singing. But they could only sing songs acceptable to the adults in charge of ministering childhood; otherwise, they would not be acting as model children. At the same time, the singing of the

5   Two primary school boys pose for a photo. The bag is from an upscale Kampala book-
     store. Photo by the author ca. 2001.

youth anthem and the school song reminded them that they were also
expected to be aware of their responsibilities as schooled individuals
for the development of the future nation. Every productive citizen was
"once a child." Levinson and Holland have argued that these are some
of the ways in which schooled identity "builds students' allegiances to
'state culture' and the hegemonic project of national identity which the
state advances" (Levinson and Holland 1996, 28).

Pedagogies and practices like these narrowly define the norms of an
educated person's behavior and their purpose. The ways in which the
larger society constructs children's subjectivity in the context of social
forces and historical circumstances thus both enables and restricts children's agency. At one school club meeting, Teacher Elizabeth encouraged
the children to show respect for their nation. One way they could do that

was by singing the national anthem. She asked them to stand and sing it and then had children criticize others who were not respecting the anthem. This effectively alienated some children who failed to enthusiastically participate, but there are spaces for resistance and negotiation: children formulate their identities across many different social spaces, including family, peer relations, and public life. They may therefore get diverse cues about the kinds of "educated persons" they should become (Levinson and Holland 1996, 15). The Obonyos, for example, formulated a very particular set of expectations for their children and the schools they attended. The older children at the assembly resisted the "child" label and were warned against referencing popular culture by singing any disco or reggae songs.

In these instances, children often become discursive subjects over whom various adults claim authority as they are producing educated citizens. Teacher Beatrice often lamented in our conversations the gulf between the school and the home environment. She claimed that this existed because parents did not reinforce whatever the teachers tried to impart. "Our parent-teacher association doesn't even meet regularly," she said, "and whenever we try to call individual parents to discuss their children, they refuse to come, thinking that the teachers want to bug them about fees." Beatrice was not sure how significant the role of poverty was, but she did say that salaries at children's homes were often stretched too thin because people had more children than they could care for. Even parents who have few biological children often have quite a few dependents for whom they are financially responsible. This leads not only to a decrease in the number of children who can stay in school, but also to a sacrifice of quality due to lack of parental involvement. Schools are left with the burden of shaping citizens.

The inculcation of schooled comportment is often coercive. Children complained of abusive teachers who beat children too much when they failed to learn a topic. Jill ultimately defended the beatings from teachers and parents, though. "They beat you for what you have done," she said. In other words, she had learned the consequences of failing to meet or resisting teachers' expectations. Though many children were resigned to it, it took a heavy toll on them, both physically and psychologically, and at times confused them. I saw one teacher pretending that she was about to kick a student whom she had made sit on the floor in the front of the classroom for being disruptive. She repeatedly made him flinch as she hovered over him with her leg pulled back. Meanwhile she had the rest of the class singing and clapping "Jesus Loves Me."

Though adult society has created restrictive categories for educated child citizens, children themselves are working hard to stay in the educated category. Even if their parents and teachers were not looking out for their individual interests, children like Jill would do what was necessary to stay in school. They know firsthand the social and economic consequences of dropping out and becoming marginalized, like their former classmate, the boy in the window.

Education: An Attainable Right?

Just what does the right to education mean? Urban children and their parents are not the only ones with educational aspirations; they are common throughout the country, indicating that more is at stake than individual class mobility. Given generally adverse conditions, the difficulties of enforcing UPE raise the important question of whether education is indeed an enforceable right.

At the World Vision Gulu Children of War Rehabilitation Center, repatriated child soldiers attended workshops on the right to education as part of their rehabilitation. Counselor Charles explained the concept and noted that in the end, children would need their parents' support in order to go to school. If necessary, Charles told them, they should help their parents to raise fees. But money was not the only obstacle to schooling. One boy asked cynically, "What should I do if my father insists I do work before going to school?"

Another boy responded, "You should leave the father, go to school, and do the work later."

"What if the father then refuses to pay fees?" a girl asked.

"I used to wake up very early to finish my father's work in time to go to school," a third boy said.

Yet another said, "The child needs to convince the father that his schooling will help the whole family."

A boy asked whether the father could be held accountable for denying his children education. Charles responded that lawyers and judges would decide that. The students did not look comforted by this. A boy stood and volunteered that the father would be wrong in that case. Others emphatically agreed. Charles summarized by saying that parents will eventually regret it if their children are not educated. "World Vision will mediate with parents on the importance of education," he assured them. One boy stood up. "I used to dig to pay my own fees, but now with my parents dead, it's useless for me to go to school."

The others disagreed with him sharply. "The government should help returned rebels when no relatives are available to help," one child offered, perhaps as a form of reparations. But Charles insisted that they could go to school through the help of NGOs such as World Vision. These organizations can help with schooling as well as vocational education, which both the state and international donors increasingly promote as a viable alternative to academic learning for rural and otherwise marginalized children, regardless of children's hopes that education will lead them away from vocational work (Meinert 2003, 179). World Vision told the children that they had to use their rights "correctly" in order to gain access to assistance. Still, these former child soldiers expressed skepticism about the resources available to them. They felt they were on the outside looking in and that their chances of securing an education were slim.

In such cases, education signifies the reproduction of class inequality and elite entitlement, despite hopes that it will provide a means of mobility. In a country where children are threatened with wars and a high chance of orphanhood due to declining life expectancies, existing practices prove even more exclusionary. It is often up to children themselves to employ creative strategies that will help them stay in school.

James: Educational Resourcefulness

James was one of the many children who placed his right to education above all else. His story highlights the fragility of children's sense of economic stability in Uganda. Due to sudden and traumatic changes at home, he was anxious about his chances if he were unable to continue with school.

At first glance, James, a spindly, twelve-year-old boy in sixth grade at Kubili Primary School, seemed to be shy and unassertive. But as I got to know James, I realized how resourceful and attentive he was, even in the face of difficult situations. And he could be quite assertive when he followed his own sense of right and wrong, usually informed by school lessons. Once he learned the harmful effects of smoking, for example, James went to his father, a policeman whom he looked up to, and said, "When you smoke, all the people in the house smoke." His father said nothing but stopped smoking shortly thereafter. In some small way, James had made a difference, and he liked that feeling.

James was born to a Pokot father and a Muganda mother in Masaka, in western Uganda. His father met James's mother, Margaret, when he was stationed there at the police post, and married her in 1983. Baganda parents were not usually very open to their daughters marrying outside the tribe, but since James's father had a steady job and had learned the language, they accepted him. They had five children together, of whom James was the third. His brother Alex, who closely followed him, was in the same grade as James when I met them, and each of them was regularly first in his class.

In a preliminary interview before the school break, he painted a picture of a very stable home with a strong and respected father of modest means but generous intentions. When I returned after break, I found James in his classroom and talked to him on the veranda. I asked him how his break had gone, and he replied shakily, "Not well. My father passed away." His father had had high blood pressure for some time, and when he started to experience pains in his chest, he sent his wife to the dispensary to get some medicine. She returned to find him slumped against the bathroom door. She could not move the door to get to him, and by the time any assistance arrived, it was too late to save him. His early death at forty-six had suddenly left a widow and five orphans. Because Ugandans frequently encounter death, the teachers at school thought it profound that James, who had consistently been number one in his class, sat for exams a few days after his father's death, and dropped to number two.

His family, who had been living in the overcrowded barracks, was immediately asked to leave to make room for families of living policemen, so they moved to a rented house just outside the barracks. With very little savings, James's mother started a small tuck shop, but it did not make ends meet. Lacking job skills and higher education, she had few other options. She had had to bury her husband and take care of her teenage daughter's newborn baby. She had opened a case against the boy who had impregnated her daughter, but the legal process was moving slowly. She was not expecting compensation soon, if it ever came at all. Her husband's brothers had no money to help her, either, so she had to do the best she could with what she had.

James suppressed his grief, but he sorely missed his father. After he would go to bed, his mother would hear him anxiously asking his brother what they were going to do to survive and stay in school. After that, James became quite sullen and reticent. It was difficult for me to draw him out, especially about his father. When he did talk about him, he described a man who always went beyond the call of duty to raise his children properly. James received countless lessons from his father, and he attributed his success in school thus far to his father's strict discipline and love. His father had given him a small allowance in hopes of teaching him the value of money. James learned well; rather than spending it on food or toys like many of his friends might have, James invested his money in a couple of baby chicks. He raised them into plump chickens and sold them as fryers. With the profits, he invested in more chicks and some building materials. He made a small coop and hoped that his chickens would start laying eggs. That way, he could sell eggs to help raise his own school fees and maybe even contribute to the family's purse.

James's struggles suggest that in order to maintain his schooled identity, he had to balance his role as a student with the need to become a wage earner and provider at home. His situation is just one example of how the loss of a parent fuels children's anxieties over the future in Uganda's current socioeconomic climate, yet I knew no other children who were quite so industrious. In fact, many urban schoolchildren, including Jill, were actively discouraged from engaging in any income-generating activity because it went against local cultural conceptions of the schooled child. This had much to do with the current investment in children's rights discourses, which extended children's dependency on their parents beyond the usual bounds of cultural norms, and which people interpreted as being against child labor across the board. Child labor tended to be narrowly interpreted, however. Chores in the home, for which children received little or—in most cases—no pay were considered acceptable. But for children to work in the public economic sector violated the adopted neoliberal development norms. James saw that he had little choice, however, and his mother admired his thoughtfulness.

James hoped to become a doctor because he liked science and he thought it was an effective way to help people. As shown by his asking his father to quit smoking, he applied his knowledge in ways that were already bettering people's lives.

I used to get sick with malaria a lot. I was young, and that year mosquitoes were so many in Uganda. People never bothered with their home compounds like that. Most people were just destroying the environment, by pouring rubbish any way, by pouring water, not even cleaning inside, not even clearing that water away. One day, a representative from NEMA [National Environmental Management Agency] came to our school and told us about ways we could reduce such illnesses in our community. I went home and introduced this program of NEMA. So people started cleaning. They were educated how to keep their community clear. That helped me not to be sick. And my younger brother stopped being sick also.

James's story seems to indicate that the Ministry of Education's development mission for state education is working as planned, but his predicament of having to ensure his own access to education highlights the fragility of such success claims. Regardless of continuing issues with access to education and quality, it is clear from these children's stories that schooling matters deeply to the country's development agenda as well as to individual and family class aspirations. Sometimes achieving and maintaining a schooled identity can be more important than actual learning. While being enrolled in school and being educated are not always one and the same, children who cannot attain them may suffer dire consequences; either they are socially marginalized, or they miss out on gaining knowledge that, like James, they can transmit to their communities, thereby participating in the grand narrative of national development. Thus, despite disjunctures in schooling's perceived objectives and actual accomplishments, the desire for education in Uganda remains widespread, transcending age and class. Pedagogies that produce educated citizens profoundly affect class definitions, which in turn affect possibilities for children's agency, especially outside of the established social construction of the schooled individual. But the children I met also attest to the high hopes students hold for what their educations will do for them and their families. The next chapters detail some specific aspects of children's identity formation around these aspirations.

THREE

"Speaking the English of a Ugandan Person"

The Intersections of Children's Identity Formation

Having examined the effects of international development and educational discourses on local understandings of children and childhood, I turn now to a discussion of how children's national subjectivities are constituted by and constitutive of the broader national character in Uganda. Most theories of agency and subjectivity are overwhelmingly adultist in their purview (Wallace 1995, 295). Childhood is usually defined negatively, as "not adult." As Allison James notes, "Childhood is, simultaneously, the cultural space within which children learn not only what they are but also what they are not and what they will become" (James 1993, 29). This is one reason why the study of children's identity formation is slippery at best: recognition of children's social lives is circumvented by the notion that childhood is a process of becoming rather than a state of being in its own right. Because children have very fluid and dynamic identities formed within the boundaries of what childhood should and could be as a category of identity and experience, we must try to account for this in social theory by no longer privileging the notion of essentialized, singular, individual identities (Ackroyd and Pilkington 1999, 449). Commonly circulated ideas about childhood—and the social policies based on them in the name of protecting children—often only obscure children's lived experiences (James 1993, 30).

The already contested concept of nationality becomes intimately entwined with culture and identity in the Ugandan context; culture is employed as a means to create national political unity through individual socialization. But social collectives change as much as individuals do, and change in collectives is achieved by group social processes (Corsaro and Molinari 2000). As sociologist William Corsaro has pointed out, social science needs to make better attempts to understand children's roles in group identity processes developmentally, over time, and across social institutions. This chapter is an ethnographic contribution to that discussion. During my fieldwork, I saw that children were interpellated by dominant discourses of national identity while they also questioned the gaps between ideology and their daily realities, thus making children's identities particularly complex and often inchoate. Children do not lack identities; their identities metamorphose rapidly with each new, formative experience.

Drawing from students' essays and interviews, I identify the major elements of identity that children themselves found to be most important in their conceptions of themselves in relation to their country. I start with Asir's life story to give a sense of the experiences that can inform children's identity-formation processes. Recognizing two themes in children's responses to queries regarding national identity, namely, ethnicity/tribal affiliation and language, I move on to discuss children's interpretation of the teachings and symbols of nationality that permeate their daily experiences.

Asir: A Troubled Path to National Identity

When I asked sixth-grade students at Kubili Primary School to write essays for me, Asir was the only one who offered me his paper in an envelope—one elaborately decorated with his own graphic art. Later, he wanted his paper and envelope back, and he kept after me until I returned them. While I sometimes had trouble drawing other children out, Asir chattered on at length about past or present events, his opinions about them, and his plans for the future. He was not afraid to ask me questions, either; he was curious about my research and asked me a lot of questions about America in general. Though other children may have kept their answers to my questions concise out of deference to adults, Asir was uninhibited and was therefore a good conversationalist.

Asir was born in 1989 in a village outside Tororo, in eastern Uganda, the youngest of thirteen children. His parents are both Japadhola, a Nilotic tribe that settled amid Bantu groups in eastern Uganda several hundred years ago but were never conquered or assimilated. The events that shaped his infancy made Asir aware of how children can become targets for political violence. Fighting came to Asir's village on the Kenyan border when he was a baby. He told me of the war between Alice Lakwena's Holy Spirit Movement and Milton Obote's last fighting forces, who had been ousted in Museveni's 1986 coup. When the shooting started, his mother grabbed him, and the family ran into the bush. "They took a lot of young children," he explained. "When an Obote soldier sees a young child, he takes the mortar used for grinding groundnuts, and he just beats the child. He used to put children there and then [beat them because] if they grow up they will be soldiers to fight against him." Lakwena's soldiers were also very bad. They would padlock people's lips for speaking against them, which, Asir pointed out, Kony's Lord's Resistance Army was still doing in northern Uganda. His family hid in the bush for four months while his father would go back to the house to dig cassava or fetch hens and then bring the food to them. "When we returned to our house after the fighting," Asir said, "it was spoiled by bullets, so we had to move to another house in the village. Recounting the story made him sad. "It was just a chance to survive." Asir made it through without getting hurt, but his uncle was abducted by Lakwena's forces. The family heard that he was killed, but they never received his body for burial, so his spirit was not at rest. This conflict was one of the last insurgencies that threatened the area's security. Today, "it is better there in Tororo," Asir told me. "Now Museveni has sent soldiers there to protect us."

Asir came to Kampala when he was four years old. At the time, his father, Mr. Owora, worked in the city for the telephone company. Despite the ethnically motivated political violence that had shaped his infancy, Asir did not learn about his ethnic identity until he came to the city and learned that people spoke languages that were different from the one he had learned in his village. It took longer to realize his nationality because, as his father put it, "When you're young, you only know your mother and your father."

Asir is another of those children for whom being educated meant a great deal. When he was a toddler, Asir always wanted to follow his older sisters to school when he saw them leaving in the morning. When he was ready to start school, his parents tried putting him straight into first grade. "I was fifth in my class," he declared proudly. "In P2, my father thought I would fail to pass. Then I would have to go back to P1 again because I did not go to nursery school. But I was tenth!" His father was surprised by how well he did, but Asir credited his success to his sisters, because they prepared him for school by teaching him some reading and writing. "But I am also thankful for my teachers," he added, "because they have taught me English, and this is very important." As the medium of instruction in most city schools, Asir would have been lost had he not learned English well. He also recognized education as an essential achievement that allowed him to participate in cosmopolitan society and in the world and understood the importance of the historical moment that made it possible. Asir wrote, "Since I was born in 1989 I got when President Yoweri Kaguta Museveni [was in] power and the country is secularized, united, [and democratic]. I also have some right and freedom like freedom of writing and speech at school." He signed his paper, "Learner Asir Owora."

Though Asir's process of identity formation was not always conscious or deliberate, in retrospect, he was well aware of the experiences that influenced him, sometimes confrontationally (war) and sometimes opportunistically (language). In rising to challenges while embracing advantages like the freedom of expression, Asir's identity was taking shape both actively and passively.

Identity: Student Essays

My conversations about tribal and national belonging with children like Asir revealed the complex ideological interrelations of these elements and how children were negotiating them. To assess these interrelations, I asked the sixth-grade classes at Kubili to write essays for me. I asked them to write down their responses to either of two requests:

1. Write about a time when you really felt like a Ugandan.
2. Write about a time when you really felt like a member of your tribe.

I got eighty responses—a representative sample. Most children responded to only one question, but some answered both. Their answers not only reveal the experiences on the basis of which children interpreted their identities, but also highlight the very different constitutive elements of national and ethnic identities and how they differ (table 3). Further, the responses illustrate the contested nature of national identity. While responses to the question of national identity were somewhat diffuse, children's answers regarding ethnic identity were much more uniform,

Essay Responses

Response	Nationality	Ethnicity
Elections	8	0
Schooling	3	0
Parents/self born in Uganda	11	3
Being citizens	5	0
Universal Primary Education	3	0
National anthem	2	0
Race (black)	2	2
Swimming in Lake Victoria	1	0
Parents/relatives told me	2	6
Visiting village/home district	3	20
Traditional ceremony/holiday	1	13
Language differences	2	12
Learning about culture	0	2
Contact with foreigners	6	0
Grandmother giving nickname	0	4
Other mention of grandmother/elders	0	5
Bloodline	0	1

referring most frequently to village visits, traditional ceremonies, and language.

The most common responses to what made children feel Ugandan were that their parents or they themselves were born in Uganda, that they had just experienced national elections, and that they had come into contact with foreigners. This highlighted some of the diverse ways in which children experience their national identities: through location, politics, and social situations.

The national elections took place during the same month that I requested essays on ethnicity and nationalism, which may account for the particularly political responses from children. In the elections, Museveni ran for his second elected term, looking to extend his fifteen years in office, and was challenged by Colonel Besigye, a former Museveni ally critical of the National Resistance Movement's "no-party" state. Some feared violence, but in March 2001 the elections took place peacefully, and Museveni won by a vast majority.

For many children, their connections with the nation were a transparent matter of lineage. Several children wrote about parents telling them that they belonged to a certain tribe or were Ugandans. One girl said she knew her nationality because she knew she belonged to one of Uganda's tribes. Social memory plays an important role in imparting knowledge about identity. A girl's parents told her stories of British rule as a time of suffering, for example. The stories that parents and grandparents tell about their own communal suffering—either at the hands of the colonial regime or during the civil wars that followed independence—transmit important signals not just about experiences that have molded the identity of the group, but of the *value* of that identity; how the assertion of identity and unity were fought for and won—and therefore deserve continued preservation.

Some children, like Asir, also mentioned contact with foreigners or people of another ethnic group that reinforced their identities. In his seminal article on the Kalela dance in the labor camps of Rhodesia, J. Clyde Mitchell claimed that the urban experience engenders a sense of ethnic affiliation through interethnic contact in the labor centers of southern Africa (Mitchell 1956). Stories that children wrote about their own identity formation also clearly reflected this. One boy wrote, "I felt like a Ugandan when they said that no Europeans to vote [in the presidential elections], only black Ugandans are to vote." In this configuration, nationality is not only a political but also a phenotypical designation. Many children in subsequent interviews also insisted that Ugandans had to be black, mainly by virtue of descent from a black, African tribe that had been in Uganda at least since the demarcation of the nation-state by colonial powers. Sometimes these responses contained latent stereotyping and connections of race and nationality with political events and socioeconomic conditions. For example, one child wrote, "The people of Uganda are called Ugandans and they are black. I felt well like a Ugandan during the time of elections. I was so happy that there were no wars going on." This girl obviously knew a bit about the political violence of the past and might in some way have been trying to dissociate Ugandanness and blackness in the first part of her statement from political violence that some come to consider endemic to Africa because now, in her time, "there are no wars."

Another student was similarly critical in his examination of race and national identity. He wrote, "The time how I really felt like a Ugandan I saw that our country Uganda is very poor and I saw that for us Ugandans we are black and I saw that Europeans are white and I said why did God make us Ugandans black and I said why didn't God make us all the same colour?" This student associates poverty with race and national identity while contrasting black Ugandans with white Europeans; he does not reinforce stereotypes but questions them and their efficacy by pondering God's plan.

Such views also reflect Gregory Bateson's classic "one-hand-clapping" theory of ethnicity, in which—just as it takes two hands to clap—contact with people different from oneself helps one to define oneself and others in terms of that difference (Bateson 1972). Students' responses illustrate the extent to which children can be confused regarding different identity allegiances (nation, race, tribe) and respond by questioning, creatively appropriating, and reinterpreting messages about their own and their countrymen's identities. In the era of globalization, Eriksen notes, "Many people in the contemporary world are structurally placed so as to have multiple loyalties in ethnic terms" (Eriksen 1993, 153). Children, by virtue of their formative status, may be more successful at integrating those identities than others. They also situate Uganda within a global configuration of geographically located race and respond critically to perceived injustices based on these differences.

Understanding Tribal Identity

The term *tribe* is still commonly used to describe a particular type of ethnic affiliation among Ugandans and other Africans. Scholars have shied away from it because of its colonial origins and its tendency to exoticize Africans; indeed, the notions of race and ethnicity expounded by many children were codified during colonial times, and tribal systems of classification were frequently used to exercise hegemony (Reynolds 1995, 230). Colonial administrations often registered people as tribal members to allocate resources, usurp the power of locally legitimate authority figures, and use one tribe to dominate another—all under the guise of "customary authority" (Mamdani 1996, 21–3). Because of this usage, however, the concept of the tribe remains very important to African identities. According to Chabal and Daloz,

Ethnicity is commonly considered in Africanist circles as a problem: either because it is seen as an inconvenient leftover from a previous "traditional" age and a hindrance to modernization or else because it is viewed as a divisive political weapon used by unscrupulous political operators. Both these views, however, are themselves throwbacks to mechanistic interpretations of African realities, casting ethnicity as a simplistically "tribalist" form of identity or as a mere tool. (Chabal and Daloz 1999, 56)

Today, *tribe* is seen in Uganda as signifying an identity that must be acknowledged and respected in the formulation of new political systems. Ali Mazrui writes, "Behind it all is the simple preposition that European colonialism destroyed structures rather than attitudes, undermined traditional monarchs rather than traditional mores. Indigenous empires were annihilated, but tribality triumphed.... While colonialism succeeded in destroying most of Africa's traditional political institutions, it fell considerably short of annihilating African traditional political values and ideas" (Mazrui 2001, 98). Though Mazrui talks of tribal identity as a political concept, it is one with filial ties and values that bear heavily on Ugandan identity formation.

When writing about their tribal identities, children overwhelmingly respond that they feel most like members of their tribes when they visit their villages or home districts. As discussed in chapter 5, most of them were not actually born in those places, but their parents come from them. In Uganda, families are traditionally patrilineal and patrilocal. Social realities, however, often cause children to move among and between both sides of their families, and, with the number of single mothers increasing, children may actually grow up around their mother's extended family. Thus, although children may often share more with their mothers' kin and tribes experientially, they tend to associate more with their fathers' tribes and home villages when it comes to personal identity construction, even though they may not know their fathers' kin or have visited their fathers' home villages.

For many children who wrote essays, however, ethnic identity only became operationalized through attending a traditional ceremony or holiday celebration. Answers to the question of tribal identity were especially gendered: girls overwhelmingly chose to deal with the question about tribal identity, and they almost exclusively cited village visits and traditional ceremonies or holidays as significantly formative of their tribal identities. Even though the most recent formulations of citizenship for national development tend to transmit gender-neutral messages, these answers indicate the alignment of gender with particular cultural spaces.

A great deal of pride and nostalgia usually accompanied recollections of these events, whether children related them to me in writing or verbally. A girl once described a Kiganda introduction ceremony in great detail for me. For her, it was particularly memorable because she was a key member of the bride's party. An introduction ceremony is a traditional celebration in which two people engaged to be married present their future partners to the other's family. I had been to one that resembled the girl's description.

Since the woman will leave her home to go live with the man's family, introduction ceremonies are held at the bride's father's home. The
groom's entourage (usually his parents and key male members of his
family) must come to the bride's father's home with a skilled negotiator
who tries to convince the representative of the bride's family that the
groom will make a suitable husband. He does this with clever wit and
a stack of envelopes containing small gifts of money that he pulls out
at key moments during the negotiations. This bantering can last hours
and usually produces a few laughs from the audience, depending on the
negotiating skills of the families' representatives. If the bride's family
wants to be really hard on the groom, they test him by making him
pick out his bride from a lineup of disguised women. Once the groom's
negotiator has convinced the bride's negotiator that they have a deal,
the groom's party presents brideprice that usually consists of staple foods
and household goods such as salt, soap, goats, cattle, and soft drinks. One
girl wrote,

We waited [for the groom's party] while taking drinks, both local and industry-made
drinks. We the young took sodas while the old slowly sipped local beers and [we
danced to] some music.... I danced but in a special place since I was the bride's
sister.... I was treated like a princess, so important and generally special. That whole
day made me feel like a member of my tribe and I am proud of that.

The girl expresses pride in assuming her cultural place as the bride's sister.
It also makes the point that cultural tradition has evolved to include such
"modern" items as sodas, but that the choices of different generations,
for soda or beer, indicate their varied approaches to and roles in the
ceremony. These practices also vary by tribe. Her classmate described
feeling like a member of her tribe when attending a wedding. For her,
it was a moment when homogeneity meant comfort: "The good thing
was we were all of one tribe. No one complained about the way we were
told to dress."

The Question of Language

Students' responses show that language is another very important marker
of ethnic difference for children in Uganda, as well as a potential unifying
force. It is, of course, closely linked to ethnicity, but it is a much more
complicated identity component than lineage. Asir, relating the points
of his social studies lessons, explained to me that there are more than fifty

different tribes in Uganda, a figure commonly accepted in the literature on ethnicity in Uganda. These tribes belong to three different major ethnic groups and thus three major language groups: Nilotic/Sudanic, Hamites, and Nilo-Hamites. Though members of tribes within the same language group can usually understand each other, communication is typically a problem for those from different language groups.

At independence, the colonial debates about instituting a national language repeated themselves. There was another push to choose a native Ugandan language as the national language, the most popular choice being Luganda. Even though the Baganda constituted less than 20 percent of the population, they were the largest single tribe. And their favor with British colonial administrators lent them more political power than any other indigenous group. Later, the British colonial government under Governor Sir John Hall tried to enforce Kiswahili as a medium of instruction in schools in order to develop it into an East African lingua franca. They reasoned that, since it was a Bantu language, the majority Bantu tribes in Uganda as well as Kenya and Tanzania would be able to learn it easily. But the missionaries battled the decision, declaring that they had already set Luganda, a local vernacular, as the medium of instruction, and since language was a medium of cultural transmission, it was important to keep teaching in Luganda to preserve local custom and cultural tradition–even as the missionaries were transforming it through their educational philosophy.

Other Ugandans noisily protested the suggestion to adopt Kiswahili in Parliament and on the street, and it never won favor. Later, the establishment of the East African Community reopened debate about adopting Swahili as the national language and the East African regional lingua franca, as it was already the national language of both Tanzania and Kenya. But Swahili had become unpopular with Ugandans during the 1979 war, when Obote's Swahili-speaking mercenary soldiers, who had trained in Tanzania, returned to Uganda to oust Amin and terrorized the public. People abducted in the night by Swahili-speaking soldiers were often taken to barracks or bushes and tortured or killed. Swahili thus came to be associated with brutality, and though the Ministry of Education under Museveni tried to reverse that trend, people avoided speaking Swahili in favor of English or a Ugandan native language. Though the topic of an indigenous national language is still revived every once in a while, English, the colonial language, remains the least contested as a national language.

Unification through language has been an unintentional but valuable marker of identity formation for educated Ugandans. David Jacobson's

1973 study in Mbale, eastern Uganda, concluded that educated Ugandans had friends of all different ethnic groups because they could converse in English (Jacobson 1973, 49). By contrast, uneducated workers in town tended to congregate in ethnic enclaves because of language barriers. This continues to be true in urban centers, especially for children who grow up in Kampala. Speaking English and—to a lesser extent—Luganda downplays ethnic difference and allows for easier association.

The use of different languages can create confusion for children trying to determine their ethnic identities. Jill faced initial uncertainty about her ethnic identity because most residents of Kampala, including her family, regularly spoke Luganda. She wrote, "There is a time when we went to a clan party but before, I thought that I was a Muganda. But when we reached the party, people started speaking in Langi and my father was the guest of honor. When I heard him and my elderly sisters [aunts] speaking Langi, I realized I felt like a member of my tribe." Once Jill had straightened it out, she liked the fact that everyone spoke English at school; it helped her make friends. Another student wrote, "A time I really felt like the member of my tribe was when I went to visit the city of Kampala. When I reached there, there were so many tribes. After two weeks I could not find a person [who could] speak with me." Another had a similar story about trying to socialize in his new city environment: "The first friend I met was speaking a different language I had never heard. Then I failed to understand her yet she was speaking Luganda. That's when I felt like learning Luganda and time came I also learnt Kiswahili. From then I felt a Ugandan and now I proceed to be a Ugandan."

The flipside of learning a common language for the purpose of belonging is that children may forget their tribal languages, even when they are spoken at home. One student told me that because she grew up in the city, "I do not therefore know my language very well. I speak Swahili and Luganda plus English language and very little Madi language."

Jill expressed a great deal of anxiety over language's alignment with ethnicity and its implications for national unity. In conversations about presidential and parliamentary elections, Jill always considered how ethnicity was a factor and how it might affect her. One presidential candidate in particular worried her. "He said that if he was elected, he would make everyone speak Luganda," she said. "And I do not think this is fair." She explained that most people in Uganda do not speak Luganda. At the same time, "A child of P3 doesn't know English." She wanted everyone to speak English because in her opinion it was the only language that would bring unity. Yet her comments indicate that she was aware of the huge logistical problems involved, namely, the important role that education and language unification will have to play in this transition. The city and the English language actually become the focal point for many children's personal identity formation as educated national citizens. Because her parents came from different tribes with no linguistic overlap, they tended to speak English at home. At school, Jill spoke both English and Luganda with her friends. Many others mentioned local language as something that made them feel like members of their tribes, but as one girl wrote, "I really felt like a Ugandan when I am speaking the English of a Ugandan person." In this configuration, the use of English not only binds Ugandans together above tribal affiliation; it distinguishes Ugandans from other nationalities by virtue of the unique ways in which they speak English. English, like national identity itself, is often learned in Ugandan classrooms.

Nationalist Discourse in the Classroom

The National Goals and Objectives of Education listed in the government white paper include forging national unity and harmony, and upholding and maintaining national independence and patriotic feeling. "This includes development of a sense of love for all citizens, and a feeling of patriotism in the citizens as well as a readiness to make important sacrifices in defence of Uganda's unity and sovereignty" (Republic of Uganda 1992, 6). This was to be achieved through the typical rituals of patriotism, such as a daily hoisting of the national flag at each school and the singing of the anthem at assemblies. The classroom, however, is the site for most traffic in formalized ideas about nationhood and citizenship.

We have seen in chapter 2 how the well-established link between nationalism and schooling reinforces bourgeois notions of citizenship. Schooled identity itself actually becomes a unifying component of national identity. Children are crossing ethnic boundaries in school that others in alternate social arenas do not cross. Even though they recognize some divisions between children in school (children speak many different languages amongst themselves on the playground), they are much more positive about the unity of their school environment than they are about that of the country.

Children revealed that school was often the place where they learned about being members of their country. As one boy wrote, "I knew that I am a Ugandan when I started schooling." Another girl talked about how she learned to sing the national anthem in nursery school, but no one explained the meaning to her until third grade. "[In] P3B, we were learning geography, science, maths, English, and we were learning the meaning of the national anthem, and that's how I knew that I am a Ugandan."

One day, I sat outside with some teachers, escaping the afternoon heat in the shade of the school block awning. I asked them about issues of unity and ethnicity in the school. "It is true that the school can be unified while the country is not," they told me. One gave the example of two boys we had seen together that had been friends for years. "One is a Karimojong while the other is a Muteso. But get their fathers together and tell them to be friends," she laughed, "and they cannot." They chalked it up to ingrained ancient ethnic hatreds, but I asked, "Then why are these boys friends?" They paused and thought a moment, unable to come up with an explanation. "I remember when I was in school, we had a lot of Arabs there," one recalled. "We got on fine with them—even many of the African students were friends with Arabs. One day we learned about the slave trade. We were taught that Arabs traded African slaves. The teacher showed us pictures of slaves who were brutally beaten. It was shocking! Suddenly, we started to hate the Arab students in the school, even though they were not to the ones who had done this to us."

Such stories became part of a fabric of social memory that children, once they had heard them, came to identify with and internalize. The essays children wrote for me and the comments they made reflected similar themes. They were helpful in determining how children thought about their identities vis-à-vis the state and public political discourse.

Social Studies Class: Interpellation or Interpretation?

Though children's responses to questions of identity are instructive, the top-down, discursive process of institutional learning offers insights into the daily practice of national identity formation in children. Schools often act as "contested and heterogeneous sites for identity formation" (Skinner and Holland 1996); but even when teachers agree about the message of national unity that they wish to impart to their students, their discursive paths to that goal can differ significantly, sending messages about the multivalent nature of nationalism. Further, how their students receive and interpret those messages is beyond their control. To see how schooling in Uganda created this discourse in everyday practice, I sat in on many fifth- and sixth-grade social studies classes. In fifth grade, children learn a very formalized hierarchy of social affiliation,

6   Uganda's national coat of arms.

from smallest to greatest: family, clan, tribe, ethnic group, and nation. They also study Uganda's formation as a nation, its government structure, and national symbols. In P6, pupils study the East African region: Kenya, Tanzania, and Uganda. P7 covers some greater African history and geography. Students do not learn much African or world history until they reach secondary school.

One day, I sat in on a double social studies lesson with Sumayiya, in which Mr. Setunda, a young and charismatic teacher whom the children found entertaining, talked at length about the symbolism on the national coat of arms (fig. 6). Students had drawn pictures of it in their exercise books during the previous lesson, along with pictures of the national flag. When Mr. Setunda asked for a definition of the coat of arms, a student replied by reading from the book, which stated, "It is a national symbol depicting significant items." Mr. Setunda spent the next hour and a half meticulously listing the features of the coat of arms and what each item represents. I took notes along with the students:

- Sun: shows that Uganda is along the Equator and gets sunshine throughout the year.
- Drum: symbolizes communication, culture, entertainment, and a call for unity.
- Crested crane: represents the "gentility and gracefulness of the Ugandan people." The fact that the crane stands on one leg indicates that Uganda is moving forward. It also implies one government, one Parliament, and one leader for the country.

- Spear and Shields: these symbolize defense and protection
- Cotton and Coffee: these are traditional cash crops and exports. They were both introduced by the British.
- Blue Stripes: the wavy blue stripes on the shield symbolize the waters of Uganda, including Lake Victoria and the Nile River.
- Uganda kob: an antelope unique to Uganda, it shows that Uganda is rich in wildlife.
- Green vegetation: indicates that Uganda is a fertile land.
- Motto: "For God and My Country." Indicates that Ugandans respect and fear God.

Although the students were a bit rowdy and undisciplined throughout the lesson (when they were discussing the symbolism of the crested crane, a student shouted out "Krest is a type of soda!"), Mr. Setunda often invoked heritage and tradition, referring to "long ago" when explaining the significance of some items, like drums. "We used to beat drums to indicate danger or to call people to come," he said. To that, children started tapping out rhythms on their desks. Today, Mr. Setunda said, drums are still used to call people to Sunday services. Different drums belong to different ethnic groups, too. "Today," he said, "you kids go to discos to shake your bums. But long ago, drums were used to entertain people." He hummed a rhythm and danced a little dance that delighted the students.

Later, Sumayiya and I talked about the lesson. She said she had only thought about the symbolism on the coat of arms when she went to read about it in her book just before the lesson (she likes to get a preview of lesson material beforehand). She identifies with the items, even though she's never seen some of them, like the kob, a large antelope only found in Uganda.

Sumayiya also felt compelled to tell me about the flag, since they had learned about it that week. "The national flag was designed by Grace Ibingira," she explained, "who became famous for designing that flag. It has six stripes and three colors and a crested crane in the middle. The yellow represents that Uganda receives sunshine throughout the year. The black one represents that all Africans are black, then red represents that Ugandans are related by blood."

"You can't be a real Ugandan unless you have descended from other Africans?" I asked.

"Yes, that is correct."

"Do you think the Indians who live in Uganda are Ugandans?"

"I don't think they are Ugandans because they came from their countries and came in Uganda. There are some true Ugandans . . . but some people are just coming in."

This assumption of ethnic indigenous citizenship is a result not only of the national symbols meant to codify race, but of the ways in which colonial history was taught. I witnessed a number of lessons on the topic and noted the racialized language teachers used to convey this history. Mr. Setunda gave a lesson one day entitled "How Uganda Became a Nation." It was partly a review of what they had learned the previous quarter, with some new material. First, Mr. Setunda asked children to define a nation. Several offered answers, which varied only slightly. The general idea was that "a nation is a group of people within a political boundary, under one government." Mr. Setunda pointed out that a nation can have many different ethnic groups, like Uganda. Mr. Setunda then talked a bit about the history of colonialism, starting with the legislative council, formed to make laws and advise the government. It was established in 1921 but did not include Africans until 1945. There were also political parties that formed at that time, mainly to fight for independence and self-government from "the whites." Notably, in this context Mr. Setunda referred to colonists and native people as "whites" and "blacks" rather than using labels like "British" and "Ugandan." He described the Kabaka Crisis in 1953 when Sir Edward Muteesa II of Buganda wanted more power within his kingdom from the British governor Andrew Cohen. "Why did he want more power?" he asked the students. They answered, "The King didn't want whites to take over." "They ruled badly." "They were taking many things [natural resources] from Uganda." Mr. Setunda affirmed all their answers. "Suppose we are a nation here in this classroom. We have a leader—our prefect—whom we elected to represent us. What if the leaders from P5 Green classroom came and took over our class, so that the prefect in our class loses power to them? How would you feel?" The students whooped disapprovingly. "Wouldn't you try to regain your power over your own territory!?"

"Yeah!" they shouted.

Mr. Setunda related how Cohen had refused to share power with Muteesa, and even had him deported for asking. "He was sent away! Organizations formed and demonstrated for the return of the king!" Mr. Setunda pulled children out of their seats, told them to hold up papers and march around the front of the classroom to illustrate what a demonstration looks like. The children were all amused by it, laughing as they marched or looked on. The Namirembe Conference was held in 1954 to plan the return of the king, who was repatriated in 1955. The students soon started to mimic Mr. Setunda's racialized language, also naming "whites" as antagonists, rather than a national affiliation such as "British." Mr. Setunda did not correct them, reinforcing, however justifiably, racial associations with colonial power. Some students turned to look at me critically during the lesson, as if I had personally banished their kings.

"It was time for Uganda to rule herself," Mr. Setunda said. Britain sent a certain officer named Mr. Wild to organize elections in 1961, because "the British couldn't leave Uganda without a leader," and he returned with the Wild Report. By now, students were getting the idea: "Was he white?" one student asked.

"Yes, of course," Mr. Setunda replied, continuing his explanation of events that led up to independence in 1962, including the Munster Report of 1961 that laid the groundwork for full self-rule. "Uganda was now in the hands of the local Ugandans—real Ugandans," Mr. Setunda said. The Union Jack that had been flying on Old Kampala Hill since 1894 was lowered while the new Ugandan flag was raised up. Mr. Setunda made the motion of raising a flag hand-over-hand and asked the students to repeat it. "Did you know that Old Kampala is a very important Ugandan historical site?" he asked.

"No," the class replied, riveted.

"You don't know enough about your country! Your parents should take you to such places on holidays to teach you something about your country."

Mr. Setunda reviewed the information, and invited students to ask questions. There were some issues on which they still were not clear. One student stood and asked, "How did Ugandans know they should have independence?"

"Can anyone answer that?"

A girl raised her hand. "Because Munster wrote a report."

"They were skilled enough to run their own country," another suggested. Mr. Setunda corrected them: "They were tired of colonial rule."

"Did the British speak Luganda?" a student asked.

"Maybe some did . . . " Mr. Setunda replied skeptically, and started the review.

Later, I watched Malik's teacher take a slightly different approach to the same lesson. Mr. Atepo was an older gentleman with salt-and-pepper hair. He started out reviewing what they had learned last time: that a nation is a group of people living within the same geographical and political boundaries under one government. From there, his lesson departed from that of Mr. Setunda. The class talked about some of the major ethnic groups (Bantu, Nilotics, Nilo-Hamites, Hamites, and Sudanic) that comprise the Ugandan nation. According to Mr. Atepo, an ethnic group is the next biggest social unit after a nation. Then there is a tribe, a clan, and a family. Before the British, there were communal types of government, mainly organized in clans and kingdoms. Mr. Atepo asked students to give some of the names for leaders of various tribes, like the *rwot* in Acholi. The kingdoms that exist in Uganda are Nkole, Bunyoro-Kitara, Buganda, and Toro. "In Bunyoro-Kitara, the leaders called on the gods to perform miracles," he explained. "They descended from the Bacwezi, cattlekeepers and iron smelters who spanned most of East Africa and were joined by the Babito (Luo) people from the north. This is when the Bunyoro-Kitara broke off from the Bacwezi and formed their own kingdom." The Buganda Kingdom also broke away, in the sixteenth century. They continued to expand until 1884, when British settlers and missionaries arrived. Their success was due to powerful leaders and the early arrival of foreigners who traded guns with them. Those colonists found the Buganda kingdom fairly organized and used Baganda leaders to conquer other regions in the area. Students knew the names of quite a few former Buganda kings—though only the current one has been in place in their lifetimes, the kingship having been reinstated in 1993 after being banned by Obote in 1967.[2]

Mr. Atepo spent quite a lot of time talking about the kingdoms rather than the nation and colonial politics. Children were restless throughout this lesson. Several students were falling asleep, and Mr. Atepo pinched the chin of one sleeping girl sitting in front without losing a beat in his lecture.

The teaching styles of the two teachers did not vary greatly, but the topic of colonial rule seemed to interest students a lot more than pre-colonial history and ethnic division. These divisions were exacerbated by colonial rule, Mr. Atepo pointed out, leading to the civil wars of the post-independence period. However, Mr. Atepo, a Musoga, inadvertently drew attention to something that Mr. Setunda, a Muganda, did not: that there was no nation called Uganda before colonists arrived. In his lecture, Mr. Setunda had shifted attention from the tension between regional ethnic groups to the colonizer/colonized dichotomy.

Textbooks also tended to water down or gloss over conflicts, creating sterilized versions of history; they explained all the post-independence changes of government like clockwork, with little reference to the violence and struggle with which those took place. Even the conflicts of colonialism were greatly simplified, though they pointed out that there was a peaceful method and a forceful method of colonization. As C. N. Nganda notes in her study of Ugandan primary school textbooks,

"Social learning from the various channels of socialization in one's childhood lays the groundwork that significantly predisposes people towards holding or not holding stereotyped opinions and attitudes" (Nganda 1996, 45). Textbooks might have mentioned that some ethnic groups did not "get along," but those statements were rarely accompanied by an explication of why. This textbook approach, however differs significantly from the kinds of messages teachers convey in their presentations of the material. These strategies, coming from adult authorities, also undoubtedly influence how children view their society and their places within it, as well as their ideas about others.

This elision of local ethnic tension in the formulation of the independent state may be a product of the present need to downplay ethnic tension once again for the sake of creating a common national consciousness out of still disparate tribal identities. Mr. Atepo, an older teacher who remembers well the devastating effects of tribalism during the 1970s and 1980s, let it creep into his explanation of early nation building because it had been important to his own identity formation. As a result, he always approached the topic of national political unity with an obvious skepticism. When explaining the formation of the legislative council, he said that no Africans were involved because the British and the Indians did not care about African interests, and because the Africans had no interests in state government. "They were still politically ignorant," he explained, "and so didn't really know what they wanted from a legislative body." Mr. Atepo would proceed in subsequent lessons to express his political skepticism, stating that the current government is a military dictatorship no different from previous ones. Mr. Atepo concluded one of his lessons ranting, "Politics are *dirty*, and politicians are *liars!*" Students repeated the words *dirty* and *liars* with their teacher, and he muttered that politicians kill their opponents. Yet, national sentiment still had a certain appeal to him that he tried to instill in his students. At the close of the lesson on independence, he led the children in a rousing version of the national anthem—all three stanzas. The students sang enthusiastically, dramatizing their rendition with the sweeping arm gestures of symphony conductors.

The National Anthem: A Key Symbol

One sunny afternoon, I sat under the giant mango tree in the school courtyard with Asir and James. We were picking at fallen leaves and talking about everyday things that reminded them that they were Ugandan.

Of course, there was the flag. "There's also the national anthem," James mused.

"Oh yeah?" I replied, feigning ignorance. "How does that one go?"

They looked at each other for a moment and then simultaneously broke into song:

Oh Uganda! May God uphold thee,
We lay our future in thy hand.
United free for liberty,
Together we'll always stand.

I had heard the anthem many times, at assemblies and special events, but the boys, who had learned the anthem in third grade, explained its meaning and significance to them. "It's a special song because it helps people have respect for the country," James explained. Their explanations also gave way to social commentary. Noting the mention of God in the first line, I asked, "Is Uganda a religious place?"

"Yes," James said and related the story of the Uganda Martyrs burned for failing to renounce their Christian beliefs. "Those people who believe in God, they have much more power than those who believe in traditional doctors. The Christians want to unite the children to the word of God, so they tell us that the traditional doctors are just trying to make money. They say they can cure AIDS, but it's not true, so Ugandans are trying to avoid them. Some traditional doctors have natural medicines like herbs, so they're not bad."

"The next part is about the land of freedom," James said. They continued with the second verse:

Oh Uganda! The land of freedom.
Our love and labour we give,
And with neighbours all,
At our country's call,
In peace and friendship we'll live.

"Why do you think they wrote that part?" I asked.

"Because Ugandans love each other," James replied. "They don't like fighting, but other people like wars. But Ugandans are tired of wars. These people like Amin Dada, they were bringing wars."

"I told you Amin Dada brought a lot of wars," Asir reminded me, scolding me for possibly forgetting his important lessons.

"I know he did. I have heard a lot of stories about him. But the person who wrote the anthem, he wanted people to love each other?"

"Yes," they both nodded.

"What about labor? Why is labor in there?"

"Because our people need love and labor," James said. The next part would reveal more about that because it was about fertile land. They had trouble remembering it, they said, because they only sing it when the president is around or an important person dies. But they tried to recite it:

Oh Uganda! The land that feeds us
By sun and fertile soil grown.
For our own dear land,
We'll always stand:
The Pearl of Africa's crown.

"That is one thing that people say about Uganda," I said. "You think it is a very fertile land?"

"Yes."

"Why?"

"Because most things are growing in Uganda—most fresh things," James offered. "So we are growing in Uganda. It is a fertile land which can grow and you can transport those goods to the coastline and you can transport them to other countries."

Asir added, "Even the fertile lands are a sign of the people. When they do the coronation [of the tribal kings], then they plant another tree in the fertile lands. When they grow up but are still a small size and a government from outside is coming to Uganda, then they provide you, us, money."

"They export them to other countries?"

"Yes."

Students came out of their classes, and it was getting loud. A crowd had gathered around us, and others had started to join in singing the anthem. It became loud, so they decided they would tell me all about the youth national anthem later. This conversation illustrated some of the ways that children incorporate nationalist messages in their understandings of their country and the greater world. In explaining the anthem to me, Asir and James reflected not only on what it means to them to be Ugandan, but what it means for their nation to be part of the wider world of nations (Billig 1995, 4). The hierarchy of identity that the boys referenced was an idiom of relatedness that linked them not only to the nation but to the international community. Further, their conception of the country is not timeless but is grounded in history (Amin's era, for example), and in the present (trade relations).

Asir and James had to think quite a bit about the meaning of the national anthem, even though they sang it often. This forgetting of daily markers of national identity is what Michael Billig calls "banal nationalism." The term is meant to suggest that the ideologies that reproduce nation-states comprise regular habits that "are not removed from everyday life, as some observers have supposed. Daily, the nation is indicated, or 'flagged,' in the lives of its citizenry" (Billig 1995, 6). These flaggings, particularly in well-established nations, have become so common that they are forgotten, almost subliminal, messages that seep into the context of everyday activities. In the case of a young nation like Uganda, many such symbols are typically much more prevalent, structured, and consciously debated. But my conversation with James and Asir indicates that even for young people, instances of banal nationalism like singing the national anthem have so permeated the fabric of daily social life that their meanings are—at least temporarily—forgotten. It took me, an outsider, to get them to examine the lyrics' meanings in depth. Even so, they did not explain them uncritically, as James' comments on religion indicate.

The Youth Anthem

As I sat in the school library one afternoon flipping through some social studies books, I asked several teachers wandering in and out about the youth anthem (fig. 13). Most did not really know much about its origins. One teacher suggested that the principal of a primary school teacher-training college had written it. She did not know when, though. They knew that it was around when they were in school, so that made it at least twenty years old. But they said they never sang it in schools regularly until Education Commissioner Fagil Mandy insisted on it with the introduction of UPE in 1997. Here is how it goes:

UGANDA'S YOUTH NATIONAL ANTHEM

We young women and men of Uganda
Are marching along the path of education,
Singing and dancing with joy together,
United for a better Uganda.
We are the pillars of tomorrow's Uganda.

Let us now embrace to true knowledge building discipline,
Resourcefulness to rebuild a great great Pearl.
We know the way to the land of enlightenment
Across streams, valleys and mountains.
Come what may we shall overcome for the glorious times to come.
Parents and teachers and the youth of this nation rise with us to support our
    endeavours,
led by God, who is the source of light,
to uplift our motherland.

Another teacher recalled that there was also a women's anthem that is seldom sung. She tried to recall a few bars and sang them for me. The general tone was that women were hardworking mothers of the nation. The last line she sang went something like "Mothers of Baby Uganda."

Whatever its origins or intentions, reciting the youth anthem—something students do perhaps even more regularly than they sing the national anthem—cements children's place in the nation-building project and can become a core part of their identities. One sixth-grade girl gave much thought to the question I had posed to her about what makes her a Ugandan, and some weeks later, she tracked me down to deliver her conclusions. "Okay, when I was young," she started, "my mother told me—I first asked her—'Am I Ugandan?' The question she answered me, 'Yes,' I am a Ugandan. So the things that make you a Ugandan are the national anthem, the youth anthem, and how the tribes behave. They have different cultures like dances. They are not the same as other countries." The routinization of singing anthems only intensifies the association with nationalist sentiment. Billig writes, "If anything, the significance is enhanced: the sacral has become part of everyday life, instead of being confined to a special place of worship or particular day of celebration" (Billig 1995, 51). In this way nationality becomes a central part of one's identity—"nationality as a means of self-definition" as Coles calls it (Coles 1986, 310). But within those national politics are also allegiances to various other social groups, and ideologies that influence how children understand them.

Conclusions

Children talked extensively about national elections, and ethnic, racial, and national identity, but as Billig points out, nationalism does not manifest in language alone. It is a product of a much larger discursive project of mundane, embodied identification (Billig 1995, 8). It is therefore important to consider the various ways that children are confronted with—and engage—identity issues in their everyday lives. The next section details several instances in which children work through these issues, individually and collectively.

For now, it is important to note that we cannot view identity formation as a one-way street of socialization. Aside from national markers fast becoming unnoticed parts of mundane, daily social practice, I saw and heard many examples of children's political consciousness being formed through their interpretations of their historical contexts and Uganda's present historical moment. The next chapter deals specifically with children's political socialization.

FOUR

Children's Political Socialization

Engagement and Disempowerment

A nation's politics becomes a child's everyday psychology. ROBERT COLES

No discussion of nationalism can omit the processes of political socialization for children. The previous two chapters provided some explanation of the common challenges for children of this historical moment in formulating their identities. This chapter draws on this ethnographic information to show how children negotiate their own political identities, and how they try to actualize them despite their apparent invisibility in public life. Popular belief holds that children simply acquire their politics from their parents. This assumption not only denies the existence of intergenerational conflict by assuming an oversimplified cultural transmission of values; it also assumes that the household is a vacuum, devoid of conflict or history, in which children are reared immune to other political viewpoints or formative experiences. This simply cannot be true, particularly when we consider that children—often more so than adults—move across the most diverse social landscapes—from home to school to streets and local markets (James 1998; Katz 2001a). Political consciousness must be more than a simple matter of inheritance. Like adults, children are constantly exposed to and absorb a variety of outlooks, and they reach their own conclusions.

In order to ensure the social reproduction of political attitudes, their principles must be reinforced by what Pierre Bourdieu called the *habitus* within which children are receiving and processing political messages: the discursive and symbolic expressions of social structures that shape individual subjects, and which they help structure through social practice (Bourdieu 1990, 52). Bourdieu's theory of *habitus* as it relates to social practice has been criticized for being too deterministic, and thus better for explaining social reproduction than social change. But the concept of *habitus* can also allow for the possibility of agency, albeit within the constraints of the "structured structures" that subjects inhabit. In Uganda, children formulate political views from their own sociohistorical circumstances as much as—if not more than—they do from their parents' teachings, just as their parents formulated their political views from the turbulent times in which they grew up. Indeed, children at times can be objects of socialization at the same time as they are themselves social agents. Ugandan children's viewpoints challenged models that reduce children's political opinions to the products of parent-child socialization, as well as assumptions that children are ignorant of or unaffected by most social forces and public debates that constitute the political arena. On the contrary, as Coles's epigraph for this chapter suggests, these are the very forces (the *habitus*) that shape their own lives on a daily basis, particularly in a country still struggling to define its political system.

The children I observed and interviewed made informed, interested political decisions regarding elections. Despite their demonstrated competence, however, children's identity as children—people excluded from the "adult" domain of politics—often deterred them from seeking greater participation in political processes, revealing another instance where children are empowered by ideology while limited in their power to act by that same ideology.

Children's Political Views: Inheritance or *Habitus*?

In a short twenty years, Uganda went from colonized protectorate to a land bloodied by despotic leaders and ethnic warfare and then became the apple of the international development industry's eye. Many of today's parents were robbed in their childhoods of the political freedoms and personal choices that their children now enjoy as a result of these changes. As parents were constantly reminding me (and their children), things were very, very different when they were growing up.

Theories of intergenerational political inheritance do not account for such large disjunctures between generations' political experiences. In the sectarian Uganda of the 1970s and 1980s, expressing one's ethnic identity or speaking out on political issues could put one's life at risk. Having been reborn by independence and baptized by the fire of political strife, the Ugandan nation is indeed still in its political infancy. The governing National Resistance Movement's "no-party democracy" is an experimental exercise attempting to incorporate elements of various models of governance from other countries that can be "customized" to fit Ugandan society (Museveni 1997). In 2001, having been assured by the NRM of freedom of speech,[1] most children felt that the preservation of political freedom was itself at stake in the national elections. When the 2001 national elections took place during my fieldwork, I met many people—young and old—weighing these different approaches to governance and their compatibility with Ugandan society. Aside from schoolyards abuzz with debate about the merits and shortcomings of the candidates, elections brought out the ways in which children defined themselves in relation to the nation.

Uganda is thus at a very important juncture in its political history as an independent nation. Many Ugandans feel keenly that how this generation of children handles political responsibility may make or break the country's stability. To preserve the fragile national unity they perceived, children rejected the fissures that divided their parents' generation; the last few chapters indicated some of the ways that tensions between children in this generation tend to center on class and cosmopolitanism rather than ethnicity and sectarian politics. These issues still matter to children as they formulate their political views, but in ways relevant to their current circumstances and future aspirations rather than their parents' tragic pasts.

Asir and Mr. Owora: Intergenerational Political Tensions

Politics sometimes put children at odds with their parents. Twelve-year-old Asir's current situation was shaped as much by poverty as by politics, and though he shared that experience with his entire family, it caused a strain between him and his father. Mr. Owora was dismissed from his telephone company job in 1995. Since then, he had been surviving in Kampala on his pension and odd jobs. When I met Mr. Owora, his pension had run out, and he was desperately looking for help to keep his few children who were still in school from having to drop out. When we met, he brought an envelope with important documents like his pension slip and his children's school reports. His brother, who was killed in 1989, also left five children for whom Mr. Owora was responsible. One by one, Mr. Owora had had to take the children out of school and send them back to the village to live with their mother. Asir was one of the few who were still in school. "I have a major problem," Mr. Owora said of his need for school fees. "I don't even sleep at night. . . . For these children who are not in school, I feel I have failed them." His gaze dropped to the ground as his shoulders slumped, crestfallen.

Under these hardships, Mr. Owora had quite a negative opinion of Museveni. He blamed many of his problems on poor governance that had impoverished him and many other Ugandans. "Today there is peace," he explained, "but because of it, there is another war. *Poverty* is another war. Otherwise, this government of ours has given us peace, but they have no way of helping us to come up fully. Instead, they are milking us." Although ethnicity was not something Mr. Owora said he cared to stress in rearing his children, and he thought the obstacles to unity were political rather than ethnic, Mr. Owora usually went on to complain about ethnic and regional disparities, claiming that the eastern region from which he hailed had not gotten its "piece of the national cake."

Though he did not revere ethnic tradition either, Asir always seemed politically concerned with his home area's regional and ethnic interests. For a while, Asir was thinking of being a pilot so he could see other countries, but the dangers highlighted by the events of September 11, 2001, scared him away from the idea. Instead, he thought maybe he would like to be a politician so he could make some good money and help develop his home area at the same time. "I hear people saying they want electricity, they want light on the sides of the road," he said once while musing about the things he could accomplish in his political career. This would help him fulfill his duties to his own people. Corruption might be difficult to deal with, but he concluded that, like everything else, "Politics has it advantages and disadvantages." Asir had written about the elections in his essay, so I pointed out that Museveni had been in power his entire life. As I got to know Asir, I realized that he saw Museveni as a sort of national father. When I asked whether he liked Museveni, the tenor of his high, nervous voice changed to a mellow reverie: "Very much," he said with a smile. "Even if my father doesn't have enough money, Museveni has given us UPE [Universal Primary Education]." Asir once explained to me that the tribe and the nation are like the bigger, extended family. At each level, they speak different languages like Japadhola and English.

Asir's political differences with his father disprove assumptions that children merely adopt the politics of their parents. Because of the very same factors—poverty and the government's response to it—Asir and his father held opposing viewpoints toward their nation's leaders, conditioned by their relative subject positions. Mr. Owora felt disillusioned by Museveni's economic promises, whereas Asir liked Museveni because he supported Asir where his father might otherwise fail in his responsibility to educate his children.

Asir knew his father cared about him because he bought him food. However, Asir got upset with his father for promising rewards he could not deliver. In the past, his father had promised him rewards for good grades that he could not actually afford when Asir achieved those grades.

He can say, "If you become like number four [in your class], I will give you something." You try your best then you become like number two, but there is nothing he can give you. . . . I feel good because I have done well but . . . he should not promise because God said, "Do not promise." My mother does not deceive me when I am at home.

Despite all this, Mr. Owora said he tried to give his children advice for success. Asir seemed to have gotten the message, because he always studied hard and was very inquisitive and determined. Asir believed that children were expected to succeed so they could pay it forward to the next generation. "[Parents] don't want us to be poor like them." Yet he knew his father was struggling, so he, like other children, had planned for the possibility that his father would not be able to continue to pay his fees. He would ask relatives to sponsor him, he said. If that failed, he would go to the village if he had to. He had grown up there and visited often, and he knew he would do well, but he preferred to stay in the city because he believed that the quality of his education would be better there. Asir emulated his friend James, who was very good in school, and he and a friend even once skipped the school variety show to look over some old exams. He hoped he would be able to continue his education in the city for as long as his father could afford it, and he was making the most of it while it lasted.

Children and the Political Process

At the same time that children were taught to navigate the political system, they were also actively discouraged from openly expressing political viewpoints in school. Teachers were not allowed to talk about the elections in classes, and when students waved small campaign posters in the air during assemblies, they were rooted out of the crowd and punished. In these and other subtle ways, children were systematically excluded from actively participating in the country's political life. Yet children were very interested in the election and avidly watched and discussed it among themselves. When I asked them to write essays a few weeks later, many responded that the elections had reminded them of their citizenship. Their responses revealed the extent to which political participation helped define their sense of national belonging. Many had gone to polling places to see the final vote counts, or had sat around radios or television sets with their families, eagerly awaiting announcement of the results. But not being able to vote signaled their status as less-than-complete citizens. While many took an avid interest, the established, apolitical discourse of childhood undermined their confidence, often to the extent that they internalized adult assumptions of their political incompetence—a point to which I return at the end of the chapter.

However, some students used the opportunity to critique the political process and explore their roles within it. A soft-spoken boy named Geoffrey extensively explained not only how the election helped him to feel more like a member of his country but how he as a child was simultaneously socialized to become a citizen while being denied the ability to exercise his citizen's rights because of his age. He wrote,

A Ugandan is someone whose parents are citizens of Uganda. . . . I was born in Uganda implying that I am a true Ugandan. I had however not yet recognized myself as a Ugandan not until the 12th March 2001 when the presidential election was held.

On the polling day I picked up interest of being a Ugandan when I saw my fellow students though of higher institutions casting their votes. I personally had no voter's card. I looked around to find if at all I could get one, but all I could see was the sight of instabilities in case the election wasn't free and fair. I revealed my feelings to my friend but the only advice I got was to keep myself out of the political situation of Uganda.

Only a day after, the results were out but before rumors had revolved around Kampala that the candidate of my choice had won. I found myself guilty for not voting for him yet I had interest in him. However, I was as happy as any Ugandan I could see nearby. To my surprise, I heard it after two days that my candidate had lost. I was so sad but being a Ugandan, I had to play it cool and wait for the next election to be had some few years to come where I will vote for a candidate of my choice.

In conclusion therefore, the prevailing politics of Uganda has forced me to acquire citizenship of my own country and currently I treat myself as a Ugandan though [I] am still very young.

Through this experience, Geoffrey learned not only about the nature of his nationality but about the political process itself and its limits for children's participation.[2] He saw what he thought was a violation of the democratic process and wanted to address it, but he was dissuaded by his friends who implied that as a child he had no power to change the situation. He learned from the experience that restraint ("playing it cool") is as important a strategy as action in the local political climate.

Geoffrey was one of many children who used his essay as an opportunity to express dissent about politics and subtly reveal his own political leanings. One girl wrote, "Politically I really realized that I am a Ugandan when I recently used to see and hear people campaigning for presidential elections for the year 2001. *Unfortunately*, his excellency president Yoweri Museveni Kaguta became the president of Uganda [my italics]." Another boy also described the elections as a time he felt Ugandan while questioning the political process and how that potentially compromised his own convictions regarding his national identity: "I wondered if this was a peaceful election or an election of cheating and in fact this was the day when I felt like a Ugandan."

When talking to children about the elections, I found that they had strong opinions about which candidates they liked and why. Most of their reasons for liking a candidate were directly related to issues that affected them as children. Many told me that they liked Museveni because he instituted UPE. They described political debates within their homes and communities, and others talked about learning about the candidates from listening to the radio or reading newspapers. It was apparent from their responses that children saw their choices as very individual and personal decisions, and that many of them had done at least some comparative research in order to reach their conclusions about candidates they preferred.

The Obonyos encouraged open political discussion at home. The whole family turned out to be very politically opinionated, for various reasons. "Children tend to side with their mothers on political issues when they are young," Mrs. Obonyo believed, "because they spend more time with their mothers and identify with them more closely." She also assumed that children made political decisions based on trivial matters. For example, Michelle, at five years old, preferred President Museveni to Colonel Besigye because she thought Besigye was ugly. But Jill and other children regularly took on the real issues, and paid attention to how they might benefit or be disadvantaged under certain candidates' rule.

When I once asked Jill to talk about some of the important events in her life, she automatically interpreted the question as meaning national, political events. All of her examples were of a tribal-national significance: the *kabaka*'s coronation, presidential elections, Bill Clinton's recent visit, the *kabaka*'s wedding. She emulated these leaders, along with the child king of Toro, King Oyo—a rare example of a child who held some kind of political power. She told me how he acceded to the throne at age six after his father died. He was nine years old at the time of our conversation. She was pleased that there was a child king, but she surmised that she would not want to be a queen because "there are jealous adults who might threaten your safety. Some of the big people want to be the king, and if they challenge you, you can't beat them." There were also a lot of royal responsibilities that Jill suspected she would find cumbersome.

James was also very interested in the electoral process as it unfolded. I originally became intrigued by James and his family when he explained to me that his father had held a mock presidential election in his house shortly before the 2001 national election date. Despite the appeal of the democratic exercise, James said, "My father told us he would not support any family members unless we voted for Museveni." Naturally, all seven voted for him. Despite this coercion, James maintained that he had formulated his political opinions independently; he was a fan of Museveni because of his implementation of universal primary education: "I am a Ugandan by birth, tribe . . . most important of all time when I really felt like a Ugandan is the time when our dear president Yoweri Kaguta Museveni introduced [universal] primary education in 1997 of which I am benefiting." Though James was surely somewhat influenced by his father, he had his own reasons for supporting the same candidate, and, while he directly benefited, he was also well aware of the ways UPE placed Uganda in a global development context: "The introduction of universal primary education has earned both our president and the country a name in the world. . . . Ugandans who are [now living] in other countries of the world are now happy to be called Ugandans which was not the case [before]."

James followed the elections on the radio and became unusually animated when we talked about it. When I asked him how he thought children should participate in the political process, he said, "Children should go ahead and support a candidate, even if they cannot vote. They can put up posters, wear T-shirts, and sing songs about candidates. They can influence older people with their support." He personally planned to vote for candidates whom children like when he is old enough.

Political Violence and the Power of Social Memory

Political identity formation in Uganda cannot be removed from the context of historically recent political violence. Adults' political disinheritance helped throw into relief the political freedoms that children now had through a "transformation of knowledge across generations" (Reynolds 1995, 226). Today's children, raised exclusively during the Museveni regime, were more openly critical of the government and politics because they had freedom of expression that their parents had lacked as they were growing up. Against this backdrop, children were shaping political values around freedom and the knowledge that, without vigilance, it can be revoked.

Mrs. Obonyo said her children's lives were very different from hers because they were growing up in the city and because she went to school during Amin's time. She remembered people being killed for failing to produce bribe money. And many women were raped. In short, Mr. and Mrs. Obonyo argued, their children have more security than they did when they were young. In many ways, this was true for children in Kampala; political violence was only a vague possibility rather than a daily occurrence. In southern Uganda, they could also move more freely without fear of violent confrontations with soldiers or rebels. Children in northern regions where the Lord's Resistance Army was wreaking havoc were not so lucky (see chapter 7).

Security is one of the conditions that enables even the possibility of public political engagement by children today. Children's broad conceptions of violence had therefore shifted from seeing violence as politically rooted in ethnic affiliation to seeing it as directed at children specifically. Their fears had become very personalized because they had been inundated with what Americans would call "stranger danger." Children worried about all the dangers present for them, especially kidnapping, child sacrifice, abuse, and defilement.

Despite the apparent security, the issue of violence was always at the forefront of children's minds at election time. Rumors abounded on the playgrounds that if Museveni's main opponent Colonel Besigye lost the election, he would "go to the bush" and start another war. Presidential elections took place only nine months after an important June 2000 referendum in which Ugandans voted against the restoration of political parties, supporting the current government's rejection of political parties in favor of a "no-party state" with progressive development goals. The referendum was the culmination of a long process of political reform in Uganda. While some saw it as a long-awaited opportunity for Ugandans to determine directly their own political future as a nation, others believed that the referendum only served to consolidate the National Resistance Movement's power over Ugandan politics for years to come. Though the ban on political parties was later lifted after a 2005 referendum, political restrictions instigated by the NRM have been justified by President Museveni and the government on the premise that Uganda's past political violence was mainly due to divisive sectarian politics. The National Resistance Movement's ability to stay in power while repressing political activity has relied partly on the threat that the return of political parties would mean the return of the horrific violence that is still fresh in the memory of older Ugandans. People who survived the eras of Obote and Amin are not keen on going back to their methods of rule.

Children were well aware of this recent, sordid past, not only from having learned about it in school, but also from stories that family members had told them of their own personal suffering. Whether or not the introduction of multiparty politics today would necessarily break down into the divisive tribal politics of the past, Museveni has effectively used the social memory of these atrocities to endorse his position of power by claiming that the country has moved beyond the violence inflicted by sectarian politics. Dickson Eyoh writes, "With the mutation of anti-colonial nationalism into state ideology, postcolonial ruling elites have been inclined to public vilification of popular movements organized around subnational loyalties as backward and sectarian" (Eyoh 1998, 293). During the 2001 elections, Museveni's campaign relied on voters remembering personal tragedy and contrasting it to the relative peace and prosperity that the NRM government had brought to Uganda. This discourse manipulates history, using it as a threat to stability and welfare at the same time as it erases current ethnic differences that continue to plague the actual cohesion of national sentiment. Declaring everyone an automatic member of the government's Movement System by virtue of Ugandan nationality supposedly subsumes all differences under the rubric of national identity and the Movement System's platform of progress. Ethnic differences that were at the center of post-independence violence are supposed to have been resolved under the Movement System; the claim is, in effect, that it has already succeeded in its goal to bring people together in a cooperative system that facilitates national development. To his critics, Museveni was using undemocratic means to promote a disingenuous form of democracy as an ideology. To his supporters, he was maintaining the peace.

Though criticism was fair, it was hardly valid to the children who shared their thoughts with me about the elections and the political process. The notion of democracy was vaguely familiar to them, but it did not seem to hold their interest. I had initially assumed that the concept was too abstract for them, but when I questioned children, they assured me that it was not a confusing idea. They understood it; they just did not think of democracy as an important issue. Even the democratic tenet of "one man, one vote" was of lesser interest to them than the preservation of peace. They considered peace, freedom, security, and education most important, and they just wanted any political system and leaders who would guarantee these hard-earned rights. "You can choose a leader who can still fail to guarantee those things," one student pointed out to me, so freely electing people was not the issue; keeping the peace had become the most crucial issue in choosing a candidate. This played into the NRM's campaign strategy.

The elections provided one of many incidents throughout my fieldwork that demonstrated how social memory invokes a common political consciousness in students' narratives. Despite Jill's fairly stable upbringing, she still worried considerably about possible threats to personal and national security. Unity and diplomacy were very important to her, as they were for most of her age mates. "You protect yourself from wars by being united with all the people in the country, your neighbors, your friends, your enemies," she told me. "The best thing is to try to be peaceful with everybody."

Having taken into account both their country's past and its future, children felt privileged to have grown up without experiencing the level of violence that their elder family members had. This was not only a relief, but a point of national pride for young people. One student wrote, "Now I love my country too because there is peace, unity and modernization and [at] the same time the government has provided my rights. There is free primary education and therefore I am appreciative for all those and I am praying that may the Almighty God bless my country Uganda now and forever and [I] will also remain a citizen of a Uganda now and forever."

Children and Political Expression

Adults typically assume that children simply "absorb" the world around them, yet children are not mere sponges soaking up nationalist ideology and political consciousness. Though children are unduly acted upon by adults, they engage politics in distinct ways based on their own positions in the social hierarchy. We have seen that children, like anyone else, actively construct their political identities, selectively taking cues from the world around them. While children have different competencies, many formulate their political identities no less critically than adults. They receive information from teachers, but also from parents, their friends, the media, international organizations, and any other sources available to them.

Children can be similarly critical about the things they learn in school—and in some cases about the things they *do not* learn. Despite the authoritarian structure of schools, designed to homogenize schoolchildren into national subjects, students found ways to communicate their identities and to discuss their political concerns with their peers.

Finding a Political Voice: Exercise Book Covers and Schoolyard Games

As I sat in a fifth-grade classroom one day, it occurred to me as I looked around the room that the children had a lot of interesting articles showing on the newspaper pages they had used to cover their exercise books. Exercise books tend to have very flimsy covers, so students wrap them in a second layer to extend their lives. They rarely use anything thicker than newspaper, which is in fact flimsier than the actual covers and so cannot do much to protect the books. Yet, I suspected that most children had access to at least limited amounts of higher-grade paper. The school tuck shop sold exercise book covers for one hundred shillings, but they were plain and students did not like them. Instead, students consciously chose certain newspaper pictures and articles as book covers to establish social positions, gain status among their peers, and as entry points to conversation topics that they did not otherwise get to discuss in school or at home.

Many had used pages with color pictures of top celebrities, both local and international. But many books were covered with pictures from the latest news stories, and especially the post-9/11 war on terrorism, bin Laden, and the Taliban. My students reported that none of them had discussed the terrorist attacks at all in class, though they had individually followed the news stories with some interest and had even heard teachers discussing them outside of class. Stories of Afghanistan were a popular choice with boys for several months after the attacks, and they circulated their book covers to share information. I often saw distracted children pointing to each other's books during class and launching into hushed discussions based on them. A lot of students chose gory pictures of violence and weaponry. Malik said, "They choose articles about Afghanistan because they want to abuse bin Laden," calling him names for having orchestrated the terrorist attacks in the United States. In fact, bin Laden had instantly become the nickname of anyone who misbehaved. Malik and his friends played war games between Bush and bin Laden on the playground as a way of working out their opinions on the issue. Malik told me, "I am usually Bush. I tell my army to attack bin Laden." Despite making play of international crises, Malik was confident that the American army would get bin Laden eventually, but as a Muslim, he believed that the United States should stop bombing Afghanistan, at least during Ramadan.

Sumayiya also talked about the news topics of the day during breaks. Exercise book covers helped her and her friends find topics to debate. She and some of her friends had even started a club to talk about the conflict between America and Afghanistan. "The teachers have discouraged it because they don't like children to talk about political things," she said. The boys still discussed political and military solutions, anyway. Sumayiya often joined them, though she was teased for being a girl who liked to hang out with boys. She responded that she did not like how girls "backstab" and talk about inconsequential topics. "They cause too many problems amongst themselves, whereas boys will tell you straight away when they have a problem with you," she said. The boys usually welcomed her into the group, and together they tried to make sense of the issues.

Government Accountability: The Children's Vision

Covering exercise books was a clandestine way to introduce political discussion to children's institutional spaces, but there were also public outlets for such expression, and children regularly utilized them. The children's section of the *New Vision* newspaper, called "Children's Vision," had an editorial section that published children's letters every weekend. To my surprise, many printed letters were written in a highly critical tone directed at parents, government officials, and fellow children. Most called for an end to undesirable and unbecoming practices, asking for government accountability or for parents and teachers to respect children's rights. Here is an example from Julius Wamala Katumba of the Green Hill Academy from the July 28, 2001, issue that cleverly asks members of Parliament for social accountability:

MPS PLEASE HELP

I read a story in the newspaper about a boy and girl who are suffering from proteus syndrome (that makes the legs swell as though one is suffering from elephantiasis). These poor children need sh3m each for treatment but they have no money. I again read in the papers that each Member of Parliament is going to earn sh4.5m per month.

We have 291 MPs, so if each MP could only contribute sh30,000 these children could be treated at Mulago hospital. I request all our MPs and caring Ugandans to help these children. I have tried to help them by paying in sh10,000 to account number 4-430-7 at Centenary Development Bank, Entebbe Road.

The writers also called for children to be accountable for their actions and for people in positions of authority to enforce rules on children. These letters often re-created in some way the public discourse on childhood and children's rights. One letter asked parents to teach children to do housework so that they did not suffer later in life.

Rather than simply mimicking the language of adults, these strongly worded letters acknowledged the power structure in which children lived their lives; as Coles puts it, "Power also enforces behavior on the power-less" (Coles 1986, 211). In addition, when children asked adults to stop certain negative treatment of children, the reason they gave was usually that "you can go to jail," not that children's rights are or should be the same as those of adults. By employing such logic, children subtly ack-nowledged that the threat of punishment through adult institutions of power is a more effective deterrent than any ideology of children's rights or argument that children themselves could issue.

Letters to government officials addressed various topics, not just those related to children's welfare. One letter called on the government to en-courage Ugandans to build small-scale industries. Some of them could be highly opinionated. A letter printed September 22, 2001, caught my at-tention. The headline read "Donors Are Just Like Stepmothers!" It states,

I really want to inform Besigye's supporters that you cannot stop donors from giving us help when we are very poor. This is madness!

I see Besigye's supporters suffering because of this. So who will be losing? It will obviously be you who will be losing. You who are supporting this kind of thing. I am very concerned because my prayer is that Uganda is among the best countries to live in. I also do not want corruption. Actually these donors are like our stepmothers, so we have to depend on them. Please donors do not accept this. We still need you. I heard this on the radio.

The author's point was that reliance on donors was a bit of a necessary evil at the moment, and Besigye's attempts at the time to discourage donors from investing in Museveni's government would only "orphan" the country. The letter suggested that even children knew that Uganda still depended on other nations, and that it had an uneasy relationship with donor countries not unlike that of a subservient child to a sometimes reluctant stepparent.

Even when children had personal problems, they did not hesitate to call on the highest authorities to help solve them. A primary school student asked President Museveni to tell his vice president to stop supporting sex workers:

I would like to tell President Yoweri Museveni Kaguta to advise the Vice President to stop encouraging sex workers (prostitutes) to expose themselves on Kampala streets.

They have made our parents become hostile. Our parents go to disco halls, dance, drink and end up abusing and beating our mothers and yet they are not in the wrong.

Our fathers drink a lot and forget that they left a family behind. Fathers are responsible for all things needed in a home.

One can only imagine the experiences that led this student to write this letter, but it illustrates two important points: one about gender, blame, and authority; the other about the accountability that children expect from adults in making their own lives better. Vice President Specioza Kazibwe had recently made news for supporting sex workers in their efforts to organize in order to gain better access to health information and HIV prevention. Aside from the logic that the girl who wrote the letter used in placing blame for prevalent gendered behaviors, it is interesting that she asked Museveni (a man) to tell Vice President Kazibwe (a woman) to stop her support of sex workers rather than writing to Kazibwe directly. As progressive as it was for Uganda to have a female vice president, this letter said a lot about the persistent patriarchy of the power system. It also delineated and appealed to the hierarchy of authority; this child recognized that state leaders had social influence that affected the way her father behaved. At the same time, it reminded fathers of their responsibilities as heads of households.

Despite regular appeals to adults, letters to other children were the most common, indicating the importance of formal peer socialization. However, this peer socialization was often modeled on prevalent adult-child socialization messages. They typically asked their fellow children to study hard, use their time wisely, respect parents and teachers, and stop wearing miniskirts or watching indecent movies; in other words, to behave as obedient, idyllic children. This, they usually pointed out familiarly, was for the child's "own best interest," though from a distinctive children's point of view. One child wrote, "I would like to advise my fellow pupils that parents are very useful to us with school fees which enables us to be educated. You are lucky if you know the value of your parents but if you do not know it, it is high time you changed. We need our parents, my dears." This scolding tone was not uncommon, but it served an important purpose. Through peer-to-peer communication, letters such as these reinforce a code of conduct meant to insure social gains for all children, even as they reinforce adult discourses about children. In the following example from the August 4, 2001, issue, Jacqueline Mutumba of the Joy Primary School reprimands her peers:

DO NOT EAT TATTOO GUM

I am advising you to stop eating tattoo gum because they will spoil your future and your success. These tattoos have meanings for instance the tortoise means laziness, the frog means greed, the he-goat means immorality, etc. If any of you has been eating tattoo gum, please stop it.

Children's Political Disenfranchisement

Today's Ugandan children, because of their position in relation to national history, have substantial contributions to make to the formulation of national political identity. Rarely did any adult but myself actively solicit their ideas about political issues, however. In fact, when I asked children whether they thought that young people like themselves should be able to vote, most emphatically replied that they should not. I was surprised by their answers; I pointed out that they had just shared their decision-making process with me, and that it sounded like they had done it as well as any adult. But they merely blushed and shook their heads. When I asked why they felt that way, James told me, "Even at eighteen years old, people's minds cannot know what they're doing."

"You're twelve, right? Don't you know what you're doing?"

"Yes," he laughed nervously.

"Us children," another student added, "we don't know much things which are going on in the world. . . . We can vote a person who is just famous, but he is not interested in politics."

It seemed incongruous that children so articulate in expressing their beliefs had so little confidence in themselves to activate them. One girl went so far as to claim, "We don't even know how to tick the box on the ballot."

In 1986, the year of Uganda's liberation by Museveni, Bob Franklin published *The Rights of Children*, which exposed the fallacy of relating age to competence when discussing the extension of political rights to children. Most children are denied the right to vote, for example, on the basis of arguments that could as easily be applied to adult voters. Such treatment of children violates democratic principles because they are subjected to laws that they could not participate in making, and their political rights are entrusted to others (Franklin 1986, 24). This denial is attributable to those same childhood and children's rights discourses that Ugandan children so thoroughly endorse. These discourses construct children as valuable yet powerless, and they are powerless because of a legitimate and justifiable adult hegemony, generally called "the best interest of the child." The same discourse that argues that we should listen to children also tells them they are incompetent to make decisions independently, yet many find this contradiction perfectly justifiable. "A child is denied the right of self-determination," David Archard writes, "in order that it should be able to exercise this very right in adulthood. Indeed the argument can be expressed more strongly. Children will only acquire the rights of self-determination if they are denied them now" (Archard 1993, 55).

I would add that this is significant in that it has serious repercussions for children's self-esteem and sense of competence. Herein lies the irony of Ugandan children's *habitus* serving as a space for both social reproduction and social change: though rights ideologies were empowering to children's future inheritance of the country, they effectively deterred children from having any faith in their abilities to execute social change as children. The argument I make here, that children are in fact very competent beings, does not necessarily mean that we should consider them to be small adults, but when children's rights discourses define the political value of children in terms of their future potential, which must be protected for "natural" growth, the inherent contradictions damage children's confidence in their own abilities to shape the society around them.

Actualizations

Part 2 presents several "sites" for applying the principles of ideal childhood discourses, as well as children's skillful negotiations of them. As I continue to situate global discourses of childhood through their local invocations and incarnations, I show how children are both affected by and engage with the cultural politics of development, relief aid, and cultural production. Throughout, I argue that children are indeed skilled social agents, maneuvering through the often contradictory nodes of discursive childhood categories that might otherwise serve to constrain them. They find possibility in protective prohibitions and carve positive spaces for self-expression from adverse—and sometimes desperate—circumstances.

Chapter 5 explores children's spatial conceptualizations of development practices; urban schoolchildren are coming to imagine "the village" both as an integral, imaginary space where ethnic identity originates and a location for the fulfillment of national citizenship through development that children hope will allow them to solidify and put into practice their identities as national citizens. The chapter therefore explicates the ideas in part 1 through an examination of place, with a particular focus on the urban-rural dichotomies that have been the subject of much literature on African life, including the diverse body created by anthropologists of the Manchester School (Schumaker 2001). Chapter 6 discusses how children in northern Uganda disrupt discursive categories of normative childhood. The child soldiers of Lord's Resistance Army pose major threats to the social category of childhood and to the overall security of the nation, and have thus become the focus of international children's aid organizations in Uganda. I argue that the universalized and normative views of childhood espoused by such organizations serve to further alienate repatriated child soldiers from citizenship and civic participation in their communities. Chapter 7 examines children's active participation in the production of national culture and development discourse through the national Primary School Music, Dance, and Drama festivals. In spite of strict adult direction of the performances, children are actually quite skilled at using the opportunities of the festival to launch cultural critiques of the state of children's rights in Uganda and to forge new possibilities for reconfiguring national culture, development, and rights discourses in locally relevant ways.

FIVE

"Village Life Is Better Than Town Life"

Identity, Migration, and Development in the Lives of Ugandan Child Citizens

During my fieldwork at primary schools in Uganda, I frequently ran across primary school students passionately engaged in formal debates. One popular topic to debate was "Village life is better than town life." Debaters argued forcefully both pro and con, and it was usually difficult to pick a winner. One day, a classroom of fifth-graders was having a particularly lively debate, and a student adjudicator kept order with a big stick. The children followed academic debate protocol, calling for points of clarification to the cheers and jeers of their classmates. A pro speaker stood and said, "Village life is better than town life because there's more food and there are no discos." A con speaker claimed that town was better because it *does* have entertainment such as discos. "Town schools also have enough supplies to provide quality education," she said.

Many urban youth studies presuppose youths' affections for the city, while others record rural young people's desires for a taste of city life and all it has to offer. My research with Ugandan children, however, revealed a phenomenon rarely discussed in the literature: urban children's desires for village life and affiliation. But as the primary school debate I witnessed forewarned, there are many contradictory

145

opinions and ideas about what the village and the city have to offer to young Africans today.

This chapter considers how urban Ugandan children have come to imagine their identities against the African rural-urban migration history and contemporary development trajectories. By situating my own ethnographic research historically in the context of the Manchester School of social research and its intellectual descendants, I hope to contextualize current debates about urban-rural migration to show how it figures in life strategies for urban families and individual children. Based on conversations with my very bright ten-year-old informant Jill, her family, and her classmates, this research suggests that many urban children imagine "the village" in a way that differs qualitatively from the views of their parents, aligning it more closely with ethnic nationalism and development, largely as a result of their symbolic position in Uganda's national development efforts. Urbanites' views of villagers have thus shifted with this generation from inherent backwardness to an appreciation by urban children of the potential to use rurally situated knowledges in their own personal and national development strategies. Children thus formulate their identities in ways that make rural connections essential to both their ethnic and national identities as productive citizens. In this configuration, I argue, "the village" becomes an integral imaginary space of both children's identity origination and their fulfillment of development trajectories.

The Manchester School and African Rural-Urban Relations

Much of what we know about African rural-urban migration in the social sciences today is derived from a body of work that has come to be known as the Manchester School. Many of its scholars did their important work not in Manchester but in field sites across southern and eastern Africa. Under the tutelage of Max Gluckman at the Zambia-based Rhodes-Livingstone Institute, they explored emergent urban-rural social networks among migrant workers and their families in the early days of African urban industrialization in the 1940s and 50s (Schumaker 2001). Taking anthropology out of the African bush and into the city, they employed innovative, field-based methodological approaches that challenged the more conventional research of current British social anthropology in Africa (Kuper 1997). A. L. Epstein, J. Clyde Mitchell, Victor Turner, Godfrey and Monica Wilson, and others developed a *dual spheres* model of social organization to explain the massive rural-urban migration of the period. Their main argument was that "under colonialism, industrialization with labor migration reinforced tribal political and kinship systems rather than breaking them down. Within the total social field there were two spheres, one urban and industrial, the other rural or tribal, and a functionally complementary relation held between them" (Werbner 1984, 167). They interpreted migrant workers' connections to rural kin communities as essential to their potential as financial supporters of their families.

For today's children, who are now a couple of generations descended from those migrant laborers the Manchester School studied, attachments to the village must obviously be of a different nature, since few work to earn money before their teens. Yet a sense of rural connectivity remained surprisingly strong for many of the urban children with whom I worked. In many cases, they had never been to what they considered their "home villages," but they had imagined them extensively, and these imaginings formed a strong emotional bond with home villages, which figured prominently, both in their pasts in the form of identity association, and in their futures in terms of development and migration. Much of this sentiment, I argue, has to do with children's desires for strong ethnic identity ties, through which children hope to concretize and actualize their identities, as both ethnic and national citizens. Further, these ties give them ways to fulfill ideals of national belonging through prevalent development discourses.

Anthropologists have traditionally explained the strength of African kinship ties as a result of the need to stay together for the sharing of resources, security, and protection. With the twentieth-century transition to a cash economy, however, kinship in Africa also came to signify security through *financial* support, because access to the earnings of wage laborers—especially for women and children—depended on strengthening relationships with them that would withstand the influence of new patterns of urban migration and settlement (Ferguson 1999, 205). In the 1950s and 1960s, most Manchester School scholars predicted that migration patterns would disrupt urban workers' ties with rural kin and communities (Parkin 1975; Southall 1975). The African industrial revolution and the post-independence search for employment and national development dislocated people from their agrarian ways of life, so that they were constantly renegotiating different social systems to keep up with the changes at hand (Kilbride and Kilbride 1990). This necessarily involved shifting and contradictory relationships with home villages. Scholars therefore argued that the new social networks being formed in cities would eventually usurp rural kin relationships in importance.

The dual spheres model eventually lost its hold on social theory, however, as it proved inadequate to explain "extremes of stratification associated with economic boom or bust" (Werbner 1984, 167). Still, hometown associations and urban-rural travel have persisted into the present, and may even have gained importance in this age of political and economic insecurity (Trager 1998, 10). In his 1999 ethnography *Expectations of Modernity*, James Ferguson argues that due to African industrial and economic decline in the 1990s, rural kinship networks remained important as "fallback" resources for urban workers for whom the dream of African modernity had failed. By examining the outcomes of African labor migrants' aspirations in the wake of the copper industry bust in Zambia, Ferguson's ethnography shows that the predicted decline of rural kinship ties was to an extent overridden by the decline of industrial wage labor, requiring workers to fulfill their roles as migrants by returning to rural villages after retirement.

A common thread in these approaches is their premise that material concerns are the crux of kin relations, effacing the affective sentiments in African society. Given their poor economic conditions, the children I interviewed indicated that material reciprocity was intricately linked with emotional reciprocity in their configurations of family and community obligation. When I asked Jill about the most important people in her life, she named her mother and her father, because "They give me enough care. They give me school fees and shelter, clothes and food." Examining the experiences and desires of children may help highlight the incredible complexity of negotiations across dichotomized domains such as urban and rural, traditional and modern, material and emotional. It is therefore relevant to consider what rural and urban spaces mean for children in Kampala (and elsewhere in Africa) today.

Citizenship, Locality and "Home"

Ugandan concepts of citizenship have long been connected to ethnicity, and ethnicity to locality. They overlap with organic notions of nationalism and ethnicity to produce a conception of the necessity of citizenship by birth (Barya 2000). Legally, citizenship is defined as an individual right, but the 1995 Constitutional Assembly concluded that in Uganda it is also defined collectively, for "it is when the individual is located in the collective, his community or nationality, that he assume[s] identity" (Barya 2000, 44). That identity is rooted further in historical ancestral locality, giving precedence to a notion of indigenousness, or what some have called the "villagization of national politics" (Geschiere and Gugler 1998).[1] Thus, being linked to one's indigenous, ethnic or ancestral location within Uganda also links one to the nation. Children I surveyed about being Ugandan commonly and transparently stated that they were Ugandan because they belonged to a Ugandan tribe, or because their parents were born here. Jill told me this the first time I met her in a conversation with her and her classmates: "My tribe makes me feel Ugandan," she said, "because it is a Ugandan tribe. If you are from a Ugandan tribe, you are Ugandan." Jill's classmate Andrew told me he felt Ugandan in his home district, but he felt like a Muteso tribe member when in Kampala because being among other Ugandan ethnicities confronted him with his own. This outlook reflects social theory on interethnic contact as explained by Mitchell in his ethnography of the Kalela Dance in northern Rhodesia (Mitchell 1956), as well as Gregory Bateson's "one-hand-clapping" theory of intercultural contact (Bateson 1972): people do not confront their ethnic identities until they come into contact with people different from themselves.

In addition, my conversations with Ugandan children soon revealed that if ethnicity is a main component of national identity, "the village" is the specific locus of that identity. Children often referred to the village where their fathers were born as "home," even when they had not been born there or had never been there. Like many children, Jill claimed two homes: that of her nuclear family or domestic unit in the city, and the seat of her ancestry in a rural village. Although children are sometimes second-generation prodigal sons and daughters in relation to their home villages, these still matter deeply to their identities. Most Ugandan cultures are patrilineal, so people tend to identify more with their father's tribe. When I asked her why she felt drawn to the village, Jill said it was where her grandparents resided. When I asked Jill about important people in her life, she also named her grandparents. But when I asked her to elaborate, I found that this was due less to personal association with them than a strong sense of generational continuity. Indeed, I discovered that she had never actually been to her father's home village, where her grandparents lived, and she had only been to her mother's home village once, when she was very young. Of all her grandparents, she had only met her maternal grandmother, on that particular visit.

K: When someone says "home," do you take it to mean here [where you live], or do you take it to mean in the village—or does it mean different things sometimes?

J: Okay, it may be both.

K: How do you tell? What is the difference?

J: This way is where you are born and in the village is where your father was born.

K: That place is home because you have that family, your ancestors?

J: Yes.

K: What does it mean to you if this place you call home is a place you have never been to?

J: You feel you want to visit it and see how it looks like.

Despite the gradual shift in emphasis from extended family to nuclear family life in Africa, elders in Uganda are still respected for the cultural knowledge they impart to young people. Epstein has written at length about how this alternate-generation relationship has long been important in many African cultures and even around the world due to its function as a metonym for one's ethnic affiliation (Epstein 1978, 140). Epstein claims that grandparents are "the repositories of ancient wisdom" and "symbols of continuity of descent" because of their stories of the past (145). Thus, relationships with grandparents, and particularly those located in rural "homelands," can come to be seen as crucial "anchors" for children's ethnic identity formation (142). Children's longings for relationships with their rural grandparents may also have to do with the ways in which relations with grandparents are often constructed as more egalitarian, lacking the strict authoritarianism that exists between parents and their children. Epstein believes that nuclear family tensions discourage ethnic identification between adjacent generations (child/parent). Within the family, grandparents can dispel tension between parents and children because the bond with grandchildren is developed through mutual respect, and without coercion and force. Relations with grandparents are thus stronger and more affective. Further, grandparents often play an important supportive role for children through joking relationships; according to Radcliffe-Brown, such a relationship "always includes elements of incompatibility" such as the age and social differences separating children and their grandparents (Epstein 1978, 145). Epstein knew that his conclusions were predicated on contact between grandchildren and grandparents, but he did not account for its absence among urban children with whom he worked.

In Uganda today, relationships with grandparents are not always possible for children raised in the city, who often do not know their grandparents at all because they reside in a remote village. But it is notable that so many of them, like Jill, *want* to have closer relationships with their grandparents. Children who lack this connection but still desire it sometimes develop an imaginative vision of what it must be like to visit grandparents and other extended family in the village. Jill and her friends once described at length the types of interactions children shared with grandparents on village visits: sleeping in grass-thatch huts, learning to cultivate crops, and listening to their grandmothers tell stories. They admitted that they personally had not had many such experiences, but to have them was to feel more connected to home villages through blood relations and situated experience. One of the girls said, "It is interesting to participate in the traditions. They make me feel like a Muganda."

Like many urban children, Jill experienced a lot of confusion about her tribal identity when she was very young. Though city life has altered its importance, children still learn that ethnicity is an important axis of difference. Only a generation ago, in the 1970s and 1980s, ethnicity was a matter of life and death in the civil wars of Amin and Obote. In the multiethnic city, some children reinvent their ethnic identities for the sake of fitting in; though their playmates are from different Ugandan tribes, they typically speak in Luganda or English to each other. Being among many Luganda speakers in the city, both Jill and her older brother Michael assumed when they were toddlers that they were Baganda. When Jill was in second grade, a teacher once asked her "what she was." Knowing that her mother was a Mutoro, she replied that she was a Mutoro, a tribe from western Uganda. Because her surname derived from her father's tribe, the teacher retorted, "No, with a name like that, you must be a northerner." Since prevalent regional prejudices tend to marginalize northern tribes, Jill was very upset by the incident, both because the teacher implied that she didn't know who she was, and because being called "northern" had a negative connotation, given the infamous tyranny of dictators Obote and Amin, still fresh in Ugandan public memory. Jill ran home from school crying.

At ten years old, Jill accepted her ethnic affiliation and looked forward to learning more about what it meant to be a Langi like her father. Her father had not told her much about Langi culture because, as he explained to me, "I want them to know about all aspects of their identity." Teaching them to be Ugandan was most important to him. Mr. Obonyo was acting on the assumption that since ethnicism was a major factor in the civil strife of his generation, emphasizing ethnicity with his children might reintroduce socially destructive prejudices. But today's children experience ethnicity differently: since Jill saw her ethnic identity as constitutive of national identity, telling her more about what it meant to be Langi would likely help to facilitate that positive identity formation rather than hinder it. Unlike her father, Jill suspected that knowing more about her ethnic background could give her a more complete sense of self, especially by locating herself in the indigenous ethnic landscape, just as national citizenship debates have decreed. As one of Jill's classmates wrote, "I [will feel that I] am a member of my tribe when we [are] gathered with elders sharing ideas."

Migration and Rural Connection

These attitudes are evidence of a social pattern having come full circle. Labor migration was prevalent in Uganda before independence and followed similar patterns in Uganda and in other African countries at the time (Parkin 1975; Southall and Gutkind 1957). The colonial government increased villagers' dependence on money and wage labor by imposing hut taxes, and families needed money to purchase basic household goods such as clothes and soap. Since Uganda had been—and largely remains—reliant on subsistence agriculture, most people who came to the cities looking for work in colonial times hoped to fill administrative positions in the colonial government. Thus, rural ties were not necessarily broken; urban Ugandans were considered the breadwinners in the new cash economy and were obliged to contribute financially to family "back home in the village." In the aftermath of the civil wars of the 1970s and 1980s, poverty in the countryside drove another wave of job-seeking migrants to Kampala. Among these migrants were many of the parents of my child informants, including Jill's parents, the Obonyos.

The Obonyos' family history mirrors that of many contemporary Ugandans, but their relationship to the village is actually a very contradictory one, in which parents and children have formulated some similar and some distinct views. Mr. and Mrs. Obonyo alternately claimed that conditions had deteriorated in the village and in the city, and though they were more critical of village life than their children, they became sentimental at times about their own rural upbringings, even amid their complaints about the problems they faced today as parents in the city. I asked the Obonyos why they didn't just stay in the village if city living was becoming so difficult, and they replied that they were doing it "for the children." Educational opportunities are better in the city, and they wanted to give their children that advantage. Though they often complained about the developmental levels of the village, the Obonyos' comments also revealed a subtle and complicated critique of the historical development and modernity of city living, which going to the village helped to alleviate, at least for a short time. Urban poverty today makes some aspects of village life more appealing to both parents and children, although the statistics do not support their claims that poverty is worse in the city. Fifty-seven percent of Uganda's poor live in rural areas—almost twice that of urban areas (Kabadaki 2001). Yet the wealth of the village is not measured by monetary standards so much as the ways in which it offers relief from them. Aside from building a connection with family, visiting the village can provide parents with a release from the economic hardships of the city, in which "everything costs money." The village is a reserve of "free food" not readily available in the city, where there is little land for cultivation. Many urbanites believed that people in the village, who grew their own food, did not require so much money. In reality, many rural homes have trouble meeting their own basic subsistence needs (De Coninck 1992; Kabadaki 2001). In the city, however, both parents and children complain that food costs money. It is one of the reasons Jill's father maintains a farm in his home village. Some of the attitudes that parents shared with me echoed the sentiments expressed by Leonard Plotnicov in 1967: "While the home village is thought of nostalgically, especially for the abundance of good food, a return home would involve the immigrant in an intolerable situation. It is difficult to readjust to 'uncivilized ways' after one has become accustomed to town amenities" (Plotnicov 1967, 297). City parents and children thus prefer to think of the village as a place they go only during holidays.[2] Children who have not lived in the village have no direct experience of this "free food," however, so it becomes a romanticized component of their imaginings about village life, validated by reports from parents and other children who have visited the village.

The village thus acts as a reservoir of both cultural knowledge and material necessities. Ferguson (1999) discusses the village as a fallback for migrant workers upon retirement, but the Obonyos' example shows that the village can also serve as a temporary back-up or support system for urban families who encounter difficult economic times, even before retirement. Further, the village is a fallback in ways that involve families' strategies for their children. As it is for migrant workers, the village is a last resort for children who fail to make it in the city. Mrs. Obonyo said, "We always want to take them [to the village] in case—you never know—you can die, then the children are taken to the village. When they have never gone, it will be very tough for them. That's what we do: We take them to learn their hometown." The Obonyos, as working-class parents living on the edge of poverty, want to prepare children for an alternate life in the village in case they cannot "cope up" to city living in the long run. Yet the village is seen as a place with a different, very practical kind of knowledge. These things may be important for children to learn because they may need to relocate to villages if their parents die or they cannot make enough money to continue living in the city. This was not uncommon: Jill's classmate Asir was the last of his thirteen siblings still in school in the city; the rest had already been sent to the village to live with their mother after his father was dismissed from his job with the telephone company. Yet children tended to view the village as a different resource. Though it was a place they wanted to know, they did not want to live there.

Development and the Urban Imagination of Rurality

Many Ugandans find themselves caught up in the failed promise of African modernity. Ferguson writes, "A return to modernist teleology, a new grand narrative that would trace the hopeful signs of an Africa once more 'emerging' out of the gloomy ashes of Africa's 'development' disaster, is neither plausible nor desirable. The modernization narrative was always a myth, an illusion, often even a lie" (Ferguson 1999, 253). Though people I met in Uganda during my fieldwork were critical of the dream of modernity, I never got the sense that they had given up on it. In some ways, the end of decades of civil war with President Museveni's takeover in 1986 and his courting of the international development community gave the country new aspirations for modernity's benefits. However, many felt that, as one parent put it, "Poverty is almost like another war." Those who flocked to the city to receive education and benefit from postwar reconstruction were often disappointed by the lack of opportunities. Yet they preferred to stay unemployed in the city rather than return home to the land. Now the government ideology being spread through the education system encourages their children to invest in the same project: to raise the country from the ashes of underdevelopment.

Parents' Attitudes

In Uganda, today's parents are the first main generation to benefit from mass formal education. Shortly after independence in 1962, President Obote launched a major government initiative to "Ugandanize" the education system by making what had until then been largely a foreign missionary endeavor into a curriculum more relevant to the social and economic needs of independent Ugandan nationals seeking status on the international stage. Despite the ensuing decades of civil war, the educational system managed to survive and continued to function at minimal levels during the nationwide state of insecurity (Paige 2000). Education, however, continued to be based largely on British social education for civil servants, and reforms failed to make it more relevant to Uganda's agrarian society (Nsamenang 2002). A friend of mine who went to school in Uganda in the 1960s and 1970s lamented that though Uganda is an overwhelmingly agricultural state, he never learned anything about farming in school. This may be another symptom of what Bradley Levinson and his colleagues refer to as "the cultural production of the educated person" in developing countries (Levinson, Foley, and Holland 1996).

The experience of the postcolonial generation of the Ugandan educated is reflected in Stacey Leigh Pigg's work, which addresses monolithic, oppositional constructions of "the city" and "the village" instigated by international development agencies in developing countries. Where the mantras of development discourses have taken hold, Pigg claims, they have created an archetypal "city" as progressive and modern, and an archetypal "village" as stagnant and mired in local, "traditional" beliefs antithetical to development goals. Indeed, cosmopolitan development schemes *rely* on the underdevelopment of villages as the locus of their reason for being (Pigg 1992, 507). The government's education curriculum can be instrumental in creating and maintaining such stereotypes, even while attempting to instill the values of national unity and development. "At the same time this pedagogical strategy aims to make development an integral part of the village," Pigg notes, "it creates a dichotomy between the village and [development] . . . villages are placed in relation to the kinds of places they are not" (500).

The adults I interviewed who had come from the village to the city often displayed a marked lack of affinity with their home villages and a disparaging view of villagers as ignorant and uncivilized—direct hindrances to their own and the country's development. Though development attitudes that are biased against rural lifestyles are derived from international development discourse, they quickly gain resonance with urbanites seeking economic prosperity, so that even those who grew up in rural areas and then migrated to the cities—as the Obonyos had—come to subscribe to them. A discussion with Jill's parents about hygiene highlights how development categories become fixed and naturalized in urban Ugandans' conceptions of the village.

MR. OBONYO: Even up to now in the villages, people do not boil water.

MRS. OBONYO: I wish you knew. I wish you go to a village and see a local well.

MR. OBONYO: The cows are drinking from the same well; people are collecting water from the same well to go and drink, for everything.

MRS. OBONYO: And by the way, those people don't fall sick . . .

MR. OBONYO: They are either immune or they live with those germs so that it doesn't harm them.

MRS. OBONYO: Because me now if we go to the village, we don't take that water, because if you take [it] immediately you start running and vomiting. But for them you will see a child only drinking that water and he will not fall sick. So for us when we go immediately they know that you have come from [the city]; you can't take that water. You have to boil yours or we buy. Recently I went to my village and I would not drink my water. I said, "Ah no, I am not taking [it]." Then my mother would say, "Eh, you are not taking this water!? I am an old woman and I have grown on this water!" I said, "No, if I take it, I can fall sick. I can't take unboiled water now." But for her she says, "You see, I am 80 years. This is the water which I have been taking. But you these days, you are dying so quickly because of that." And she will tell you that you are dying because of that boiled water!

Mrs. Obonyos' comments point to the embodied urban-rural differences that render located development categories immutable: city dwellers cannot drink village water (and vice versa) without falling sick. In the Obonyos' view, villagers are physically acclimated to the unsanitary conditions of underdevelopment. While villages are targets of development projects, they are described by urbanites like the Obonyos as inherently *unable to be developed* due to their natural(ized) affinity for underdevelopment and their lack of knowledge about "modern" things like germs. Yet Mrs. Obonyo's elderly mother overturns this established city-village hierarchy by claiming that lack of immunity to germs is the price her daughter has paid for becoming "modern." To an extent, Mrs. Obonyo agrees: she worries that her children's bodies would be too weak to thrive in the village.

Educational access also influenced the Obonyos' decision to remain in the city, despite economic hardships; they stayed so their children could be well educated and acquire job skills to lift them out of poverty. The purported anti-developmentalism of village mentality also has consequences for children's education, sometimes characterized by development-minded adults as dire. Mr. and Mrs. Obonyo explained to me how rural people prevent their children from going to school, even though the government introduced Universal Primary Education in 1997, making primary enrollment free for up to four children from each family. They explained that children can become caught between two types of adult authority in the village: parents who will not let children go to school until they have finished their chores, and teachers who beat children for being late to school. According to the Obonyos, parents in rural areas do not see the value of education because they need their children to contribute labor to the household. Rural people, they claimed, prefer to have their children work because they will reap immediate results from the child's labor, whereas—if they invest in their children's education—it may be years before they receive any benefit. Mrs. Obonyo considered her view more enlightened than that of many Africans concerning education:

For me as far as I am concerned, when you are educating a child, you are saving; you are banking your money. But that is not really common in us, we as black people. We always aim at getting [money] very quickly; . . . when you say you plant this tree, this tree will produce fruits maybe after three years, they will say, "That is a waste of time. I want something earning right now." And yet I don't think that is the process of development.

To Mrs. Obonyo, shortsightedness becomes both the plague of the African village and the lure of the city, where poor people believe that they will be able to earn lots of money in little time and return to their villages wealthy. The result is a high rate of unemployment and petty crime in the city.

Many urban Ugandans see a fundamental conceptual rift between the practices required for development and attendant moral standards carried by the "traditional" values rooted in rural agrarian culture. Some village lifestyles are seen as antithetical to development practice, but cultural values that people want to preserve and impart to their children—like respect for elders and valuing hard work—also suffer as a result of the production of educated citizens in urban areas. This may have something to do with the increasingly lateral direction of knowledge instigated by formal education. If children are educated in technological and developmental changes more quickly than their parents (Kneller 1965), in the "time-space expansion of globalization" (Katz 2001b), "progress" breaks down the African elder tradition that is the cornerstone of African values, thus causing children to lose "respect" and "obedience," qualities still highly prized in African children (Mazrui 2001; Women's Commission on Refugee Women and Children 2001).

Children's Attitudes

Jill had already learned a lot from her parents about the struggles of their generation, but she told their story a little differently. She once wrote,

Long time ago our parents were children like us. Some of our parents didn't go to school like us because of school fees, poverty. And some of our parents went to school because grandparents were hard working, they used to grow crops and sell them eventually to get school fees for our parents. But thing was they were many and the house was small. So my mother went to her auntie's place. But the auntie was lazy and rich and so my mother before she went to school she would first dig the garden and take the cows to the farm and put the fire—do everything that was needed and go to school. But when the cousins of my mother saw that she was working a lot, they decided to take her to a boarding school. But nowadays when we are coming to school we don't take cows to the farm. And now everybody knows that hard work pays.

Though some children with whom I spoke had inherited many of their parents' attitudes, viewing rural people as a problem for development goals, their approach to development was more often to see the village as a gap they could fill in adulthood through a particular development trajectory they were currently learning in school. If rural people are a problem for development, they are also an antidote for the ways that city life breaks down certain morals, norms, and cultural understandings of heritage and identity. Part of the breakdown of these categories is blamed on the school curriculum, which naturalizes localized categories of development. According to a Ministry of Education official with whom I spoke, "National development is the Bible of education in Uganda," but this has typically taken the form of representation that Pigg has shown is highly problematic for its reification of village life (Pigg 1992). Education has thus created a demographic rift between town and village that correlates with the historical clustering of schools near urban centers. As mentioned in chapter 2, education is essentially linked to ideal conceptions of childhood promoted by international development and child rights discourses. They tend to stereotype children according to Western, middle-class standards, further marginalizing the village as a place outside of progress because of the lower proportion of children in school and the lower quality of schools in rural areas. When I served as a Peace Corps English teacher in Malawi, schoolchildren were often given punishments involving manual labor, including cultivation, slashing grass, carrying water, or moving heavy stones. Characterizing the daily activities of rural populations as "punishments" further alienated schoolchildren from them, and created disdain for rural activities among the educated. My elite secondary school students for the most part had negative views of rural people. They considered them hicks and farmers whom they saw as having less productive worth than them-selves and their parents, many of whom were urban civil servants and affluent businesspeople. In this way, negative characterizations of vari-ous childhood experiences, necessarily located in urban and rural areas, were reproduced.

As the village remained a marginalized location of "backwardness" and "antidevelopment" in Uganda, children from poor and working-class families in particular also saw it as a place of cultural value and potential investment. Children of the urban poor find that view appeal-ing and mutually beneficial. In many cases, children have no memory of the village hardships that characterized their parents' childhoods, so they romanticize rural lifestyles for their relations to African ethnic "au-thenticity." Jill's friend said she doesn't go to the village for holidays, which explains her lack of cultural knowledge. "I stay in Kampala, so I don't know many things about my tribe. If I lived in the village, I would learn more."

In my discussions with Ugandan children, I learned that idea of the village is linked not only to the children's understandings of their pasts, but also to their sense of responsibility for national development: de-veloping the village will develop the nation and simultaneously instill ethnic pride while ameliorating the urban tribalism and sectarianism that has caused instability and thwarted development in the past. One sixth-grade girl wrote, "As a member of the tribe of North (Acholi) I [feel] for what we call equal regional balance. Something should be done."[3] Educated urbanites are often seen as elite returnees to ancestral villages and are commonly given authority to set the villages' development agendas (Trager 1998). This developmental involvement tends to com-pensate for urbanites' lack of rural cultural comportment. This is the challenge for today's young educated citizens: to get a job that provides enough income to contribute to personal, familial, and home village development—which in turn contributes to national development ef-forts from the bottom up. In the past, this has typically occurred either through ethnic associations or family ties through which money and resources flow from the city to the village (Barkan, McMulty, and Ayeni 1991; Denzer and Mbanefoh 1998; Ferguson 1999; Gugler 2002; Honey and Okafor 1998). But children, who have limited mobility and almost no economic means, imagine the village as a subtly different resource for them than for their parents' generation.

While urban parents set themselves apart from the village through a critical development discourse, their children strive to identify with home villages by seeing them as merely different—but not ultimately better or worse—developmental spaces. This may be attributable to several aspects of their revised, late-primary curriculum; children were learning about the ethnic groups of Uganda, basic agriculture, and urban problems in development. Many of these elements were lacking in pre- and early post-independence curricula. Rural life may still be reified through school lessons about indigenousness and rural development, but it is more balanced today by critiques of urban problems. For example, I sat in on one fifth-grade lesson about street children, a solely urban phenomenon in Uganda.[4]

As stated in chapter 2, children's comments indicated that Ugandan national development discourse created an *educational*—rather than economic—class difference that was only loosely correlated with urban-rural divides, perhaps because they saw the procurement of education itself as an indicator of potential class mobility. Surprisingly, these children did not look down upon village children. Rather, urban children recognized and valued the hard work that village children performed, and they appreciated the way rural children typically struggled to achieve the same things that city children sometimes achieved with much less effort, precisely because they were subject to a different set of childhood ideals and expectations.[5] Children like Jill feel more solidarity with other children who are educated, whether they come from rural areas or a different socioeconomic background, precisely because they have been endowed, through the national education curriculum, with the responsibility to develop the nation. "When we know about education, we shall be tomorrow's pillars of Uganda," she explained, quoting the national youth anthem. .

Second-generation urban children also realized how their families saw investments in their educations as investments in the future. Children and their parents hence placed great emphasis on education because it supposedly would produce children who could find employment and survive in the city and who might then go on to contribute to kin in rural areas with their discretionary income. Such participation in the development of a cash and wage labor economy was the ideal path to full participation as citizens among urban schoolchildren. The children to be pitied most—whether they live in villages or cities—are those who cannot go to school. Jill knew that she was growing up in a very different situation than did her parents, but she believed that as long as she had her parents, she would not have to work for her school fees. Still, she would be willing to do so if it became necessary—"Any work which there is."

7   Rural Ugandan children fetching water. Photo by the author ca. 2001.

Urban children I spoke with viewed children in rural areas as laborers
for the family first and foremost (fig. 7). But, significantly, city children
also saw villagers as stewards of cultural and environmental knowledge.
Urban schoolchildren tended to naturalize villagers' knowledge, but in
very different ways from their parents, by assuming the accumulated
knowledge of villagers to be essential to understanding their own identities, and by learning the value of hard work, especially in agricultural
production. Jill implied that village children could still get by in their
own environments, even without being educated because, "They have
their own natural knowledge," she explained. Cindi Katz's research on
children in rural Sudan shows that they possess substantial environmental knowledge and social skill as a result of their central economic roles

in household labor and production (Katz 1991; Katz 2001a). Ugandan children thus tended to conceptualize their relationships with villagers as complementary, envisioning them as potentially reciprocal and mutually beneficial: they could exchange development knowledge with villagers in exchange for cultural knowledge.

The urban children I spoke with actually had positive things to say about rural children and their contributions to society. However, they expressed doubt about their own childhood competencies. When they envisioned making their first trips to the village, they anticipated learning a lot of practical things from villagers, but they rarely spoke about knowledge that they might possess—about development practices, for example—that they could impart to villagers in return. James, a bright and resourceful twelve-year-old boy at the top of his class, described his recent first trip to the village to me. "The children in the village taught me to shoot a bow and arrow," he reported excitedly. Earlier, he had told me about how he taught his family and neighbors better sanitation and environmental practices that he learned in school, and how he had used his allowance to raise chickens and start a small egg business. But when I asked him if he had taught villagers anything, he shyly said no. They were teaching him so much about being a Pokot tribesman that he felt he had little to offer them.

Children's self-deprecating attitudes toward their own knowledge and ability indicate the extent to which they have internalized Western concepts of idealized childhood through educational indoctrination and international children's rights discourses, which imply that all child labor is exploitative (Robson and Ansell 2000). Yet they also notice that local values involve a different set of expectations, especially for rural children. African concepts of childhood hold children to be useful, productive members of households; they are laborers and thus sources of wealth. By contrast, Western childhood ideals hold children to be precious objects to be invested in now for the sake of their productivity as adults; they are valuable and yet powerless. These divergent values get too easily mapped onto children living in rural and urban environments. As Pigg writes, "Childhood defined as work is the childhood of the village laborer; childhood defined as diligent study and carefree play is the childhood of the landowning or professional, largely urban, elite" (Pigg 1992, 501).

For this reason, city children's configurations of situated knowledges tended to characterize the forms of knowledge they possessed as pupal in nature—merely training them for adult citizenship—whereas they codified rural children's knowledge as both practical and practicable in the

8 Urban elementary school girls playing a game at break time. Photo by the author ca. 2001.

present. James, for example, once explained to me that because rural children often have more responsibilities, they are more independent—especially those out of school. "Kids who don't go to school [in the village] feed themselves," he explained. "They are always working be-cause they have to graze their father's cows. But [rural children] who go to school are fed because they don't earn money." They may have to watch their father's cows and do other chores, but even rural schoolchil-dren have more geographical mobility and autonomy as a result. Urban schoolchildren, on the other hand, must rely more on their parents for everything and do not learn applicable life skills early on, thus extend-ing their dependency (fig. 8). The result is what Katz calls a "de-skilling" of children educated through academic rather than production learn-ing (Katz 1991). According to the children, this was not necessarily a bad thing, because it afforded educated city children "more time to be children"—in global normative childhood parlance—as it allowed rural children to be more productive citizens in the present: each experience of childhood had its advantages and its disadvantages.

Thus, children themselves acknowledged that children everywhere experience childhood differently and have different contributions to make to their communities. My interactions with Ugandan children confirm Berry Mayall's assertion that "children learn what it means to be a child and about varieties of childhoods, by comparing experiences, discussing emotional responses to events, and debating values" (Mayall 2000, 133). In other words, children executed a subtle contextualization of diverse notions of childhood by paying attention to the influence of various locations and situated knowledges that shape childhood experience.

Children's Development Trajectories

Urban schoolchildren feel connected to rural roots through development as much as through ethnic ties, but development discourse also throws into relief how children should value their positions as "city kids" who were receiving an urban education. Asir believed that in order to achieve full membership in his tribe, he would have to contribute meaningfully to the development of his home area: "I [will feel] like a member of my tribe when I qualified to have grown up and complete my degree and get employed to get enough money to help my tribe to move towards development. . . . When I also give them good ideas and contribute unity, peace, and democracy within the tribe." He spoke with me many times about his plans to initiate development projects or small businesses in his home area, where most of his family stayed, when he was old enough.

Though many children had romanticized images of the village, they were also aware of the hardships of village life. When I asked Jill about the difference between herself and village children, she said, "They work a lot, so they get thin." James learned a lot about his ethnic identity—and his place in the social order. "The place was nice," he said. "I liked to be there, but we had to come back." Urban children's interest was not in living in the village, but in identifying with it (for a sense of ethnic belonging) and contributing to its development (for fulfillment of their national development role), which they could only do if they stayed in the city and successfully completed school. "They do not pay school fees [in the village]," Asir pointed out, "but the teaching standards are not very good." If these children could avoid ending up in the village now and got an urban education, they believed that they would be in a better position as adults to contribute to the village's development later, possibly making it suitable enough for them to eventually retire there. Ethnic and hometown associations provide common avenues for initiating and funding such development projects in home villages (Gugler 2002, 23). For these reasons, they wish to maintain ties to their home villages and thus to their ethnic identities; though Asir's father had failed to make it in the city, Asir thought he might still have a chance to become "elite" in the eyes of villagers.

Jill's interest in visiting her home village continued to be learning more about her identity, but her interest extended beyond genealogy. She also wanted practical information about how villagers live and attend to what Jill has come to consider basic needs, such as education:

к: What are some things you want to know about when you go there? What will you ask them?

J: Their clan, their brothers and sisters, how they went to which school and how they live and how they manage to get the school fees.

Jill's comments indicate that she sees the village as a potential source of knowledge that will not only educate her about her identity, but about important life strategies such as acquiring school fees. Like most children who did not have particularly close ties with the village, Jill saw it not so much as a fallback position as a place from which to gain a different kind of knowledge for survival, some of which may be even applicable in the city.

Conclusion: Shifting Locations of Family and Home

It is clear that even if obligations to home villages have eroded in importance over the course of twentieth-century African urban migration, Africans' sense of obligation to family has not. Urban Ugandan children knew that their parents were making great sacrifices for their educations and that they were expecting great payoffs and accomplishments in return. Many children I talked to said that they would one day like to build a house for their parents. Some located these in the village, but others said they might build them in the city. If it turns out that rural connections have indeed weakened enough that today's city dwellers no longer find it viable to return to rural areas, many of these children may end up taking care of their parents in the city. If so, kin networks may continue to become more urbanized, but in ways that may relocate family obligations and affective relationships (like those with grandparents) to the cities at the same time as development efforts continue to focus on raising rural living standards.

In the age of AIDS, however, many grandparents in Uganda are becoming primary caregivers for their grandchildren because AIDS has decimated a generation of parents, afflicting the most productive members of society—those in their twenties and thirties—and creating a generation of AIDS orphans for whom no effective government social safety nets exist. Hence Kilbride asserts that alternate-generation relationships need to be restored in order to help "children in crisis" (Kilbride 2000). But grandparents were never meant to be primary caregivers for children, and this modern phenomenon in turn deepens the economic crisis, because grandparents are often too old to work to support children in their care, whether they live in urban or rural areas. Given the far-reaching effects of the AIDS pandemic, children must be better equipped for the possibility that many of them will end up being reared in rural communities by extended family.

In this chapter, I have tried to contextualize Ugandan urban-rural relations through children's knowledge, imagination, and experience in order to show how urban children's senses of urban-rural connectivity differ qualitatively from those of their parents, mainly by virtue of being sociohistorically rooted in the present moment of Uganda's national development-through-education agenda. The ways that city children envision "the village" and their potential relationships with it help to ground issues of class, ethnonationalism, and citizenship in a more integrative notion of national belonging and development. Children with little actual connection to rural ancestral homes imagine them as integral to their attainment of ethnic and national identity. They incorporate villages into their personal development strategies as places which—once personally experienced—will help define them and which they will eventually help define by bringing development to them, thus fulfilling the national development trajectory through personal life strategies. This reciprocal relationship demonstrates how children actively engage dominant social discourses—such as those on national identity and development—in creative and responsive ways that contribute both to the inclusion of the rural in national development and to their own sense of national belonging through locally situated identity formation. It also reveals that children hold themselves responsible for the social obligations they have as educated children toward their various communities, be they familial, ethnic, or national.

SIX

"Our Children Have Only Known War"

The Predicament of Children and Childhood in Northern Uganda

I would say that you should help to see that every child gets her rights, all over the world. . . . The government never reacts about citizens having their rights abused. The rebels have done the worst things, which must be stopped as soon as possible, or else the meaning of life will be no more—only hatred, disunity, and grief will fill this nation.

SIXTEEN-YEAR-OLD NORTHERN UGANDAN GIRL IN A LETTER TO PRESIDENT MUSEVENI

A full understanding of the predicaments of children in Uganda must include an account of the tragic events that have made northern Ugandan children an exception to the paradigm of ideal child citizenship. While the last chapter dealt with the ways in which Kampala schoolchildren conceptualized their mobility, this chapter deals with a very different set of children who find themselves in circumstances that pose even greater challenges to their ability to escape the tyranny of place. This is because they are being exploited for the purpose of destabilizing their own communities. They are the children of northern Uganda who are still caught in the midst of war.

Children abducted by the rebel Lord's Resistance Army (LRA) challenge the social category of ideal childhood and the overall security of the nation as a sentimental space in which children are encouraged to grow into responsible adult citizens. In this chapter, I share two more life histories of children who were abducted by the LRA. From their examples, we see how regional disparities in wealth and security affect the lives of the Acholi children of northern Uganda through poverty, displacement, and the breakdown of family life. This analysis leads us to critically question normative concepts of childhood as aid workers and children try to achieve some degree of normalcy amidst continuing violence and insecurity. Notions of childhood deployed by the international aid community often reduce children to victims who need to be resocialized and reintegrated into society through a normative yet unrealistic discourse of childhood. Children in turn respond by strategically utilizing international childhood discourses to actively aid their own reintegration in their communities.

"Child Soldiers"?

Ugandans and the international community alike tend to view LRA children simultaneously as victims and perpetrators of political instability. Much of the literature on child soldiers focuses on their involvement and demobilization within a framework of international rights discourses (Bennett 1998). With the spread of hegemonic, Western notions of childhood through media, aid organizations, and United Nations declarations, many adults cannot conceptually reconcile violence like that of the LRA with the purported innocence and purity of childhood (Jenks 1996). They typically lack situated analyses of these discourses in local circumstances (de Berry 2001). On a theoretical level, the prevalence of unique types of child combatants produced in the rebel LRA complicates efforts to end war and to aid child soldiers' social reintegration. War becomes a context in which disparate and contradictory notions of childhood are negotiated by various actors in the conflict, and these notions, when locally situated and implemented by government and international aid organizations, reveal the complexity with which the situation in northern Uganda confronts children and the nation.

On the other hand, many adults laud the child soldiers who participated in the current government's guerrilla war to liberate the nation in 1986. Museveni's National Resistance Army retained about sixty-five hundred child soldiers.[1] Most were orphaned in the fighting, and the NRA provided for their basic needs. Though they played auxiliary roles in the conflict, much was made in the international media of the gun-toting children on the front lines on the eve of liberation (Dodge and Raundalen 1991). President Museveni argued that the NRA was justified in enlisting children to fight because their social, cultural, and religious futures were at stake (Okumu 1997), but he quickly removed underage soldiers from combat, and many blended back into society. Recent literature on the proliferation of child soldiers suggests that the use of children in combat situations is a new, "third-world" phenomenon, but David Rosen proposes that the practice is actually enduring and widespread (Rosen 2005). Others have claimed that child soldiers are a natural extension of the African traditional age system in which young men were warriors (Bennett 1998), but the argument rests on more pliable African definitions of youth that range from adolescence to any adult not yet married.

These divergent notions of childhood and children's agency obscure amelioration of the situation for northern Ugandan children, though; LRA children are not conscripted into armed conflict in the stereotypical child-soldier scenario; they are literally kidnapped and sacrificed.

A Brief History of the Conflict

Colonial Origins

Today's conflict in northern Uganda has its roots in the colonial period. Externally, the LRA conflict is seen as an extension of post-independence civil war strife. Since independence in 1962, Uganda has had seven changes of government, all of which have been violent. Ugandan historian A. B. K. Kasozi writes, "Inequality . . . has been the main source of social conflict in Uganda, generating the structural violence from which all subsequent political, military, and civilian violence would erupt" (Kasozi 1994, 7). This violence is a characteristic outgrowth of ethnic division. On the basis of the British colonists' "noble savage" belief that the Nilotic and Sudanic ethnic groups of the north were part of a great pastoral warrior tradition, much like the Maasai of Kenya (Martin Shaw 1995), they were recruited for positions in the army and police, while those from southern ethnic groups were recruited for civil servant positions, and their lands were targeted for economic development. Northerners continued to hold primarily military jobs after independence in 1962 under first president Milton Obote. By 1969, Uganda's largest ethnic group, the

Baganda, comprised 16 percent of the population and 5 percent of the army. The northern Acholi and Langi, on the other hand, comprised 19 percent of the population and 61 percent of the army (Kasozi 1994, 54). Northerners were thus economically disadvantaged but controlled the instruments of violence: the armed forces. They would be alternately courted and betrayed in the subsequent overthrow of President Obote by Idi Amin (1971), and then Obote's retributive coup against Amin (1979).

When Idi Amin, a military commander, overthrew Obote in 1971, he assassinated many Acholi and Langi soldiers and replaced them with those with whom he had close ethnic ties. Obote returned to power in 1980 (with the help of a coalition of forces that included Yoweri Museveni's guerrilla followers), and with him the Acholi and Langi soldiers returned to dominate Uganda's military. According to people living in Kampala at the time, this was the worst period of oppression; Obote's military sought to avenge the deaths of colleagues and punish Amin supporters, including civilians. According to the International Red Cross, several hundred thousand people in the Luweero Triangle region (Baganda territory) were killed during this period (Human Rights Watch/Africa and Human Rights Watch Children's Rights Project 1997). Museveni's guerrillas, the National Resistance Army, continued to fight against Obote after he rigged the 1980 elections, receiving popular support for their commitment to protect civilians. Eventually, Acholi army leaders took advantage of Museveni's weakening of Obote to oust him in July 1985, replacing him with Acholi General Okello. Museveni's NRA persisted and took Kampala on January 26, 1986. Okello's soldiers, fearing another Acholi massacre, this time at the hands of the NRA, fled north, some across the border to Sudan. A new Acholi rebellion began when they merged with other opponents of Museveni to form the Uganda People's Defense Army, or UPDA (Human Rights Watch/Africa and Human Rights Watch Children's Rights Project 1997, 64).

The NRA did not kill Acholi soldiers, but widespread misconduct by NRA soldiers stationed in the north was reported, including the looting of Acholi cattle, a serious offense, given cattle's centrality to Acholi livelihood and their cultural symbolism of wealth and security (Women's Commission on Refugee Women and Children 2001, 33).

Rise of a Prophet: Alice Lakwena

Under the threat of ethnic extermination during the Obote and Amin eras, Acholi soldiers had gradually turned to atonement under a religious indoctrination that was a mixture of Acholi animism, Christianity, and militarism. This Acholi revival ultimately gave rise to the Lord's Resistance Army.

By the time Museveni took power in 1986, prophet Alice Lakwena had raised a holy army from northern UPDA soldiers. Lakwena, an Acholi healer and prophet whose name means "spiritual messenger," was given a battalion of the UPDA in November 1986, which soon became known as the Holy Spirit Movement (HSM). Alice was a spiritual healer claiming that her *lakwena* (possessing spirit) was the ghost of an Italian who had died near the Nile during the First World War. She enjoyed great support from the Acholi, and when they were threatened by the NRA, Lakwena became the spiritual and military leader who would protect them. One of her early followers explained,

The Lakwena appeared in Acholi because of the plan drawn by Yoweri Museveni and his government to kill all the male youths in Acholi as a revenge.[2] . . . so the Lakwena was sent to save the male youth. . . . The good Lord who sent the Lakwena decided to change his work from that of a doctor to that of a military commander for one simple reason: it is useless to cure a man today only that he be killed tomorrow. So it became an obligation on his part to stop the bloodshed before continuing his work as a doctor. (Behrend 1999, 165)

Lakwena set about cleansing the Acholi of their evil ways as she led soldiers into battle. Purging the Acholi of past wrongdoing and having them swear on the Bible, she promised the newly righteous Acholi that they would be protected and grow strong as a people. She became possessed by the spirits of various warriors and gave great sermons before battles, convincing soldiers that if they purified their Acholi hearts and minds by smearing themselves with shea tree butter, bullets would bounce off of them. They therefore ran fearlessly into battle, causing Museveni's army several embarrassing defeats. If HSM rebels died, Lakwena explained that they had retained sinful thoughts and allegiances to powers other than God—and therefore deserved death by God's own authority (Behrend 1999). Even abducting people into the movement was justified as being for the good of the abductee. This united the Acholi in a popular millenarian movement that for a brief time seriously threatened the power of Museveni's army in the north.

Acholi Apocalypse: Joseph Kony

Though Lakwena's movement was crushed by the new National Resistance Army after several months, commander Joseph Kony remained

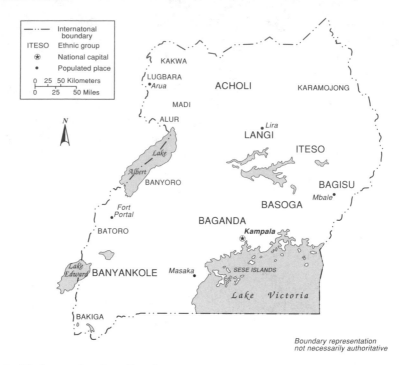

9   Ethnic map of northern Uganda.

in the bush with a group of HSM soldiers. As one of Lakwena's ritual assistants and her distant cousin, Kony claimed that he had inherited her powers, and his small band of followers continued to harass civilians and government installations. Kony soon usurped Lakwena's mysticism through elaborate rituals, founded the LRA, and declared that they would overthrow Museveni's government to run the country according to the Ten Commandments.

The National Resistance Army's continued misconduct toward people in the north engendered support for Kony's rebels until the early 1990s, when Kony's brutality began to exceed that of Museveni's army. The Acholi were becoming tired of war and had started to trust that Museveni, unlike his predecessors, would guarantee their security. With waning Acholi support, Kony felt that the older generation of Acholi had betrayed him—and themselves—by turning away from their "ethnic imperative" to wage war against the NRA. In the early 1990s, the LRA began a spiritual purging of Acholi through large-scale attacks on civilian targets in Acholiland (fig. 9) and increased abductions, especially of children, who were said to be easier to control and indoctrinate (Dodge

and Raundalen 1991; Coalition to Stop the Use of Child Soldiers 2001).
According to Acholi historian Heike Behrend, the Lord's Resistance Army
began to abduct children to

rescue them so that they could live in the New World. The old world was too corrupt
to be saved . . .

Kony's programme to make angels out of human beings and to build up a sinless
world has turned into an apocalyptic vision: "God said in the Bible, 'I will unleash
my wrath upon you and you will suffer pain. And in the end you will be killed by the
sword. Your children will be taken into captivity and will be burnt to death.'" (Behrend
1999, 182, 195)

Kony is thus using children to destroy Acholi culture and rebuild it
according to his own design. It is estimated that the LRA has abducted a
child from every extended family in Acholiland (Behrend 1999).

Children in LRA Captivity

Survivors' stories of LRA captivity tell of extreme brutality, fear, and
hunger. When children are abducted, they are typically tied together
and forced to march without rest or food while carrying stolen goods for
rebels. If they talk or show any resistance, they are beaten or killed. Until
recently, many were force-marched across the border into Sudan, where
they were trained as soldiers or—in the case of girls—given as "wives" to
commanders. Children who are caught attempting to escape face death
at the hands of other captives, who are gathered around and ordered to
beat the accused about the head with a log or a machete until they are
dead. It serves as a lesson to all other abductees that if they do as they
are told and do not try to run, they will live.

Through the performance of various religious rituals, Kony and the
LRA indoctrinate their army of children with an alternative discourse of
redemption and the possibility of recovering a national identity for the
Acholi. Rituals involving elements of both Catholic and Acholi animist
beliefs—and even some Muslim practices like banning pork and kneeling
to pray—are carried out to initiate new "recruits," and to purify soldiers
before they go into battle.[3] A fifteen-year-old girl told Human Rights Watch,

If they've just abducted you, they smear you with oil in the sign of the cross, on your
forehead and on your chest. They did that to us on the third day after we were abducted. They said it was their custom . . .

After we had been with them for three weeks, they drew a picture of a large heart in the ground, and divided it into thirty squares. They told us to bathe and to remove our blouses and remain bare-chested. They told each of us to stand in one of the squares. They dipped an egg in a mixture of white powder and water, and drew a heart on our chests and our backs. They also made a sign of the cross on our foreheads and across our lips. Then they poured water on us. The commander, Lagira, told us to stay without our blouses for three days. He said what they were doing was written in the Bible. Another man told us they were doing this for our protection. (Human Rights Watch 1997)

Often, however, the rituals end up being tests of the recruits' loyalties. Other escaped abductees have described similar rituals, but they were told that white markings made on their bodies could not wear off during those three days. If they did, the rebels claimed that it signified spiritual impurities and lack of allegiance to the LRA, and the abductees were severely beaten.

After abductees are trained as soldiers, they often go on missions where they are ordered to attack their own villages. They must burn huts, loot food and goods, beat, torture, or kill people, and abduct more children there. Once they have participated in brutal attacks such as these, their commanders argue that they cannot go home again without reprisals by the community. Many come to believe it, and their fate as LRA rebels is sealed.

The Sudanese government began supporting the LRA after failed peace talks between the Ugandan government and the LRA in 1994. Sudan's support for the LRA was a response to Uganda's backing of the rebel Sudanese People's Liberation Army (SPLA) in Sudan's civil war with the Arab Khartoum government. Sudan heavily armed the LRA and enabled them to slip away from the army by crossing the border back into Sudan between raids on northern Uganda. The LRA also received land, food, and weapons from the Sudanese government in return for helping to fight the SPLA in southern Sudan. Thus, children and their families in northern Uganda have borne the brunt of interregional as well as ethnic and national conflict. The limited information available indicates that the LRA continues to pursue a policy of Acholi purification, a large part of which is indoctrinating abducted children with rhetoric about religious purity and moral behavior. But even these claims seem to have diminished over the years, and the LRA's purpose becomes more vague as their attacks on civilians have become more brutal.

World Vision

Luckily, children have managed to escape from the LRA and return to Uganda, but they require assistance with their transitions back to community life. Most receive assistance from the World Vision Gulu Children of War Rehabilitation Center. World Vision, a Christian nongovernmental organization (NGO) that manages various development and relief projects throughout the world, has often been criticized for the hegemonic economic and evangelical dynamics that its programs create and perpetuate—between Western middle-class sponsors and the impoverished Southern children that they sponsor, for example (Bornstein 2001). Despite my misgivings based on knowledge of such practices, I appreciated that World Vision was one of only two organizations that were taking on the important work of receiving escaped LRA captives at the time (the other being a local NGO called Gulu Save the Children Organization, or GUSCO). I found that World Vision's Children of War Rehabilitation Center had a wonderful and accommodating local staff in Gulu, and after a few phone calls from the head office in Kampala to the center in Gulu, I was invited for a visit in the spring of 2000.

I got a ride from a friend of friend—a northern Ugandan journalist who often traversed the dangerous road from Kampala to Gulu in his ancient, sky-blue truck. I was a bit apprehensive about making the four-and-a-half-hour journey because of rebel ambushes. The army performs a security sweep of the road every morning before allowing people to pass from the Karuma Dam on the Nile to Gulu. To be honest, I was even a bit anxious about arriving in town. Before one goes to Gulu, one tends to imagine it as a sort of otherworldly hell on earth, where rebels are plundering, raping, and burning, and where the rest of the population is walking around in terror. Many of my friends in Kampala refused to even consider going there. They had certainly tainted my imagination as well. "The north is another country," my Muganda roommate said dismissively.

But once I arrived in Gulu, I was surprised and somewhat relieved to see none of the tension and fear I had anticipated. It was actually a fairly sleepy, friendly town, with few cars and a lot of Chinese bicycles. People were oddly serene, gracious, and welcoming. The calm atmosphere was not all that it seemed, though. When I was introduced to people, they often brought up instances of extreme violence and threat quite casually, as if such things were comfortable and familiar: "Oh, things in Gulu are fine. There have been some deadly robberies in which people have been killed in their homes, but the army caught the perpetrator and shot him."

Or someone might say, "Please come to visit us at home, but be sure to follow the worn footpath, since there may still be some landmines here and there." Staff at the World Vision Center talked of the war and its effect on their clients and communities in similar ways. Though people were weary of war, that weariness could manifest itself in frustration, resignation, or rebellion. At the center, I was introduced to some of the staff members and shown around the grounds. The Ministry of Works had sold the compound to World Vision in 1995.[4] The center operates on funds from World Vision offices in other countries, most recently Australia, Denmark, and Canada.

World Vision has assisted about fifteen thousand former captives to date with counseling and resettlement. Because the nature of the war is constantly changing, staff members accomplish much of their work through contingency planning. They have nurses and counselors on staff. Though conventional counseling and psychotherapy are considered to be "outside" local culture, trauma counseling and other psychosocial services have proven beneficial. They also employ nonverbal and traditional healing strategies such as drawing, music, drama, ritual, and prayer.

The walled compound consisted of four main permanent structures: an administrative block; a long building housing some staff offices, a counseling room, quarters for the matron, and a fourth room sometimes used as a dormitory room for female clients; a storage facility for food and supplies given to clients upon arrival and departure at the center; and a building at the opposite end of the compound that was the boys' dorm. The latter looked just like a school dormitory, with two rows of bunk beds stretching down the long room, a few foam mattresses, and the meager belongings of the boys neatly assembled either on or under their beds.

When I visited in the spring of 2000, there were about twenty children at the center, most between twelve and fifteen years old. When Uganda and Sudan signed the Nairobi Peace Accords in December 1999, part of the agreement was that Sudan would cooperate with UNICEF and other aid organizations to help secure the release of the children. Counselor Violet told me that they were preparing to receive up to three thousand children estimated to still be held captive in Sudan. UNICEF managed to locate a few wounded LRA child soldiers in hospitals in Khartoum and Juba and evacuate them by air back to Uganda, but they were never released in large numbers.

Counselor Daniel explained that children start in group therapy and eventually move to individual counseling while they undergo medical treatment and attend educational classes. Meanwhile, the center's staff tries to locate their families. They try to keep children for as short a time as possible, but they found that they needed to keep them for at least two to three months for security reasons as well as medical or psychological ones. Children also stayed longer for vocational training or if they required prolonged medical treatment for injuries or sexually transmitted diseases. The center had transitioned from vocational training to training community caregivers and finding local artisans to mentor children. These activities had heightened community involvement and so facilitated resettlement.

LRA Life Histories

Chancy—A Lifetime of War

Chancy was fifteen years old when I met her in 2001 at the World Vision Children of War Rehabilitation Center. She was abducted by the LRA in 1999 and was with the rebels for about thirteen months before she escaped. She had been at the center for two weeks.

Counselor Violet called her into her office, and she sat meekly in a chair. Though Chancy was a big, healthy girl, she was painfully shy, always staring down at her hands in her lap, which were usually fiddling with small objects like blades of grass or paper clips. She had a gracious but nervous smile, and it struck me how submissive these escaped children usually were, especially considering the assertiveness that an act of escape required. It was almost as if children's experiences with the rebels remade them—through extreme trauma—into the types of children their parents found ideal—with the exception that they usually were not happy. Chancy wore a T-shirt and a skirt picked from the center's second-hand storehouse along with an issued pair of rubber sandals. Violet picked lint out of her combed hair as she explained to Chancy who I was and what I was interested in. Chancy agreed to share her story with me, at first perhaps because she felt she had no choice. But as we talked, her voice gained strength and momentum, even if she continued to stare into her lap.

Though it is easy to assume that abducted children like Chancy suffer disproportionately at the hands of the LRA, Chancy's story illustrates how Acholi children are subjected to the violence of poverty and abuse that mark their lives on a daily basis. As I spent more time with Chancy at the World Vision Center and later, after her return to her family, I would come to recognize that her suffering did not begin or end with her LRA captivity.

Chancy was born in 1986, the year Museveni came to power. It was also the year that Alice Lakwena started the Holy Spirit Movement and attempted to march on Kampala to overthrow Museveni. Chancy was the third of six children. Her parents subsistence-farmed at their Gulu District village home, and her father occasionally got work as a farmhand on commercial farms. She explained,

My father and my mother were staying together, but after the sixth child was born, they separated. So we the five older children were left to stay with our father, and our mother went away with the youngest child. Our father took another wife, but in 1996 he went to work in Masindi and remained there without my mother. My stepmother was always beating us, mistreating us because our father had gone to Masindi. My mother was at least properly married to our father; at least he took dowry to her family. But they didn't take dowry to my stepmother's family, and I think she just felt that she didn't want to look after a co-wife's children. When my father would send money for school fees and uniforms, my stepmother would use the money to buy things for her own children. So my studies were disturbed. She would refuse to give us food if we hadn't done certain chores. We sent word to our mother to come and collect us, so she came and took me to her sister and took the other four children with her to stay in the village. I grew up with my aunt, the sister to my mother. At least life was easier because she had three children and I was able to go to school.

I stayed with my aunt at Karuma and in 1998, my mother called me to her. So I went to my mother and started school there. We were living in a camp [for internally displaced persons] at Anaka. . . . We stayed in that camp because the rebels were disturbing people in the village. Because in the camp there are no gardens, you have to go sometimes to the village to collect food from your home garden. So we had gone to dig cassava. We could not come back immediately, so we slept in the village. Sometimes we would hear that rebels are around, but that day when we went home, we had not even heard of the presence of rebels, so we stayed there thinking nothing would happen at night. We were not sleeping in the house; we were sleeping in the bush. When people go back to the village, they don't sleep in the house whether the rebels are around or not. We thought it was safe to sleep in the bush and wake up in the morning. But the rebels got a certain lady who knew where we were sleeping, so she led them to us, my mother, my elder sister, and me. They walked around us with torches as we were sleeping. They told us to get up and they started asking us why we have slept outside. They asked, "Are there government soldiers around?" And then they asked, "Is there a trading center around?" So that's when I knew they were rebels. So my sister was made to carry luggage a distance and they set her free, but I was the youngest so they took me away.

Her abductors joined up with the rest of their battalion and reported their new acquisitions. Chancy estimated there were about one hundred rebel soldiers, and she was one of fifteen children abducted that night, bringing their total number of recent captives to about fifty. Unlike many previously abducted children, Chancy was not taken to Sudan right away, but she was trained to shoot a weapon over the course of one month and forced to loot villages and homesteads as they made their way through Gulu and Kitgum Districts. She said that at one time they tried to enter Sudan but were shot at and so retreated. She was relieved.

I was thinking that if they took us to Sudan it would be difficult to come back or to escape.

I found some children who were from the same school, and I found some others who were from our village. I knew them. When we could, we talked about our experiences with the LRA, home and school, but we were not supposed to talk about wanting to go home, or escape, because if you do it you are going to be beaten or killed.

We moved from place to place but sometimes we stayed in a place and made shelter. Sometimes we stayed among the villagers deep in the village. We were always guarded by soldiers, even when we were going to fetch water or we were moving anywhere. They were always watching. And whenever you do something wrong you are beaten, and sometimes when we meet with the government [army] and they start shooting, we run away and we throw our luggage. If you leave your luggage you are beaten, so you have to run with your luggage.

You are told to kill. One day a boy escaped and they went to his home, and they got him there so they brought him and told all the captives to come and kill him. A few of us were called to the well, so I didn't kill the boy. I came and found they had already killed him. They used clubs or big sticks and they beat and hit him. They always hit the back of the head. After that, those who have participated in the beating, they will do a ritual ceremony for cleansing. They sprinkle water on them. They say [it] is to cleanse them from that killing.

Shortly after she was abducted in 1999, the rebels told her group that the angels had said they would overthrow the government in 2000. When nothing happened in 2000, they revised their projected takeover for 2002. That's when Chancy knew they were lying. "I did not feel good," she said. "All the time I would think if there was a way I would escape . . . but it was very difficult because of the soldiers looking at us, watching us all the time. So life was hard with no peace, no happiness."

Chancy was under the direction of a certain commander who ordered her to do work when camped and to carry things when on the move. In January of 2001, he told her to go to a twenty-three-year-old lieutenant to be his wife. Unless a girl is explicitly given as a wife, soldiers are not supposed to touch them. "I was so scared," she said, "but I could not refuse because I had seen a girl who refused to go to a man get beaten so badly. She was tied to a tree to be shot. Then she just accepted him and went to him." She remembered that incident when she was called to the lieutenant's bed and chose not to protest. The lieutenant had no other wives, and he did not beat her, so she was relieved. At least he was gentle. He was later given another captive girl, and together the two cooked, washed his clothes, made his bed, and went to him whenever he called.

Life remained difficult, with constant hunger, fear, beatings, and intimidation. "I escaped because of the suffering you can't imagine. They can kill you anytime. They don't care about people. They don't really care about anybody." Chancy and others finally found their chance to escape in the summer of 2001. When they came close to a small town, government forces ambushed their camp.

When we had gone in the villages to loot chicken and some food, we didn't know that the government soldiers were there. So one boy as he entered a house to loot, the government soldiers caught him. But for us, we ran away. And then this boy led the government soldiers to where we were. We were already camped and were trying to look for firewood to cook. All of a sudden, another rebel group—the one which had gone to loot—was also coming back. The government soldiers saw them before they saw us, so when they started shooting is when we realized they were there, so we all started running. And as we ran I branched away from the main group. They continued to run in one direction as I was running in another direction. I was alone.

As I was moving ahead I saw my friend with two other boys. So I ran to them. As we were moving the government soldiers again saw us because they still had that boy they had captured. And so they asked the boy and I think he told them, "These are part of the rebels." So they followed [us] and they started shooting guns at us but they were shooting high. They wanted us to stop but we were already running. As we ran we also separated again from the two boys, who went on their own. My co-wife and I went on our own, but they were still following us. So we went to the village, we got the chairman of the local council, and we were asking him to show us the way to town. The chairman refused; he said he wanted to take us to the government detach, so we accepted. As we were still moving, the rebels we were with were also looking for us. As we crossed the road to the detach, they had also come. So we went and reported to the army. The rebel lieutenant whom I was given to as a wife came up to the road and the government again shot him and I heard they broke his arm. The government brought us to the main barracks in Gulu Town, and then they brought me to World Vision.

Chancy was in the barracks for a while as the army debriefed her about her rebel activities. She was then handed over to World Vision for re-habilitation, and the girl she escaped with was taken to Gulu Support the Children Organization (GUSCO), a local NGO doing the same work. Chancy was one of a half dozen girls at the rehabilitation center when I met her. Others had had children by their captors and had escaped with babies on their backs. Now that she and the other girls felt they were safe, they were trying to put the past behind them and look forward to the future. "At World Vision," Chancy said, "We don't talk much about the bush, but we talk about home."

Girls' Double Stigma of Captivity

Sexual assault and the risk of contracting sexually-transmitted diseases in the LRA often compounds girls' suffering. When they bear children, their chances of escape diminish. I met a young woman named Mary a day after she arrived at the World Vision Center with her bouncy, one-year-old daughter. She had quickly befriended Evelyn, a shy girl who was abducted at twelve, married to a high commander, and escaped several years later while pregnant. She had just had a little boy at the center, whose name meant "Trust in God" in Lucholi. I listened as Mary first told her story in a group counseling session. She was abducted in 1994 when she was fourteen and was one of the "pioneers" who was first marched to camps in Sudan. She was immediately given to a commander as a wife and gave birth to a boy when she was seventeen. She was also trained to shoot a gun, and she and others talked about marching hungrily to raid villages of the starving Dinka people for food. These fights between two starving factions were particularly fearsome.

At the time of her escape after nearly eight years with the LRA, Mary was cultivating fields at a camp located three miles from Kony's main camp. Because of security concerns, Kony ordered all but the women who were tending their fields to retreat to the main camp. This left her and some others virtually unattended. She hesitated to take the opportunity to escape because they had taken her son, who was five years old, to the other camp. She only had her daughter with her because she was still breastfeeding. But she knew it was her only chance, so she ran. She managed to walk from Sudan back into Uganda with her daughter, but she could not escape her guilt at having left her son behind.

One of the most famous LRA abductions involved 139 female students from St. Mary's Aboke, a Catholic secondary boarding school. The story is chronicled in Els de Temmerman's book, *Aboke Girls: Children Abducted in Northern Uganda* (de Temmerman 2001).[5] Sister Rachele, the Italian headmistress, pursued the rebels through the bush and negotiated the release of 109 of the girls, but the remaining 30 were marched to Sudan. Sister Rachele contacted the presidents of Uganda and Sudan and made a visit to LRA camps in Sudan to try to rescue the girls, but could not secure their release. Her efforts brought international attention to their plight, but reports from escaped children indicate that this made life even worse for the Aboke girls. Kony told them they had brought negative press and diplomatic pressure on the LRA. After several managed to escape, the remaining Aboke girls were put under constant surveillance and were told that if any more of them tried to escape, the rest would be killed. They were doled out as "wives" to rebel commanders, including Kony himself. In 2001, twenty-one Aboke girls still remained in LRA captivity. I learned later that Counselor Violet's daughter was one of them. Violet received news of her every once in a while when escapees who knew her came to the center. She had heard that her daughter had become one of Kony's thirty-five wives and had borne him children.

Even when girls manage to escape the LRA, they experience gendered obstacles to their reintegration. Rose, eighteen, was at the World Vision Center for several months while they worked out where to place her upon rehabilitation. Her only living and locatable relative was her uncle, with whom she had been living at the time of her abduction. While the children slept in the bush, the rebels dragged him from his house and told him to lead them to the children. He showed them where the children were hiding, and she was taken away by the LRA. Once she was given to a commander, she endured repeated sexual assaults and finally gave birth to the little girl with whom she eventually escaped. She did not want to go back to her uncle, both because she was still angry with him for having aided in her abduction, and because she had told her LRA "husband" where her home village was. Her uncle still lived in that location, and she feared her "husband" would come looking for her there. She eventually had no choice but to go there, and even though she received assistance with her school fees, she complained to World Vision staff that her relatives neglected her child while Rose was at school because the child had been born to a rebel father.

Girls like these are particularly difficult to reintegrate in their communities because of the multiple stigmas they bear for having been rebels' wives, having borne them children, and in more than 90 percent of the cases having contracted a sexually-transmitted disease, usually HIV (Amnesty International 1997, 17). This brings shame to the families and renders the girl undesirable for marriage within the community, thus burdening the family financially. Having children makes it more difficult for them to return to school, even with sponsorship; like Rose, they cannot find anyone willing to watch their children while they are in class. They therefore utilize different reintegration strategies than boys, trying as quickly as possible to blend back into society (Shepler 2002b). Many of these girls thus become beneficiaries of the World Vision vocational training programs, especially in tailoring.

Richard—Resilience Despite Obstacles

The signing of the Nairobi Peace Accords in 2001 strengthened Uganda-Sudan relations and fortified the border. Many detachments in Uganda were cut off from Kony's command, changing the nature of LRA abductions; namely, they became shorter, and it was easier to escape. Children were abducted mainly to carry looted goods in the Ugandan bush, and few were taken to Sudan to be trained as fighters. Richard was one such child abducted for a short period in 2001.

Richard was thirteen years old, though he looked and acted more like he was ten or eleven: he was skinny and slight for his age, and, like Chancy, painfully shy and nervous, behaviors I was coming to see as manifestations of post-traumatic stress. Richard and I sat down with an interpreter—a university student doing his internship in social work—to talk about his experience. With dirty bare feet and skinny, scarred legs, worn and faded shorts, and a second-hand, black nylon jumper with a red Nike stripe that traversed his distended belly, Richard fidgeted nervously, so I was extra careful to explain my intentions to him.

Richard contradicted himself often, probably out of confusion rather than any intent to deceive. We were uncertain about the timeline of his abduction and length of captivity, but we were able to discern some basic information. He seemed to have lived with his mother while his father, a soldier, had been largely absent from his life. As the third of seven children without a supportive father, he had had to work since he was young to support his mother and managed to afford to go to school on and off by selling paraffin. He was abducted from his grandfather's home in the village. We visited his mother, who lived within walking distance of the center, to clarify some other details.

Though Richard did not have a handle on the duration of his abduction (we did not know from his account whether he had spent three weeks, three months, or three years with the rebels), he was eager to tell us his story. He did not speak of his emotions as he went through his ordeal, but he spoke rapidly of the experience as he continued to look down at his hands and pick at dry skin. His eyes glazed over with tears as he talked about being in the village on holiday from school and having soldiers come and loot the compound.

When they came there was a troop which passed by our home, and seven of them branched to our place; they came at home. So two entered the house and told my brother who was listening to the radio to hand it over. When the rebels came they met me with my brothers, so they took the radio and from there they arrested [abducted] me. One of the rebels said, "This boy, should we take him or we leave him?"

They said, "Let's go with him," and they took me.

My brothers were not taken; they are older than me so the rebels, they claim if they take someone who is mature—who has got all the tactics of knowing their movements—he can plan and easily escape. So with a child like me, they move with him in the bush and he gets confused and lost, so it is better to take children.

Before I was abducted, I knew the details about the rebels. The way they behave; the way they mistreat people when they get you; they can kill you, they can beat you, they can do any sort of thing to you. So I at least had that sort of idea. Once abducted, I was sure of such things to happen to me. I heard it from my friend when we went to school. He was abducted before so he was telling me at school when we were playing, so that's how I came to know the bush experiences.

At first I was beaten because I was walking slowly. They wanted me to direct them where there are more children so they were moving with me so they get more children. But wherever we would move, those children were all in hiding, so they didn't get those children. I was the only child in the group who was taken. The first day they abducted me, they started walking at eight or nine at night, then we stopped somewhere and slept there. The next day we started walking at seven up to one, daytime. Then we stayed there again. We moved from there and slept and went to some village on the eastern side of Gulu District. It is something like thirty kilometers, maybe more than that, from the village where I was taken. That is where the rebels staged their camp there, but there are other camps in Gulu District. I carried some beans and some *posho* [cornmeal] which was looted, and I also carried a bag on my back. The bag contained clothes which were robbed from other people.

The rebels were telling me the reasons why they abducted me. They abduct people and they mistreat . . . tribe mates because they claim that the people used to report them to the government troops; maybe they have shot one of their rebels, their commanders, so they mistreat people seriously. They are doing that to [get] revenge. They wanted me to go to the bush to have a hard life so they could train me to become a soldier like them, doing what they are doing. When we moved, the government troops stormed us four times. So I had some experience of gunfire between the rebels and the government troops. When they were fighting, they put me up in a tree to monitor what was going to happen. So my work was just like an informer.

Richard was also forced to fetch water when they made camp but was rarely allowed to bathe or eat much of whatever was prepared. He never trained as a soldier, probably because they were constantly moving through the bush to avoid capture by the army. He knew some of the areas they passed through, but he never had the opportunity to get away. At one point, they reached a place that was familiar to him because his uncle stayed nearby. But they luckily passed by and did not attempt to disturb people there.

The children they had abducted before trained me on how to stay with those rebels. I was with my friend and we started planning to escape. When we were moving in the bush we reached an area which was not so safe. The rebels were fearing the government troops, so they told us not to move in lines but to disperse and each one should move in the same direction but not following each other so that our routes cannot be traced. While we were moving, the soldiers were ahead of us maybe twenty-five meters. We had heavy luggage, it was bushy, and we are very short, so we could not easily be seen. We remained behind. We pretended as if we were for a short call [to urinate]. So the rebels moved a bit as they were not seeing properly. We dropped our luggage and started running away, but following where we came from because we were very sure it was safe behind us.

We escaped at night, around nine o'clock. We moved like that until it was too dark. Then we slept and waited for morning hours to start moving. As we slept in that place, the next day we were planning to move to another place. We were very tired and we went under a certain tree to rest. By surprise we heard the rebels passing by. It seems they slept in the same area. So we had to take cover within that place so we could be safe. We hid there until they passed the road, then we had to cross the road where they had passed. We survived, and they didn't get us again! We moved a very long distance until we came across some man who was burning charcoal. We asked him the name of the area, so he told us and then the man took us to the local authority.

It took us two weeks because we used to move short distances and then sleep because our legs were swollen. For my friend it was more serious, but I could not leave my friend because we escaped together and neither of us knew the area. So we had to assist each other. We used to get some wild fruits for food. The day we escaped, we escaped with a five-liter jerrycan of water. So that is what we used to get water.

After we reached the local councilman, he took us to the barracks. The day we were taken to the barracks, I was escorted by my grandfather. I was very happy to see him. He said he was very happy to see me, too. He told me that everybody thought that I was killed. They were worried but they had forgotten because they thought I was dead.

Several factors made escape easier for the more recent abductees like Richard. First, rather than being marched to Sudan to be trained as soldiers, they often stayed in the countryside within their own districts and had some idea where they were in relation to their homes. Second, they often ran into army ambushes as they traveled, so in the middle of a firefight, many found opportunities to drop whatever they were carrying and run. Third, newer abductees knew that the army would attempt to rescue children abducted by the rebels rather than shoot at them.

Richard had been at World Vision for a short while when I met him, and he was enjoying himself. He had since seen several family members, including his mother, who lived close by. He said that initially, he was angry with her because "she is the one who made me to be "arrested." I was in town, and she told me to go to the village, and yet the villages are insecure, and she was very aware of that. Anyway," he added, "I know adults are not protecting the children because there is no alternative for them."

Locality and Structure

The LRA's cruelty remains incomprehensible to Uganda's political elites and other nations, who believe that to understand the LRA's logic, they must step outside of their own codes of civil society—a move they are not willing to make. But the structures and discourses of the LRA and the government bear remarkable similarities, especially in relation to the formation of children's political identities. The LRA adopts normative structures—family and school—within which children typically form their ethnic and political identities (James 1998; Kiros 2001). The LRA tries to communicate high morality through vicious discipline and seemingly senseless violence. Elizabeth Rubin writes, "The moment they were snatched by the LRA, they entered a moral universe where everything they had been taught was flipped on its head. Killing was good. Kindness was bad" (Rubin 1998, 63). But children are punished in the LRA for some of the same things for which schools often punish them: disobedience to elders and inappropriate association with members of the opposite sex, for example. The difference, of course, is that the LRA usually takes punishments to the extreme, even killing their offenders (or making fellow children kill them). In the LRA, children are still subjected to adult authority, but their obedience and discipline are suddenly in the service not of fulfilling state discourses of productive citizenship, but of the destruction and death that the LRA deems necessary to achieve their concept of ideal citizenship: Acholi purification through violence.

It is not coincidental, then, that the LRA tends to abduct children from schools, which are not only obvious places to find large numbers of defenseless children, but also among the few material symbols of state presence in the north outside of military installations. They are also important sites for children's national identity formation (James 1998; Levinson and Holland 1996; Mayall 1994; Stambach 2000). LRA commanders even refer to themselves as "teachers," perhaps in an effort to earn respect and deference from children who are reared to respect teachers. Richard told me, "They nicknamed themselves teacher, so when they call you to do something, you must respond in a respectable manner. They are saying they are disciplining. They are teaching people yet what they are doing is not really humanitarian."

Given that the family is traditionally another main site of children's identity formation (Christensen, James, and Jenks 2000), the LRA also maintains control over children by using the idiom of family to hierarchically structure their society. Commanders who are given "wives" act as heads of families in which all abductees are placed as "siblings." They have the authority to instruct, punish, and kill members of their "families" as they see fit.[6] Despite its apparent cruelty, this form of organization succeeds in cementing relationships between captives, if not always between captives and their captors. Chancy's close friendship with her "co-wife" is one example.

Children reported that they constantly had to demonstrate allegiance to the LRA's code of conduct to keep from being killed. One girl said, "A little girl tried to escape, and they made us kill her. . . . Then they made us lie down and they beat us with fifteen strokes each, because they said we had known she would try to escape" (Ehrenreich 1998, 92). Meanwhile, in Ugandan primary schools, children were being punished by caning for skipping classes. As in Ugandan society, LRA children who obey and excel in the given conditions advance in the ranks. Thus, while people outside the LRA tend to view it as a horrific exploitation of children, it is often successful because of the very ways in which locally valued attributes of childhood subjugate children to adult authority. One child said, "Elders are older people with authority; they carry sticks, as do teachers, and require respect from young people" (Women's Commission on Refugee Women and Children 2001, 10). Such statements lead us to see how local cultural expectations of children's behavior are precisely what enable Kony to coerce children to do his bidding.

Many quietly resist the LRA's tyranny when they can, but others come to fully subscribe to it. Acholi children have grown up in a war-torn environment and inherited their parents' sense of political disenfranchisement. In her study of female soldiers in the Tamil nationalist struggle in Sri Lanka, Yamuna Sangarasivam writes that "people living in these extreme conditions realize that survival in war is not fully congruent with the notions of survival in peace . . . to survive and live with dignity amidst the crisis of war may require one's participation in the very same violence that destroyed one's sense of dignity and integrity" (Sangarasivam 2003, 60). Children are not immune to the ironies of survival amid political insecurity. Younger children, when forcibly abducted, often come to identify with and depend on their captors in the absence of any other parental relationship (Dodge and Raundalen 1991). Once older children are faced with the horrible situation of submitting to the LRA code of conduct or dying, many rightly see acquiescence as the only option for survival. On occasion, though, some children even see the rebel life as an escape from their unpleasant realities: A teenage boy at the Gulu World Vision rehabilitation center said that the uncle he lived with was so cruel to him that he hoped that the LRA would come and abduct him. At least in the LRA, he figured, he could become the instrument of violence rather than merely its victim. When his wish came true, however, he went from one living hell to another.

Many children who do what they do in the LRA merely to survive under coercion are stricken with feelings of guilt at the atrocities they commit against their own families and friends. They eventually give up the will to live, escape, or die trying. Children commonly reported that they experienced nightmares about recapture or the people they have killed, especially other captive children. The Acholi believe that people who die by violent means create spirits called *cen*. Finnstrom writes, "The spirit of a killed person might return to disturb its killer. If you have 'killed too many people,' . . . this will have a profound and malevolent influence on your behavior. . . . The spirit of the one who died violently will also disturb the person who found the body" (Finnstrom 2001, 251). This is why the Acholi (including Kony) require ritual cleansing after involvement in warfare. Since the LRA children suffer from *cen*, perhaps they are not so far removed from their cultural cosmology as elders suppose. Many rehabilitation programs now include cleansing rituals in their programming.

"Normality": An Achievable Goal?

These children's stories give rise to concerns about the ways in which various concepts of childhood circulate and operate in northern Uganda when it comes to "rehabilitation" of LRA child soldiers. Given the intense violence to which LRA children are exposed, aid workers and government officials often lament the loss of a sense of "normality" for the children of northern Uganda. The idea of normality, however, includes an idyllic, singular notion of childhood: the 1983 Draft Convention on the Rights of the Child states, "The child, for the full and harmonious development of his or her personality, should grow up in a family environment, in an atmosphere of happiness, love and understanding" (Ennew and Milne 1990, 8). As stories like Chancy's and Richard's indicate, many northern Ugandan children have never actually experienced this construction of normative childhood due to war. A Women's Commission on Refugee Women and Children report states,

Ugandan and Sudanese refugee adolescents have identified insecurity as the over-arching preoccupation and devastating reality of their lives. On one level, the dire circumstances of war seem "normal" because they are all young people know. On another level, adolescents and youth are acutely aware that it is not normal to be abducted; forced to fight, kill, and steal; forced to labor; be sexually enslaved, exploited, and abused; go hungry; lose out on education and any hope for a livelihood; and miss the care and love of parents, who are no longer with them as a result of war. (Women's Commission on Refugee Women and Children 2001, 11)

The conditions for children in northern Uganda are not only seen as "abnormal" by UNICEF and other children's organizations, they are unacceptable to anyone who cares about children. One reason that children are acutely aware that their situations differ starkly from normative concepts of childhood—especially those perpetuated by international aid organizations—is that these concepts are based on UN-proliferated Western notions of ideal childhood that presume a certain level of security and infrastructure that is usually absent from war zones. Even UN mandates written to protect children in war cannot be neatly implemented in northern Uganda because children have already suffered the trauma from which the UN hopes to shield them. At this point, the Convention on the Rights of the Child has already failed to protect their rights. In fact, much of UNICEF's mandate focuses on post-traumatic assistance to children, precisely because "education, health services and food supplements are relatively simple to supply, compared with preventing the exploitation, torture, killing, abduction, and imprisonment of children" (Ennew and Milne 1990, 7). UNICEF's goal to help children achieve certain universal ideals of childhood is quite noble and ambitious; the problem arises when those standards effectively exclude many children from the category of "normal," further marginalizing them for being unlike the "normal," universal child of UN documents.

Like UNICEF, World Vision's very notion of rehabilitation is premised on this discourse of a "normal" state of childhood that involves experiences and material resources that are absent from a region that has undergone nearly two decades of civil strife. Basic education, for example, is the very nexus of this return to normality, and yet it is out of reach for many Acholi children. Still, World Vision staff (all Ugandan) encourages children to hope that they can rise to these ideals through certain strategic, mimetic devices. When I first arranged to visit the center, the World Vision communications officer based in Kampala called the Gulu center on my behalf. "It sounds like you have a lot of students there!" he shouted over the phone. I was surprised by the use of the term "students" to describe LRA escapees. What exactly were they being educated in?

I soon discovered that the World Vision compound is modeled on a boarding school, with boys' and girls' dorms and a timetable of "classes" that include individual and group counseling, health education, children's rights, drawing, traditional singing and dancing, debate, and storytelling. All are intended for rehabilitation and repatriation, based on both local and global assessments of child soldiers' psychosocial needs. Ex-captives did not talk much about their emotions without encouragement from counselors. I even got the sense that clients were reluctant to talk at all but felt they had little choice. Openly discussing how one feels is not culturally sanctioned among the Acholi, who prefer to bear suffering stoically (Barton, Mutiti, and The Assessment Team for Psycho-Social Programmes in Northern Uganda 1998). However, rehabilitation and psychosocial services are premised on communication-based therapy. They must thus undo quite a bit of cultural conditioning to be successful. Creative activities like singing, drama, and drawing became useful strategies for drawing out children's emotions because they are effective, indirect modes of telling. Ex-LRA captives commonly hold public dramatizations of their abduction and servitude. Children's drawings that adorned the walls of the main activity room usually depicted their abduction scenes, life with the LRA, or their hopes for the future (fig. 10). They even received marks for their efforts.

10 An LRA escapee displays a marker drawing depicting his abduction that he drew as part of his rehabilitation at the World Vision center. Photo by the author ca. 2001.

The center's director told me that they initiated the school structure because in the LRA the children had experienced such a lack of structure that the center wanted to reintroduce stability. Children's descriptions of their time with the LRA seemed cruelly structured to me, but World Vision workers saw it as a lack of structure because it was based on horrendous reversals of their concepts of childhood normality. World Vision subscribes to the idea that children are any people under the age of eighteen, but they also take older escapees—still referring to them as "students" and "children" because, one counselor explained, "When they were abducted as children, their childhoods were stolen from them." This idea configures life in the LRA as a sort of static environment that either suspends or usurps childhood. The director explained to me that World Vision policy focuses on psychosocial services for the recuperation of a sense of normalcy for "vulnerable and oppressed" children, but he could not directly articulate what normalcy meant. Like his "students," he reverted to a discourse of education and how educating children about their rights would help them contribute as productive citizens to the nation.

In sum, the World Vision mandate tries to bring disadvantaged children into line with international discourses about appropriate lives for children. Despite the invaluable work they do, I wondered whether this was fair or realistic under the circumstances. As noted in chapter 2, World Vision's young clients were highly skeptical of their counselors' assertions that they could attend school. Children in the LRA, if they were ever admitted into normative categories of cultural citizenship in the first place, immediately drop out of them by virtue of their forced participation in rebel activities that destabilize those categories. For the Acholi, this is one more contradiction in their struggle to gain a sense of full citizenship. Over the course of my visits, I was to learn the extent to which rehabilitation meant the "recovery" of a mode of childhood experience that most of these children had never experienced in the first place.

Life in Gulu

Richard indicated that he had a keen sense of the ways war and poverty had affected his family and that of others in Acholiland, but we would get an earful from his mother when we visited her the next day. Richard's family history and home life provide a detailed picture of Acholi children's alienation from "normative" constructions of childhood, yet they are representative of the realities faced by many children, in Gulu and around the world.

I met Violet in her office for a sip of milky sweet tea before we fetched Richard to take us to his home. He used terms like "my older mother" rather than typical Lucholi kinship terms, so that we were unsure which relation we would find at the home near the center. He led us out the gate and along a path that cut between a lush valley with a communal well and a thick cluster of concrete conical huts with thatch roofs. Piles of garbage burned acrid in the gardens surrounding the grounds, beaten bare and black all around the compound by the footfalls of people living there. Young children toddled in the courtyards while their mothers busied themselves with chores. I saw no men around the settlement. Violet pointed out that this settlement was only about five years old and had gone up as temporary housing for the people streaming into town once the LRA insurgency had picked up in 1996. It was turning out to be permanent, however, as people had been living there and the settlement had slowly expanded since then.

Richard led us all the way to the last hut at the edge of the settlement, where his mother stepped out and invited us in as though she had been expecting us. We entered through a door made of corrugated metal. A picture of a Kung Fu artist was drawn on it, along with some faux Chinese characters and the word "Nike." The hut was perhaps ten to twelve feet across, made of cement with a thatch roof. Richard's mother kept it neat, with two sheets to separate the sitting room from the mattresses where she and some of the children slept. She said her older boys slept in an abandoned house, which we passed on our way out. Its thatch roof had caved in, and graffiti lined the mud and cement walls. In her home, pages from an old company calendar brightened the wall behind the three locally made chairs where Violet and I were invited to sit. To one side of us were a few iron cases and bags stacked high to hold the family's few clothes. To the other was a big bag of charcoal that represented the family's entire livelihood.

After customary greetings, Violet got out Richard's file and asked a few questions to get the facts straight. Lucy was Richard's mother, and his father was a soldier who rarely came around. Lucy said that Richard was abducted on May 19, 2001, from his grandparents' village home near Palero. They sent word to her that he was abducted after it happened. "I was never at peace because I thought maybe they had killed him," she said. "I was very bitter." She lost her sixth child to yellow fever aggravated by malaria when she was a baby, so she did not want to lose another child.

By the time Lucy heard that Richard had escaped, he had been sent to the barracks. She sent a boy to collect him there and they brought him to World Vision with a letter from the barracks. "When Richard first returned," she told us, "he had swollen cheeks because he said they didn't eat food while in the bush; they just ate wild fruits and raw cassava. They just boil it and eat it half cooked. He is looking much better now." She smiled as she looked at Richard, who sat sullenly.

Lucy explained that the children sometimes went to their grandparents' place because she had trouble feeding them. "They are hungry, and Richard would say, 'I will go away.' Here they don't get satisfied, so I think he ran away because of hunger. When there is not enough food, they don't feel good." Richard's experience confirmed the imagination of Kampala children, who visualized the village as a place of plenty. Since his family had moved into town, they could not cultivate their own food and so went without whenever money was short. Violet asked him whether he liked the grandparents' house. He replied, "It's good there because there are a lot of groundnuts."

The grandfather to whom they referred was his father's father, so Violet asked why they do not bring the groundnuts home. "The man will not give even a cup of groundnuts to me," Lucy complained. "They don't give me any support. So when the child went there, the grandfather

11 Gulu charcoal seller with her baby. Photo by the author ca. 2001.

told the child, 'You come and stay here.' With children, they always like their father's side." She also sent her older son sometimes, "but he always comes with nothing." She was not happy, but she said when she sold her *gomesi* dress, they started selling charcoal (fig. 11). If she bought a bag at five thousand shillings, she could make about three thousand shillings' profit on it over two or three days' time.[7] She had been doing that to support her family for some time, but it barely paid for food, let alone schooling. She hoped to try to send Richard back to school once he came home again. "If there's no money, I don't know what to do," she sighed. "When the children get chased away from school for not paying fees, I just tell them to go anyway, hoping no one will notice them for a while."

The children sometimes did some things to help raise money. Richard told us that his older brother had started washing vehicles because he was sent away from school. He was in seventh grade. The firstborn, nineteen, was in sixth grade. He contracted measles when he was little, and it affected his ear so that he sometimes could not hear anything. Violet suggested that Lucy take him to a school for the disabled, Lucy looked a bit ashamed, saying that she had not known about it. Lucy explained that sometimes they do not go to school for a whole year.

Lucy and her children moved from the village when the army said it was no longer safe to stay there in 1995. At the time, her husband was among the rebels of Obote's regime. He went to the bush, and when

Museveni asked ex-soldiers to come back to the barracks, he joined them and became a member of the UPDF and then the NRA. Lucy said he would move around with the army, getting a new woman in each place. They were staying in a place where the LRA came and abducted a lot of children, outside of Gulu town. "They came to the hut where I was sleeping," she said, "but all the children were sleeping in another hut with the door completely open—it was where we usually cooked, so the rebels didn't know that people were in there. As they were disturbing me, the children heard and they all ran away to the bush. That's how they escaped." That's when she came to stay in town.

She had been living in this temporary shelter for six years. Still, the children's father refused to help. In 1996, people started asking her, "How do you live with this man? You will die! Why don't you go and report him?" So she went to the welfare office to report her husband for not taking care of his children. They did not do anything. The army did nothing when she reported him in 1997, either. In 1998, they gave her a letter to take to the barracks. There, she was told to go to Anaka, and then at Anaka, she was told to go to Pacwach, in a different district. She went with the soldiers who were transporting the salaries. They sent for him there, and when he confirmed that she was the mother of his seven children, they gave her his salary and drove her back home.

She bought second-hand clothes and paid school fees and the rent with the money. With part of it, she bought the paraffin that the children sold in small quantities after school. She tried again later to go back to the barracks and get more money, and they gave her half of his salary. "That's the only money I ever got from him," she said.

When they took him the other half of the money, he quarreled so much and it brought a lot of problems. I had to go there, and he said his money should not be taken out without his permission. All the wives of soldiers get their husbands' battalion and detach numbers, and they go to Loro in Apac to receive money from their husbands' salaries. I went there and stayed three weeks, leaving the children to sell paraffin and stay in the house alone. I even had to borrow money to pay for the transportation. His other wife was there, too, and when a letter came from him, he included money for the other wife. Nothing for me.

I am so bitter and I don't think I will accept him again because of what I have gone through with these children. Maybe he treats me this way because he never even paid a dowry, so the marriage was never quite official. So me, I am just staying here because I know the man hates me. Me, I have no husband anymore, because he doesn't care, and he doesn't send word, and he knew that I was going to Loro, but people who met him said he was just saying I was wasting my time. I have already suffered so much.

I went there three times but I was empty-handed. And when I am going there I have to borrow money from people with the hope that maybe this man would think of his children and will give me something. So now I have given up completely. I will not follow him. Even when I hear he is coming, I will not follow him.

The fact that Lucy's marriage was never formalized through the bride-price custom probably accounted for why the children's grandfather refused to help support his grandchildren in their mother's home. Though the custom is still regularly observed in Acholiland, such common-law marriages are becoming more typical as people get poorer. They do not have the money to pay a dowry or have a church wedding. Whatever the situation between Lucy and her husband, it was apparent that Lucy considered their long history together—and especially the fact of their seven children—as proof of marriage. Hence her bitter disappointment with his obvious neglect of his family.

Lucy fell silent and wiped tears away with the edge of her *leso*, a cotton, patterned sarong. We asked her about the future, and she said she did not know what to do because she lacked the capital to survive. She only had only a sixth-grade education,[8] so there was little opportunity for her to advance. She did not have much hope for her children, either. "With the little money I get out of the charcoal, I have to pay rent, I have to feed them, everything. So to me, if they can complete their study, well and fine. If they don't, then nothing. I will do nothing about it because I am unable. Even the parents of this man don't care, not even to give a little food for their children." Lucy seemingly had no real expectations for them anymore. She just wanted to keep them fed every day. But she wanted them to at least take a lesson from her to motivate them: "I always talk to them. For them, they can only do well if they listen to what I teach them. They have also seen how I have suffered and the way I am trying so hard to look after them, to care for them. So if they grow up and begin to do something on their own, then maybe they will be okay. If they decide to go astray, I will have nothing to do for them."

Later, I sent Richard with some *posho* and beans to give to his mother. He returned quickly, saying she was very happy because she did not have anything to feed her children and was planning to let them go hungry today. Now she would cook the food right away.

The mixture of surrender and persistence in Lucy's story characterizes parent-child relations, as do her experiences, which are common for women in Uganda. In Acholiland, war compounds existing social problems of poverty and deadbeat dads. With the sole responsibility of raising her children, Lucy was surviving in the only ways she could. But

I could also see why children like Richard were not so eager to go back home from the rehabilitation center, even though home was just a few steps away; at least he was sure to get three meals a day at the center. His mother could not guarantee that.

Resilience like Lucy's is still being transmitted across the generations, but I wondered whether school was really a helpful or viable option for a boy in Richard's situation. He insisted he should try to continue with school, and that it was his mother's responsibility to see to it. If she could not raise the money, he said he would be willing to go back to selling paraffin in order to raise school fees. "Education gives you knowledge and helps you get a job in order to assist your family and yourself," he explained. Richard said he would like to go all the way through secondary school, which he believed was the highest level of education available. He would like to work in an office or run some kind of business. He was not interested in any kind of skill training. He said he would like to get a kiosk in which to sell a few small items, because he saw one near his house and he thought it made a lot of money.

———

I went to see Chancy and Richard on two more occasions before I left Uganda. Violet and I visited them both at school. Richard was doing particularly well. He had quickly adjusted to being back at school, and his books were nice and neat. He was less fragile; he talked with more command and fidgeted less. He was back to selling paraffin, and though the money I had left with his mother to cover his school fees never made its way to the school, he was still glad to be studying. Chancy, though, was having some problems. She was doing fairly well at school under World Vision sponsorship, but she had been placed with her stepmother while her father was away, and her mother was in a remote village. She said that her stepmother was cruel to her. She explained how her stepmother cooked food during the day for lunch but did not save any for her. When she came home, her stepmother had already gone drinking and had left instructions for her to harvest something and start cooking. Her stepmother became abusive if she came home to find that Chancy had not finished cooking. The previous Saturday, Chancy came home to find only dried greens in the house. She began to cook them, but when her stepmother returned, she got angry and scattered the remaining greens all around the compound. She cursed all of Chancy's father's children and verbally assaulted Chancy. According to Acholi custom, such behavior can bring bad luck on a compound. So neighbors intervened and suggested they slaughter a goat to reconcile the two. Her stepmother rejected the idea, though, and tension worsened.

After that incident, Chancy really wanted to leave the household and go to live with her mother. But her mother lived far from any functioning school. Her father had also told her to sit tight until he returned for the holidays, but Chancy was truly unhappy. She even inquired with Violet about the possibility of going to a boarding school, but it was unlikely that World Vision sponsorship could cover the costs.

The Generational Dynamic

Within Acholiland, the conflict in northern Uganda is fundamentally explained as one between generations, where reciprocity and interdependence have broken down into fear, guilt, and suspicion. African traditional societies have strong social norms regarding the strength and hierarchy of generational stratification through age-grade cohorts, which are reciprocal and interdependent. The Acholi are no exception. Ajume Wingo writes that historically, in African societies, "Certain traditions reinforced the value of human dignity, partly through rituals such as those that honored children" (Wingo 2001, 152). Under colonialism, young Acholi were recruited into military and rebel movements, and their roles were even mysticized in Acholi spiritual revivals through military coercion (Behrend 1999). This upset generational and social hierarchies in which clan elders decided when and why to wage war, and cleansed warriors of the deaths of their enemies. The HSM and LRA further exacerbated these problematic generational relations. Lakwena effectively usurped Acholi elder authority by reengendering Acholi pride through cleansing soldiers of atrocities they committed. When Kony took Lakwena's place, elders complained that he was violating culturally sanctioned justifications for declaring war as well as rules of combat (Finnstrom 2001, 252–53), which exempt women and children (Women's Commission on Refugee Women and Children 2001, 49).

It is useful to consider the possibility of LRA reconciliation from the analytical framework of generational difference. Karl Mannheim, who pioneered the sociological study of generations in the 1920s, claimed that generations are not natural but cultural phenomena, marked by shared social and historical experiences (Alanen 2001, 15). While Wingo posits a notion of generational continuity as integral to African social reproduction, Mannheim argues that socialization of generations by historical and social forces is socially transformative. The situation in northern Uganda necessarily draws both into conversation with each other, because the LRA illustrates that both change and continuity occur within and across generational socialization. The war has exacerbated problematic, abusive social relationships between generations: "Families and communities often expect the returning adolescents to behave like adults while still having the authority to treat them like children" (Women's Commission on Refugee Women and Children 2001, 42). These circumstances victimize today's children and overturn the intergenerational social structure of the Acholi. Children blame their parents for failing to provide for and protect them (their rights as children), and parents complain that children no longer respect them and are disobedient, respect and obedience being two significant markers of ideal African childhood identity.

The very children who are affected by the war count themselves out of normative childhood categories, even as they draw on the same discourses. One girl wrote, "Why can't we children be put aside and not be involved in political affairs? Many children are being killed and dying, all because someone wants to take over the government. I think that there will be almost no future generations, as most of the children are captured" (Human Rights Watch/Africa and Human Rights Watch Children's Rights Project 1997, 87). It is interesting to note here that even captured children can consider themselves to have fallen out of the generational continuum, despite the fact that some children manage to survive and grow up in the LRA. She is aware, however, that her protected status as a child has been violated by political events from which children should be "put aside." Yet the fact that children are indeed at the center of the LRA conflict threatens the very existence of the Acholi as a people.

The Death of Culture

Acholi journalist Opiyo Oloya writes, "After more than a decade and a half of being refugees in their own backyards, the people of Acholi continue to watch school-age children waste away without the benefit of education. They weep for the new generation of Acholi children born in a culture of fear and abject poverty.... One of the biggest tragedies of this experience is the death of culture" (Oloya 2002). These circumstances now characterize Acholi children's lives and completely overturn the intergenerational social structure of the Acholi. As one parent told me, "Since 1986, our children have only known war."[9] For northern

12 Acholi children and their elders in an Alero IDP camp. Photo by the author ca. 2001.

Ugandans, security and livelihood are not the only things at stake in the resolution of the LRA conflict. Counselors and parents alike told me repeatedly that the war was destroying Acholi culture. In Acholiland, elders say, culture is literally disappearing due to the circumstances of war and poverty. Family, agricultural work, schooling, ceremonies, and rituals—all locations for the dissemination of social values and cultural knowledge—have been severely disrupted by the LRA. Parents complain that aside from making them unable to care for their children, war makes it impossible to properly guide and discipline them. Richard's mother said that one of the biggest impacts of war on her children had been that, because of the constant insecurity, she lived in a temporary shelter in Gulu town, and her children did not know their ancestral home. "The children don't know their villages; they think life is living in a camp, living in a small hut like this," she said. "And the life of the children growing is not good because there so many children in this surrounding, they are all packed up together. You cannot teach your children properly." She explained that families used to sit around the fire circle in the evening, where children would entertain elders with their antics, and elders would tell stories that helped children understand who they were and would morally guide them. Traditions such as this have broken down in the internally displaced persons' IDP camps where millions of Acholi are forced to live (fig. 12): despair is as rampant as the destitution, unemployment, alcoholism, and domestic violence that are its symptoms. Children wander in groups with other children rather than staying close to their parents.

Whether or not people who lament this loss of tradition and family are idealizing the past, their assertion of loss indicates a deep cultural anxiety over the fate of intergenerational relationships. When children become LRA rebels, the complaint that "children today have less respect for their elders" becomes the lament, "Our children are killing us" (Rubin 1998). Young people are thus considered a generation both threatened and threatening to Acholiland and the nation, a situation rarely accounted for in normative theories of childhood and family. As Stuart Aitken points out, "Mythic renderings of parenthood and childhood foster political identity formation and social placement, but they do not reflect the day-to-day work of parenting, nor do they anticipate adequately the complex changes of daily living that accompany child-rearing" (Aitken 2000, 126). Because their experiences transcend the boundaries of "mythic renderings" of childhood norms, both local and international, LRA children challenge the culturally understood social category of childhood and the overall security of the nation as a sentimental space in which children are "presumed innocent" and encouraged to grow into responsible adult citizens. In a country where ideal notions of childhood and nationhood are in states of ideological flux and are integrally linked to the country's development, the threat is especially salient. This generational upheaval in which children with guns wield power through fear creates yet another incentive for other Ugandans to marginalize the north as a dysfunctional region.

Life in IDP Camps

War and poverty take their toll on *all* children and families in Gulu. As many as two million people live in poorly protected IDP camps, relying on handouts from the World Food Programme (WFP), even though they have fields of food within several miles; with so much rebel activity, the army claims it is just not safe for them to stay in their homes. Abduction experiences have confirmed that, but the Acholi complain that if the army would just supply ample security in the countryside they could stay at their homes, cultivate, and avoid suffering in camps.

I visited a few of these camps and found droves of small children wearing rags to cover their distended bellies—a symptom of kwashiorkor and chronic malnutrition. A World Vision caregiver who guided me through

13 Idle children in a Goma IDP camp. Photo by the author ca. 2001.

one of the camps told me he thought the single biggest problem for children in the camps was the lack of food. The WFP hands out food to registered household heads, but it rarely lasts the entire month for which it is allotted. Each family receives a ten-foot wide circular hut to sleep in and another in which to cook. Huts are crowded together, but latrines and garbage pits are few and far between. Human excrement lay on top of rubbish piles within ten feet of residences.

Initially, there were no schools in the camps. Sudanese refugees in the area had better access to education than Ugandans because the United Nations High Commission for Refugees (UNHCR) provided funding for those camps. IDP camps fell outside UNHCR's purview because people internally displaced by war were not considered refugees.[10] In 1996, schools were established in many of the larger camps, but some children still do not go to school because they need uniforms and school supplies their families cannot afford, and because they are not fed there. When we asked a nine-year-old boy and a girl wearing nothing but a filthy skirt and holding a one-year-old baby why they were not going to school, they just shrugged (fig. 13). The WFP has helped raise enrolments at some IDP schools by offering a lunch program; the food gives children an incentive to go to school, and having food in their stomachs helps them to learn.

14 World Vision skills-training graduates in tailoring receive new sewing machines.
Photo by the author ca. 2001.

On the other hand, about two hundred ex-abductees who lived in the camp were doing relatively well. With the help of sensitization by the caregivers, they had been accepted back by the community and trained in various skills. On that day, about twenty graduates of a World Vision vocational skills training program were to be handed certificates and equipment to start their own tailoring or masonry businesses (fig. 14). They also received a "starter kit" before leaving the World Vision rehabilitation program which included some clothes, a wash basin, food, and a foam mattress. Few other families could afford many of these basics. Aid to former rebels has thus roused additional resentment among community members; rebels get special entitlements while the rest of them suffer. There had even been reports that young people were showing up at the army barracks with fabricated stories about being abducted and having escaped, just so they could get access to the aid resources they saw ex-captives receiving (Women's Commission on Refugee Women and Children 2001).

An End to War?

The Ugandan Government established an Amnesty Commission on January 21, 2000, in an effort to end rebel insurgencies. The amnesty guaranteed that all who had opposed Museveni's government since it took power in 1986 would be forgiven, with no charges brought against them. The signing of the Amnesty Bill was a reversal of policy for the president, who had often refused to open peace talks with rebel groups, claiming that they could only be suppressed by force. Since its inception, the Amnesty Commission has resettled more than thirty-five hundred people. The period of amnesty, originally set for six months, was extended several times as more people were pardoned and others started to see that the government was acting in good faith. But word of the Amnesty Act was slow to reach many of the LRA rebels, partly because the Ugandan government took more than a year to open a northern regional Amnesty Commission office. Kony also mocked the amnesty offer, along with invitations by Acholi religious leaders to open peace talks. Further, the government had limited ways of getting word to individual combatants, who are sequestered by their commanders in the bush. Others were told that the amnesty was a trick, and that if they were not executed by the LRA for trying to escape, the Ugandan government would surely hang them once they turned themselves in. The limited resources available to amnesty applicants also reduced the amnesty's success. Less than 10 percent of applicants have received resettlement packages to help them reintegrate. The Amnesty Commission constantly complained that lack of funds hampered their work; they could not offer jobs, land, or livelihoods to returnees as incentives for handing in their guns and leaving the bush. Several LRA peace talks had failed over the issue of resettlement because having a gun in the bush guaranteed more material security to the rebels than surrendering.

The Ugandan government was widely criticized for its military campaign against the LRA, from within Uganda and throughout the international community. Acholi leaders complained that the army's actions had not only gone against the spirit of the two-year-old amnesty but had destroyed the fragile peace they were working so hard to build. The government replied that Kony had flatly rejected the amnesty offer. Army leaders were tired of giving Kony chances and saw themselves as being at war. Museveni even came to Gulu to lead the military offensive, whose timeline kept expanding as the army failed to bring the LRA under submission. They kept claiming to be making gains on Kony, but had made no significant progress toward ending the war.

Operation Iron Fist

At the beginning of 2002, things were fairly quiet in northern Uganda. With Sudan's support for the Lord's Resistance Army waning in favor of renewed diplomatic relations with Uganda, the LRA based in Sudan were finding it harder to survive, and bands of LRA rebels in northern Uganda were cut off from Kony's control, allowing them to engage in independent peace talks with local authorities. Many IDPs living in camps had started to trickle home to tend their gardens after years of staying away. There were rumors that Kony was dying of AIDS in Sudan, and northern Ugandans were hopeful that this time the rebels would finally put down their guns and start coming home.

On Saturday, February 23, 2002, about three hundred LRA rebels attacked a Ugandan Army detachment in Kitgum district. They killed several people, abducted about a hundred more, and stole cattle and other goods. The Ugandan army pursued them and managed to rescue most of the captives, but they did not stop at that: "We are deploying effectively on the Sudan border," army spokesperson Shaban Bantariza told the media. "This is an invasion" (Allio 2002). Uganda signed a protocol with Sudan to allow its army to pursue Kony inside Sudan's borders in a military maneuver dubbed Operation Iron Fist.

With the heavy deployment of soldiers in Sudan, the LRA sent detachments into Uganda to divert the army's attention away from Kony. As a result, attacks on northern Uganda increased in size and ferocity; thousands of families fled the unprotected IDP camps and villages for towns with army detachments, and relief efforts were inhibited by LRA road ambushes (Integrated Regional Information Network 2002e). Displacement, massacres, and abductions resumed on a massive scale. The army claimed to be making gains on Kony, but after several years of Operation Iron Fist, he was still at large, and the fighting had claimed many more lives. Relief organizations claimed that abductions under

Operation Iron Fist had reached a number nearly equal to that of the previous fifteen years, and the fighting had even spread to the formerly unaffected northeastern Teso district.

In the wake of Operation Iron Fist, the LRA targeted the very IDP camps to which people had moved in order to avoid attack and abduction. Following the army's massive recruitment of local men into protective militias called LDUs (local defense units), Kony ordered an all-out genocide on the Acholi (a genocide that many blame on Museveni as well, for his government's actions as well as its inaction). A captured LRA major quoted Kony as saying, "Go out and kill all the men, women and children you find in Acholi. Leave nobody standing, for they have risen against me and none shall be spared" (Moro 2004). In one attack in February 2004, an estimated three hundred LRA rebels dressed as army soldiers attacked Barlonyo IDP camp north of Lira town. They overpowered the Amuka LDU, and, following Kony's orders, killed men, women, and children indiscriminately. The rebels burned people alive in their grass-thatch huts and bludgeoned, hacked, or shot to death civilians who attempted to flee the chaos. By the following day, more than three hundred people had been killed.

Kony's call for extermination of his own people is the apogee of his obsession with ethnic purity. Kony gave the order on the basis of his belief that those who resisted him were not "pure Acholi but a mixture of blood from Banyankole and other tribes. He said only children who [had] been born in the bush [were] the pure breed of the future Acholi" (Moro 2004). In 2004, Kony reportedly summoned all abducted children to his camps in southern Sudan to train the boys to fight while using the girls to produce more Acholi children, whom he was personally teaching—purportedly according to the Ten Commandments.

Night Commuters

Displaced people numbered more than 1.5 million with the renewal of hostilities in 2002. With no reliable security, unaccompanied children started flocking to town centers each night to escape abduction from villages or IDP camps. At the height of the "night commuter" phenomenon, as many as fifty thousand children were walking from two to ten kilometers in order to find a safe place to sleep. Gulu alone hosted an estimated eighteen thousand children per night. They slept in the bus park, emergency accommodation centers, or—when those overflowed—on the verandas of local Samaritans. These night commuters thus became even more prone to illness, hunger, vagrancy, and exploitation, despite the prevalence of international humanitarian aid organizations. Many children would forego long walks between town and their home villages and schools to remain in town during the day trying to pick up petty jobs instead. Again, girls were especially vulnerable, this time to attack by gangs of men (sometimes UPDF soldiers) and adolescent boys who sexually harassed and sometimes assaulted girls and women while they were en route to their sleeping spaces in town (Women's Commission on Refugee Women and Children 2004).

By night commuting, war-affected children in Acholiland were literally putting the problem of their displacement at the doorsteps of aid agencies. Their actions highlighted the fact that every child, not just those abducted by the LRA, faced life-threatening circumstances on a daily basis and finally put their plight on the map. Stories of night commuters finally attracted the attention of international media and aid organizations to the tragedy in northern Uganda; media attention markedly increased to document this unique response to a horrific situation for children. Jan Egeland, the United Nations Under-Secretary General for Humanitarian Affairs, visited in November 2003 and concluded that "northern Uganda must be one of the worst humanitarian crises in the world," claiming the situation was just as dire as that in Iraq (Cocks 2003), which had just endured the US-led invasion to oust Saddam Hussein. Egeland promised a stronger UN presence and pledged $128 million for IDP emergency relief (Integrated Regional Information Network 2004a).

Conspiracy Theories

Given the history of Uganda's regional and ethnic conflicts, many Acholi claim that the government just does not care about their suffering. Museveni's government and other Ugandans in general have viewed the north with suspicion, because it has produced Lakwena and Kony along with notorious dictators like Amin and Obote. Historically, Acholi frustration over historical social problems has found expression—if not support—in rebel movements, which have had quasi-religious elements emphasizing an Acholi revival, even if the end result has ironically been the devastation of Acholi livelihood and custom (Integrated Regional Information Network 2002d). Once the strife caused by northern rebels seemed confined to the north, though, many claimed that southern Uganda and the government ceased to care what happened in Acholiland. They have come to view it as its own region with its own problems. Other

Ugandans' readiness to disown the north rather than view its problems as internal to the country only compounds its marginalization. This has changed somewhat with Museveni's presence and outreach from the south, but bitterness still persists.

Acholiland is rife with conspiracy theories: that the Sudanese and Ugandan governments are somehow profiting off the war and thus contribute to its longevity; that the LRA was actually created by the Ugandan government intentionally to destabilize the north and then blame it on the Acholi themselves; that a covert genocide is being carried out against the Acholi people. Acholi who live in Kampala also complain of prejudice from other tribes. Schoolchildren in Kampala tease Acholi classmates by calling them "Kony," and teachers perpetuate ethnic "warrior" stereotypes in class. The regional prejudice against the north has even reached the point where Acholi themselves have lapsed into an acceptance tantamount to complicity. Olara Otunnu, the United Nations Special Representative for Children and Armed Conflict (1997–2005), is an Acholi who has received heavy criticism for neglecting to give the crisis in northern Uganda a higher profile. He had not even visited northern Uganda in his official capacity until 2001. Others experience guilt and abandonment issues. Acholi journalist Opiya Oloya's February editorial in the *New Vision* reflected common attitudes of guilt and conspiracy, even before the new wave of attacks:

I was derelict in not focusing attention on the issue of Protected Villages in Gulu and Kitgum districts. . . . A journalist from southern Uganda had recently condemned the inhuman conditions in the Acholi camps. If a southerner could feel the pain of the Acholi people, what was wrong with me, an Acholi writer who is directly affected[?]. . . . We in the media have become accomplices in the systematic sidelining of the people of Acholi in their sufferings. (Oloya 2002)

Children? Rebels? The Uses of Childhood Identity

One of the central questions in the debate over appropriate action for restoring order is how the army distinguishes between "children" and "combatants." Child-protection organizations and Acholi community leaders have come forth to voice strong opinions about how the army should proceed with regard to the LRA child abductees. When the 2002 military offensive, Operation Iron Fist, began, UNICEF emerged as the child advocate community's main representative, bantering back and forth with army spokesmen before the media. Their central disagreement rested on protocol in battle; on how to distinguish between abducted children and committed combatants, when the rebels they encounter could very well be both. As noted earlier, UNICEF voiced concerns that abducted children would most likely end up on the front lines. An Integrated Regional Information Network report stated,

Carol Bellamy, Executive Director of UNICEF, urged Uganda and Sudan "to conduct their offensives in such a manner as to minimise the risks to children and other civilians.". . . UNICEF appealed to both sides to "regard the children as children" and appealed for humanitarian access to the region, to save children who may be stranded or wounded. "These children may be highly militarised, but that doesn't mean they should not be regarded as children," an official added. (Integrated Regional Information Network 2002b)

UNICEF's intentions are certainly honorable in this regard, but they are somewhat unrealistic. UNICEF operates on a Western essentialist model of childhood that idealizes children as innocent and harmless. This notion fails to account for circumstances in which the child may be the aggressor. It pigeonholes children as only innocent victims of war and not as potential perpetrators. Anthropologist Helen Schwartzmann criticizes ideal social models of children like those perpetuated by UNICEF for viewing children "as 'targets' of training—passive, imitative, conservative, and accepting of adult socialization practices" (Schwartzman 2001, 28).[11] What happens when we apply such a model to children socialized into the LRA? How are we then to treat children who are socialized successfully by "bad" adults?

While UNICEF sees children under normal circumstances as passive objects to be molded, nurtured, and protected by adults, they would like to believe that children in these extremely difficult circumstances also actively resist indoctrination by the LRA. In either case, UNICEF evades issues of children's agency and culpability, whether positively or negatively utilized. Many LRA children perform acts that they know are wrong in order to survive under extreme duress, but many also come to believe that the LRA is the only possible life for them—and a desirable one at that—and they become willing participants.[12] Perhaps they are still "redeemable" according to ideal UN childhood models, but how can that process begin when they are still engaged in battles with the army? "We'd like UNICEF to show us how to extricate children from their hardline commanders," army spokesperson Shaban Bantariza was quoted as saying. "How do you respond to a 17-year-old child who is trained and only interested in shooting?" (Integrated Regional Information Network 2002a).

To the army, LRA rebels have appropriately become literal targets for discipline by the ultimate parent: the state. And the army does not want UNICEF telling them how to discipline their misbehaving children. Because the army is charged with the responsibility of simultaneously "crushing the rebels while rescuing the children," they strive to make everyone understand just what a fuzzy proposition this really is. Before long, Bantariza was trying to get the army out of this bind by refuting the categorization of LRA rebels as children: "'It is a pity that some of them are no longer children. Some have been armed and ideologically twisted. But if they point their guns at us, they become legitimate targets'" (Wasike 2002). Eventually, he became plainly critical of UNICEF's ignorance on the matter: "UNICEF has a problem. They don't know what children they are talking about. . . . Our situation is such that we cannot talk about children. Children need not simply be referred to as children" (Integrated Regional Information Network 2002c).

Bantariza has a point: he inadvertently does more to acknowledge the realities of the situation and the possibility for conceiving of multiple types of childhood than does UNICEF—even if some versions of childhood that emerge are less than desirable (Ennew and Milne 1990; James, Jenks, and Prout 1998; Qvortrup 1997). Bantariza finds it crucial to army operations to distinguish not only between children and rebels but between different childhood realities. The army does not want to violate the tenets of the UN Convention on the Rights of the Child, to which Uganda is a signatory. Yet they understandably complain that this situation defies the universality and assumed transparent characteristics of children inherent in UNICEF policy.

This incident highlights the paternalistic subtext of documents like the UN Convention on the Rights of the Child, which not only extend Western normative models of childhood to all corners of the earth, but reinforce the contradictory belief that children possess freedom of choice, while their "best interests" must be protected by adults (Archard 1993). In *The Rights of Children*, Bob Franklin distinguishes between the legal and moral rights conferred by international declarations and conventions: the latter tend to be advocated for children, while the former is denied them (Franklin 1986). African children's rights advocates and critics alike defend this criticism, claiming that, in order to be more attuned to African cultures, rights must come with responsibilities and obligations to society.[13] When such local concepts come into conversation with international conventions, however, the question of how to handle active LRA child combatants becomes even less clear. How can children be considered innocent but still culpable for the violence they perpetrate?

UNICEF's delineation appears rather discriminatory when based on age alone. One UNICEF report stated, "With some 10 percent of those abducted becoming adults in the years following their abduction and a reintegration rate of 88 percent or more, fewer than a thousand child abductees remain to be returned and reintegrated" (Integrated Regional Information Network 2002d). Why perform these mathematical tabulations in order to separate LRA children from LRA adults according to an arbitrary, eighteen-year-old dividing line? Here's where Franklin's distinction between moral and legal rights becomes especially valid: once children reach the age of eighteen, they are no longer considered children and are suddenly out of UNICEF's jurisdiction—and apparently in control of their own faculties as social actors. Thus, they no longer warrant rescue, and are subject to prosecution, even if they are still doing exactly what they did before their eighteenth birthdays. In contrast, local authorities such as the army and rehabilitation programs tend to make the distinction between child and adult, guilty or not guilty of LRA atrocities, based on individual circumstances, often through extensive interviews with ex-soldiers to ascertain levels of coercion and remorse.

In sum, those invested in ending the conflict in northern Uganda have been—unwittingly or quite purposefully—wielding divergent understandings of childhood as tools for both justifying and accomplishing their various mandates. While UNICEF employs particular conceptions of children for the protection and promotion of children's rights, LRA child soldiers are killing others. The army is also guilty of strategically deploying the category of childhood for its own purposes: army officials often refer to the LRA abductees as "children" whenever the army "rescues" them or shows progress toward doing so. But any LRA soldiers who successfully stage an attack or are killed by the army are referred to as "rebels" to play down the fact that those "rebels" are also abducted children.

Young people who have reached adulthood while actively fighting with the LRA also utilize childhood as a protective category once they escape in order to facilitate their reentry into the community. Repatriated children are often viewed with contempt and distrust in their communities because of their involvement with the LRA. In their cases, universalized notions of childhood and their influence on local conceptions actually facilitate reintegration. On my first visit to the World Vision center, I met Geoffrey, a twenty-two-year-old ex-soldier still being labeled an "LRA child." In seven years with the LRA, he had been shot three times and had become a high-ranking commander. Geoffrey escaped when a UNICEF staff member found him in a Khartoum hospital a day before surgery on his leg for shrapnel wounds. At first, he refused to be returned to Uganda because he feared reprisals—from the LRA, the government, or his own community. But he ultimately decided to take the chance and was evacuated. Now he is disabled by his injuries, but he is still willing to return to school to get on with his life. Like many in his position, Geoffrey expressed his wish "to be a child again, to go back to school" in order to recover the childhood that World Vision pointed out was stolen from him. This narrative helped engender pity and forgiveness from his community.

LRA returnees I spoke with sometimes actively embraced their identities as child soldiers, and even "performed" them for both local and international aid workers in order to claim certain protections and entitlements.[14] Others followed NGO cues and constantly reminded people that they were traumatized or victimized children. In a group counseling session at the World Vision center, I asked returnees how they would like their communities to view them. One boy said, "The community should look at us as something which is very important and receive us in a very normal way because we have been suffering in the bush. Some of us died in the bush." They are normal children, but they are important and lucky because, as they told me, "God allowed us to return." Repatriated LRA child soldiers thus embrace a potentially stigmatizing label in order to wear their survival as a badge of honor that makes them the same and yet sets them apart from other children in ways that facilitate forgiveness and even warrant special attention. Their distinction is especially valid to international relief efforts, and it makes war-affected children who have not been abducted envious of LRA returnees who receive entitlements, which range from food and material goods to educational sponsorship and vocational training (Women's Commission on Refugee Women and Children 2001). "Adult" escapees typically get none of these, so it literally pays to claim identity as a child or, better yet, a child soldier.

Envisioning a Transition to Peace

Though ex-combatant children and their caretakers are developing coping strategies for reintegration, the war must end before any massive transition to peace and rebuilding can occur. Army reports on the LRA often read like tally sheets of the dead, captured, and surrendered. These tallies are meant to reassure the public that the insurgency is gradually weakening, but inevitably another attack comes to break the relative calm. The tallies outrage Acholi parents and leaders: not only do they typically represent the number of their children and relatives killed at the hands of the government, but they are more a result of the LRA's aggression than the army's vigilance—and they disregard the whole issue of diplomatic solutions. Despite widespread bitterness, Acholi leaders remain convinced that the road to peace and reconciliation is through amnesty and the cessation of Uganda's support for the SPLA.

The way that the news media and people I spoke to always referred to Kony as a metonym for the whole of the LRA localizes blame with one man. This may help civilians to reconcile with those who escape from the LRA, because they have a common enemy. In fact, many former abductees think the war can end only if Kony and his top commanders are killed. Otherwise, rebels express a reluctance to come out of the bush (Ojwee 2002). Many of the escapees I spoke with who expressed such sentiments were very logical and unemotional, as when Richard suggested, "Bomb Kony. Kill all the rebels." To their counselors, this indicates the ingrained violence to which children have been exposed, as well as the hatred the LRA engenders in its captives.

Though Museveni's government has been criticized for doing little or nothing to stop Kony, many children who survived their experiences with the LRA still look to the national government for solutions to the crisis. They have a sense of their marginalization from national affairs, both as children and as Acholi:

I felt deeply hurt and prayed to God to help us, and especially our leader, his Excellency the President, to find a solution to liberate us from the painful experience. (Human Rights Watch/Africa and Human Rights Watch Children's Rights Project 1997, 89)[15]

When rebels attacked us, I did feel that we children from the north were not cared for by the government. (Human Rights Watch/Africa and Human Rights Watch Children's Rights Project 1997, 95)

If we are really the children of Uganda in the North, what can the government do to stop this? (Human Rights Watch/Africa and Human Rights Watch Children's Rights Project 1997, 90)

How will Uganda remain a nation if this continues? Maybe it will be a nation of the dead, and not of the living. (Human Rights Watch/Africa and Human Rights Watch Children's Rights Project 1997, 87)

15 Postings in the boys' dormitory of the World Vision rehabilitation center. Photo by the author ca. 2001.

I ask for more help from you to bring peace and children's rights to our country. We want to have a voice in our country to develop it, not to destroy it. (Human Rights Watch/Africa and Human Rights Watch Children's Rights Project 1997, 91)

Many children I observed at the World Vision center also indicated their awareness of the profound national and international implications of their situations, and they looked beyond their own borders for help. In the boys' dorm, a client had posted a drawing of a crying child next to the words, "UN save us please! What [crime have we] committed as innocent children??" (fig. 15). I had anticipated that most children's LRA experiences would mobilize them for political engagement. Instead, the majority of children I met shared surprisingly few political opinions—at least not openly. Most just wanted to go back to being children, which, I argue, can be seen as a political identity in itself. But their keen senses of justice were usually somehow sharpened, more harsh.

On my return to Gulu two months later, I checked up on Richard. I found him at home with malaria. He was still quiet and reticent, picking nervously at his hands and taking long pauses before answering questions. His younger sister was also sick with malaria. Richard was making porridge when we arrived. His mother said that he loved to cook and that he was an obedient child. She, at least, seemed in much higher spirits than the last time we had seen her. I spotted a basket of beans and a bag of *posho* flour and surmised that she was having fewer problems feeding her family.

Richard was going to a primary school several kilometers away. His younger siblings were not in school but helped with small chores like washing dishes and fetching water. Aside from being sick, Richard seemed to have adjusted well to his return home. He was glad to be back in school, and since he had been going to the same school before he was abducted, he already had some friends. Some also lived near him, and they played football together. He said his friends treated him the same, but they asked him a lot of questions about what happened in the bush. He told them how captives were always beaten and had little food while with the LRA. In the bush, he was always scared to make a move. "At home it's better because you have friends," he said. "You can talk freely with one another, you can play with other children, and you live with the family. But in the bush, you are always scared and you are always pushed to do hard work. And there is no time to play or chat with friends, so there is a big difference." At his school, there were others who were formerly abducted. One boy had had the same task of being a lookout for the rebels and was also beaten severely. They became friends because they could relate to each other's experiences.

Richard was interested in hearing news about the war. He thought that the way to stop the LRA war was for the government to go and bomb the LRA camps in Sudan. "If they had done that," Violet pointed out to him, "captives like yourself might not have survived." Richard just shrugged and replied, "Captives should run away when the bombing starts." He had not heard about the peace talks that the government was conducting with the rebels at that time, but he did not think they would end the war. At first he could not say why, but then he said that the LRA would not accept that because he heard the rebels in the bush saying they would never surrender and go back to a normal life. He was therefore certain that bombing was the best solution. "The army just isn't using the proper weapons," he determined.

I asked Richard how he felt about the government and its treatment of children. He said that the government has been helping children, but it's not enough. He thinks they send children away from school too often due to defaulting on school fees. Even with UPE, there are other PTA fees, the uniforms, and supplies that parents like his found hard to meet. He was still sullen but had some hope and was finally able to derive some joy from simple things like cooking and playing football. Before we left, I presented Richard with a care package: school supplies, stickers, soap, and a T-shirt. When he opened it, I saw him smile for the first time.

———

How might we draw on these examples to postulate some alternate approaches to peace, reconciliation of generational conflict, and national identity-building in northern Uganda? Agency and situated analysis are still at the heart of this struggle: children, like Africans as viewed from a world perspective, are often designated as objects rather than subjects, making Acholi children a marginalized group within another marginalized group. But children too make conscious decisions about their participation in war and community that are, if not always justifiable, at least understandable. Local people actually want children to be culpable in some ways, if only to break the cycle of violence. For a generation of children to recover, however, they must no longer be labeled—and thus stigmatized—according to universal categories of childhood and normality. It is hard for NGOs and aid organizations to carry out assistance programs for children in need without engaging this discourse, partly because establishing LRA children as those in difficult circumstances (hence abnormal and victimized) is what justifies their funding. The Ugandan government and its southern population must take ownership of the north to work toward lessening ethnic animosities that initially led to this conflict and have since become complicit in its continuation. UNICEF representatives have voiced the opinion that LRA child soldiers should automatically be granted amnesty by virtue of the fact that they were underaged and forcibly conscripted. The more important amnesty needs to be granted not from the government, however, but from the communities to which the rebels hope to return. Though they are not mutually exclusive, rehabilitation so far seems to be a much more worthy allocation of resources for young ex-abductees than amnesty, especially when amnesty is not coupled with material assistance for resettlement. But children's voices get lost in current rehabilitation discourses. Social workers and aid organizations would do well to reconsider idealized assumptions of childhood in light of local realities.

As Christensen, James, and Jenks have noted, "Identities are forged within a locational matrix of constraint, contested meaning, conventions of placing and avenues of possibilities. . . . Control and power are fundamentally exercised by the movements and positionings through which emergent identities are made and articulated" (Christensen, James, and

Jenks 2000, 153). Children's experiences with the LRA have reshaped their relationships to family, community, and the nation, yet their outlets for expressing their political identities remain constricted. LRA violence cannot be neutralized without recognizing the fluidity of boundaries around childhood experience and attention to attainable social realities in the context of long-standing war, especially the amelioration of generational conflict. Despite what many Acholi and aid workers have argued, I believe that effective reconciliation cannot be achieved through a cultural revival or imposed reinstitution of generational relations. Cultural revival agendas especially tend to be fundamentalist and repressive in nature, often producing new regimes of social control rather than reviving old ones. The LRA itself is a good example. Communities and aid organizations must instead design programs around notions of positive social change: a better idiom for relief work models than recuperation or restoration. Focusing on change will leave the social landscape more open to reinterpretation and collaboration, yielding new possibilities for positive intergenerational relations. Open dialogue among the Acholi can reconfigure those relations to facilitate peace and reconciliation for future generations. In this regard, models based on Acholi campfires may act as a bridge between the old and the new: they offer spaces where people of all ages can speak, be heard, and receive respect. This would be similar to what the South African Truth and Reconciliation Commission did in modeling its proceedings on the local concept of *ubuntu*, an "African philosophy of humanism," as Antjie Krog puts it, that "gives access to a new identity for South Africans [appealing to] African concepts of the harmony between individual and community" (Krog 2000, vi, 143).

What stories might be told as today's Acholi children sit around the fire talking to their own children? How might they talk of their lives and what they have made of them after surviving seemingly insurmountable atrocities? Their stories will hold important lessons—not only for the Acholi—but for many future generations of Ugandans.

On my last trip to Gulu, I attended a skills-training graduation ceremony for former LRA captives. It was a hot and sunny day in the IDP camp, but trainees and their parents came out to take part in the festivities that marked a new beginning and a hopeful possibility for each of them. Local dignitaries gave speeches and trainees sang songs about development and education for employment—not much different, I realized, from their Kampala counterparts a world away. A local councilman came forward to make a speech in support of the children and the skills-training program, which he believed was making a difference. "Everyone is working to bring peace," he said. The trainees stood and sang a song.

Violence into peace.
Killing into peace.
Raping into peace.
I believe there is power for peace and good in everyone.

Each one smiled as they clapped and marched around their parents. The parents clapped, too, smiling back at their children. I hoped that perhaps one day soon they would all know that elusive peace of which they sang.

SEVEN

"Did the Constitution Produce my Children!?"

Cultural Production and Contestation in Uganda's National Primary School Music Festivals

What we must generate for future generations is not the preservation of cultural products, but the capacity for cultural production.
MANUELA CARNEIRO DA CUNHA

At a musical performance at the National Theatre in Kampala, Uganda, the stage is packed with fifty colorfully adorned musicians and choir members, led by a charismatic female soloist in a *gomesi*, the Ugandan national dress. She moves throughout the group of attentive choir members who sit about her, swaying to the music as she harmoniously describes the basic provisions of the country's new constitution in Luganda:

I want to consider the issues about children in the constitution
    because they are the foundation of the country's development.
When you give birth to a child, don't strangle it to death.
Those are the country's gifts.
A child deserves to get proper care, health and feeding so as to live a
    good life.

The choir repeats each of her lines for emphasis and effect as the drums pound out a steady rhythm. They divided into three groups to sing overlapping rounds of phrases in harmony, the first repeating the soloist's words while the others sang:

Choir 2: Some of you say, "I'm not your parent. Why should I care?"
Pity for your unkindness!
Every citizen, please, you have a responsibility to raise the children into responsible people.

Choir 3: We also see clearly that it is very right to use this constitution to help us.
These people with the hope of leading us astray, please leave us alone.
We discovered the path to our growth.

At the end of the song, the choir comes back together, the drums quicken, and dancers move jubilantly to the front of the stage, shaking their skirted hips and smiling widely. The choir claps in support as they hoist a giant constitution up and punch the air in triumph. The crowd explodes with applause. The choir members bow and exit the stage. The topic of their song has particular resonance for them: they are all primary school students.

This performance was typical of those I saw at the Ugandan Primary School Music, Dance, and Drama Festival—perhaps the most consciously collaborative construction of nationhood and childhood that I encountered during my fieldwork. I aim in this last chapter to detail this process in order to discuss how children and their interlocutors engage common cultural identities to negotiate their places within the nation through ongoing cultural production.

By encouraging children to participate in music, dance, and drama festivals, the government positions children as important purveyors of an emergent sense of collective national culture as well as civic messages crucial to Uganda's social and economic development. This process is fraught with contestations and contradictions, however; though children are supposed to learn about constitutional empowerment through school music festivals, schools and festivals are ultimately very authoritarian environments for students. Children's rights discourses generated in festival performances encourage children's active participation in social change, while age-based authority and power prevent children from claiming those rights in their daily lives. In spite of the obstacles they face, children are skilled at manipulating their performances at the festival to launch cultural critiques of the inherent contradictions, and to forge new possibilities for reconfiguring national culture, development, and rights discourses. Because children on the festival stage occupy a very public space of national identity and its reinvention, the festival offers them an opportunity to critique the quotidian contradictions involved in children claiming full rights and citizenship.

Choosing Field Sites—Or Being Chosen by Them

I must admit that I did not start out with such assumptions about the festival; rather, I chose to do fieldwork on the festival out of more pragmatic interest. When I first visited Uganda in 1993 to do some undergraduate thesis research, I was mesmerized by the alien beauty of the place and humbled by the way in which my community there embraced me. I regularly took walks around the secondary school compound where I stayed. One evening, as I became enchanted by the play of the sunset's colors in the smoke of cooking fires that rose out of the lush green hills and valleys stretching away from the hockey pitch where I sat, I heard a wickedly delightful rhythm being pounded out on drums. It was coming from somewhere near the school's main gate. Before long, it was too captivating to pass up, so I followed the sound.

Outside the school gates was another school—a local primary school of modest means. Children playing there had often squealed with both delight and anxiety as they spotted me, the *mzungu*, approaching. On this evening, that school was the source of this indescribably complex beat. As I left the gates, buzzing swarms of young children scrambled excitedly in the half-light back and forth across the road between the schoolyard and the community center, awash in a sea of blue, pink, green, and yellow school uniforms. Others were dressed in traditional costumes and dancing apparel, and several of them struggled to lift gigantic xylophones and drums that dwarfed the musicians. Many became distracted from their tasks when they saw me—a foreigner was still fairly rare in the country at the time—and I was instantly swept up in the festivities. Children shyly practiced their English greetings on me, hesitantly touched my skin, or unreservedly stared at my strange features until their flamboyantly dressed mothers shooed them into the hall with apologetic smiles. This was my first experience of the Ugandan primary school music festival. Children and their parents and choir directors crammed into the tiny hall to hear the results of the day's competition. The drumbeat I had heard, I was told, had been the last performance of the day, a traditional dance.

Later, I described the scene to my Ugandan roommate over dinner. Being a busy secondary school teacher, she sometimes neglected to inform me of cultural events taking place around us that I, as a visitor and student of local culture, might enjoy. She apologized but assured me that "when it comes to music, the children are the best!"

On a subsequent visit to Uganda in 1996, I was browsing in the new craft village set up behind the National Theatre when groups of children dressed in costumes for their traditional dance numbers came out to practice on the patch of lawn surrounded by vendors' booths.[1] Inside the theatre, the sound of drums and jubilant singing reverberated. I stood with other tourists appreciating the acts warming up outside, and then—remembering the magic of the incident years before—went to the box office to inquire about what was going on. The woman at the window told me it was the primary school music festival national finals. "They are very good," she added. I could tell she was sincere and not just trying to sell me something, so I bought a ticket and was treated to creative dance interpretations of the meaning of the new constitution, speeches on corruption and civic responsibility that made the audience laugh and clap in affirmation, and traditional dances that brought the house down. A friend who was expecting me eventually had to sneak into the theatre and drag me out. But the scene made such an impression on me that it became the event around which I formulated much of my initial fieldwork.

Despite their high quality as entertainment, the mission of Uganda's national primary school music festivals is to engage children in mutual processes of socialization. I worked with the St. Michael's Primary School children's choir (most of whom were in the fourth through sixth grades) as they trained for and competed in the early stages of the festival. I then followed the progress of the festival up through to the national level. Speaking with performers, organizers, choir trainers, and Ministry of Education (MOE) officials, I found that the festival stage offered primary school students a place to participate in the development of a new national culture by interpreting a national development discourse with which, as detailed throughout this book, they were fast becoming familiar. But children also utilized the opportunity of the festival to highlight gaps between nationalist aspirations that co-opted children as symbols of the future and the daily realities they faced as powerless members of society, even within the structure of the festival itself.

Festivals and Child Performers

Overcoming a Troubled Past

Schools are some of the most crucial institutions for social reproduction. When the National Resistance Movement government took charge, its officials recognized the need to encourage national pride and unity among primary school students as part of educational reforms, in order to counteract the lingering social effects of years of civil war, ethnic conflict, and underdevelopment. A large part of the citizenship curriculum involves sharing cultural traditions. Christine Kiganda, a Ugandan educational specialist, says, "[The national unity effort] has been a very, very conscious fight against ethnic differences and building towards a Ugandan united culture. The children learn all the dances from Uganda and they perform them all together" (USAID and The World Bank 1999). The Ministry of Education and Sports sponsors the music festivals that arose out of this effort as part of the primary school curriculum each year.

The music festival was originally adapted from missionary-organized church music festivals. Many choir directors I spoke with, however, claimed that missionary conversion was one of the colonial elements that most threatened local musical traditions. Christian churches often forbade any dancing or use of African instruments in church services and missionary schools. George, a music teacher from Luweero, told me, "Music in particular suffered [under colonialism] because missionaries said the local instruments were those of Satan, while the piano played the melody of God." Another teacher told me about a church-founded school that still prohibits any type of traditional instrument to this day. Thus, by adapting the festival format to promote its nationalist project, Ugandans derived a means of preserving traditional culture from an activity aimed at destroying it—or at least limiting its effects on those wishing to become "civilized." Now the children of today are reviving the culture—and formulating a new national culture by sharing their musical diversity.

The MOE designates a contemporary national development theme for each festival and requires students to create songs, dances, and dramas about it using traditional instruments and dance.[2] The first national music festivals in 1985 and 1986 focused on AIDS dramas for sensitizing communities to the disease (Uganda Ministry of Education and Sports 1998).[3] According to the MOE, the festival themes are "designed to awaken awareness of the Uganda Society on the development taking place in the political and socio-economic arenas" (2). In 2000 and 2001, when I conducted fieldwork, the theme was "The Uganda Constitution (1995) and National Development." The children were to "Examine the Constitution of Uganda, 1995," and address through their performances "How [it is] likely to bring about national development" (Uganda Ministry of Education and Sports 2000, 1).

The festival is run under the supervision of the National Music, Dance, and Drama Organizing Committee of the MOE, whose members set forth strict rules for the involvement of children at all levels of primary education. Parents and the public are invited to competitions, which start at the zonal level and culminate in the national competition between district finalists. Performers are judged according to such criteria as tone, rhythm, costuming,[4] form, and authenticity[5] (Uganda Ministry of Education and Sports 2000). Joyce Othieno, coordinator of the festival for the MOE, told me that the festival started with just traditional songs, but then they wanted teachers and students to develop creativity, which might also break some monotony. They added an African original composition, and when the results were encouraging, they gradually added more creative categories. Including original songs with lyrics also helped facilitate the inclusion of a theme. The government's concern for the reconciliation of tradition and modernity is reflected in their curriculum for the festival, which requires children to use traditional cultural elements to artistically convey modern, national development messages. Festival performance, then, has evolved into a discursive project where the government and child citizens mutually invest in building new notions of tradition and its role in the modern nation-state.

Performances typically involve high energy and incredibly talented performers. People like my old roommate thought children were exceptional performers because of their abundance of raw energy, often required to sustain the vigorous styles of Ugandan traditional music and dances; their lack of formal training in, for example, Western conventions of music; and the types of creative freedoms that children take when interpreting music and dance styles.[6] In his remarks at the 2000 festival, the inspector general said about the performers, "They are committed; they are free; they are not shy." Adults tended to find these essentialized childhood attributes conducive to performance, while at the same time they co-opted children in the spread of national development messages. Yet this is not a simple process of mimesis; in his work on social dramas and performance, Victor Turner claimed that "cultural performances are not simple reflectors or expressions of culture or even of changing culture but may themselves be active agencies of change, representing the eye by which culture sees itself and the drawing board on which creative actors sketch out what they believe to be more apt or interesting 'designs for living'" (Turner 1986, 24). More than a few of the choir directors and children I worked with likened their performative work to play and said that it was fun for children because of the element of pretend. But pretend has an important visionary social function within the controlled institution of the state-structured music festival, a place where children, despite the fact that the space is highly structured for them by adult interlocutors and institutions, negotiate "a dramaturgical language about the language of ordinary role-playing and status-maintenance which constitutes communication in the quotidian social process" (Turner 1986, 76). The word *play*, far from denoting a lack of seriousness, has some important meanings, especially when we speak of the negotiation of identity (Schwartzman 1978; Thorne 1997). Play can also mean "an opportunity for action" (Thorne 1997, 4–5). In the festival setting, children accomplish some very serious and important tasks of socialization through play. Likewise, the possibilities for social change lie in such playful experimentation as using festival categories like plays and speeches to further a children's rights discourse in which the welfare of children figures prominently in national development.

Ethnomusicologist John Blacking suggested that viewing music as a cultural system helps us understand how different people think about and interpret particular pieces of music within social context (Byron 1995, 230). Through an examination of the festival's cultural production process, this chapter considers how the "cultural system" of the music festival makes it an effective purveyor of both national cultural tradition and progressive constitutionalism. After presenting some of the organizational principles of the festival, I discuss the paradoxes of children's involvement in the production of both national traditional culture and a progressive "culture of constitutionalism." Finally, I present some strategies children employ in the performative context in order to negotiate their positions in the production of a new national culture. Because of the collaborative quality of their cultural production, I argue that festivals serve as particularly productive social spaces for the reconfiguration of the nation, and of children within it.

Festival Organization

To get a better sense of festival philosophy and structure, I first attended an organizational meeting with seventeen choir directors from local area schools. A drama professor from a local arts college immediately started lecturing about how to produce a good play. He explained stage setup and efficient use of stage space, and had teachers role-playing for an hour. (The teachers later complained about the lesson's relevance because none of them even had stages at their schools.) The MOE circular on the festival arrived then, and we all perused it, discussing the theme of the constitution and national development. Teachers listed possible topics, including children's rights, child abuse and defilement, the predicament of the girl child, privatization/decentralization, the federal status of monarchies, economic liberalization, women's emancipation, and the modernization of agriculture. They brought up the items pertaining to children first, though they were not explicit about the relevance of children's rights or abuse to national development.

The teachers' discussions revealed the politics of festival performance from the outset. One teacher raised the question of whether to praise or criticize the government through their performances, and most who murmured something in response said it was not a good idea to criticize the government or the constitution. After all, the section on original composition in the MOE circular stated that "it should not convey an embarrassing message." Teachers interpreted this as meaning that they should employ only constructive criticism, criticizing the method of implementation of a policy but not the very ideas or principles found in the constitution, which are considered incontrovertible. This later resulted in many performances that highlighted the virtues of the ideas set forth in the constitution while decrying the ignorance of local people who refused to implement those ideas, hindering development, and even contributing to their own underdevelopment. But they weren't the only ones who hindered the festival's development goals: after the organizational meeting I'd attended at the beginning of the festival season ended, I joined some of the teachers for lunch at a restaurant up the hill. I listened as the teachers, who had been so agreeable during the meeting, complained about how the festival is run. Schools as a whole advance in the competition on the basis of overall scores rather than individuals or single-category winners advancing as representatives of a school. Teachers pointed out that such a structure runs counter to the MOE goal of widespread involvement, because individual talent can be eliminated quickly if the entire school does not advance. It also reinforces the elitism of some schools, as evidenced by the fact that many of the top ten schools are the same every year. But of course, they lamented, no one at the ministry listens.

"Pure" African Culture

This meeting was the first indication of the extent to which festival organizers and participants would be concerned with the nature of national cultural representation. The teachers followed the list of events on the circular until they reached traditional dance. This topic enlivened them. They fetched instruments from the music room as they listed a few traditional dances. These dances were originally created to commemorate events like rites of passage (a certain circumcision ritual has been danced many times in the past few festivals). Courtship dances are popular, as are dances created to entertain royalty.

At first, the facilitator presumed that the schools would all do Kiganda dances because they are in Buganda. But teachers, especially women, immediately objected. The dances should all be "Ugandan," they emphasized. Once the instruments arrived, male teachers got up to play, and women sang or danced along. Presumably, they were stressing the importance of accurately doing the dances; for example, if a choir chooses to do the Kiganda dance *bakisimba mwogola*, they must be sure they follow that progression of dance steps, where *bakisimba* means to step lightly with the toes first, and *mwogola* means to shuffle the feet outward to faster music that leads to a climax. So they must follow that pattern rather than starting with *mwogola* first.

Addressing some logistical issues, the facilitator pointed out that because only the performance itself is evaluated, "children shouldn't be subjected to torture by making them dance the exit. Just let them walk freely" on and off the stage, he said. Then he pointed to me and said, "It is the fault of you Western people that we do this," meaning dancing their exit from the stage. "The stage is not hell," he reminded teachers while shooting a sideways glance at me. I took this tension as a commentary on the varying African and Western performance notions of the stage: most Western performative music is characterized by distance between audience and performer (Ebron 2002, 60–1). African music, as it is traditionally performed, has a more utilitarian purpose and participatory nature in which the audience becomes intermixed with the performance (Askew 2004). When going over the guidelines for the folk songs, the facilitator noted that most related to daily activities: hunting, fishing, planting, harvesting, war, courtship, and various rite-of-passage ceremonies. When these were brought to the stage, their format was fundamentally altered from circle formations, for example, to line formations (Askew 2002, 215). The facilitator's comment may have been his way of affirming a space for African convention on the more formal performance stage.

At a division festival, an announcer filled some time by musing about how the arrival of foreigners marked a dilution of "pure" African culture. Describing the traditional folk song, he said, "They show us how we used to be organized before foreigners came,... how we used to dress and entertain ourselves before the coming of the foreigners." Though "foreigners" have been visiting Africa for centuries, colonialism, while irrevocably altering the African social landscape, in some ways actually helped solidify dances as cultural forms; by discouraging them, colonists slowed the process of innovation.

St. Michael's Choir Practice: Dedication and Discipline

At the festival informational meeting, district coordinator Mr. Balimusa introduced me to Mr. Felix Kisakye, the music teacher at St. Michael's Primary School. He was a slight man in his mid-twenties with glasses and a friendly demeanor. As I practiced saying his surname, he pointed out that it is Kiganda for "blessings," and he was indeed a blessing to me and my fieldwork. He invited me to come to the school and participate in their choir practices. Felix had been teaching music at St. Michael's for seven years and had led the choir to considerable success, their crowning achievement having been a trip to Italy several years earlier to attend an international cultural music festival, from which they brought home many honors. They had also made it to national finals once, and St. Michael's usually finished in the top five in the competitive Kampala district. Felix was also a class teacher for a fifth-grade class of 120 students. Since he was a bachelor, he had ample time to dedicate to the children he taught, even while he pursued an advanced degree in music at the university. He had also founded a cultural dance troupe in which he cultivated the talents of schoolchildren who were in danger of falling through the cracks of the system. He used profits from their performances at weddings and other functions to pay their school fees, and several of the boys even stayed with him in his tiny quarters on the school compound.

About sixty children showed up at St. Michael's first choir meeting, many of them girls. The boys who attended were a bit younger, as was typical (older boys, Felix suggested, went for pop music and preferred to lip sync or dance to hip-hop rather than learn traditional dances). The students seemed particularly interested in the theme of the constitution, since they were learning about it in social studies classes. A few asked if they could write original pieces like poems, speeches, or plays. Felix told them to go ahead and give them to him for review. He did not end up getting many submissions, but he later incorporated some of their ideas into the original numbers he composed.

The next day, they got right down to business. When Felix started rehearsal, he told them to line up in a half-circle choir formation.

"How are you today, choir!?" Felix bellowed as he stood before them with hands clasped.

"We are fine, sir," they replied obediently. "How are you?"

Felix was put off by their lack of enthusiasm. "Didn't you people eat lunch today?" he asked.

The children giggled. "Yes, sir!"

"Okay, then: HOW ARE YOU TODAY, CHOIR!?"

"WE ARE VERY FINE, SIR! HOW ARE YOU?"

They repeated the exchange several times until Felix was satisfied that he had awakened them. Then he gestured to me. "Choir, I told you yesterday that Kristen from America would be joining us this year. Here she is. She loves music so much, she loves children so much, and she wants to learn with us. Is that alright?"

"Yes!" the students replied together.

"Okay, then we will start." They did a few DO-RE-MI warm-ups and then got into the folk song. Felix explained that folk songs are "songs that have been around for a long time, and we keep singing them to preserve our culture. . . . They will die if we don't sing them and teach them to young people." He announced that they would learn "Omulya Nnakka," a Luganda folk song about the process of hunting and gathering white ants (fig. 16).

"How many of you have tasted these white ants?" he asked. Most raised their hands. "Most tribes in Uganda eat them. Is there anyone from a tribe that does not eat them?" A girl raised her hand and said that the Langi from northern Uganda do not eat them. A Tanzanian girl said they do, and the Swahili word for them is quite similar to the Luganda word.

They got underway. I soon decided it was best to join them—participant observation and all—and so fell in line with the choir. I got a few bemused looks from the students, but they quickly got used to me muddling through the pieces with them. We recited the first part of the song, about the process of catching the white ants. Then we sang about how, if we have a good catch, we can sell the white ants to buy shoes, pay taxes, and even get a wife. Felix encouraged clapping and swaying

16 A St. Michael's student leads the choir in "Omulya Nnakka." Photo by the author ca. 2001.

to the beat as well as animated gestures to demonstrate the ideas in the song. In the next part, which talks about eating the ants, Felix told us to make gestures of eating from our hands and even those of our neighbors. Then we gestured by pointing over our shoulders that we were headed home.

Felix brought interested soloists up front and some boys got out the drums to start the accompaniment. The soloists only watched and sang the choir parts because they did not yet know the words. But the drummers, including Malik (see the introduction), forged ahead with little or no guidance. They seemed to know the appropriate rhythm to play according to the words Felix sang. He only needed to cue them on when to come in.

Near the end of the song, most children either anticipated the crescendo or fell in with it, including the sizeable crowd of uniformed students who had come in to watch. The drum beat quickened, and Felix and some of the bolder soloists, mostly boys, started shaking their behinds in the typical Kiganda fashion usually reserved for women. The choir raised their voices high and also danced until the sudden two beats on the drum signaled the end. Immediately people laughed and clapped, clearly enjoying themselves.

The next day the main hall was in use, so Felix decided to hold practice on a small patch of lawn. He had a student bring a chair for me, but I told him I would prefer to sit with the others in order to continue to be involved. We began with the part that asks the gods for a big catch. Malik was trying to get the opening drum beats right but kept on throwing in one too many notes. The others laughed a bit and he blushed, but he eventually got it right, and we were underway. Felix paused to explain exactly how some lines should be sung, according to the Kiganda style called *engono*, which involves repeating what the soloist says but with tonal variation and vocal formation.

Before long, more students were lining the sidewalk watching than there were in the choir. I gathered that many were curious about whether they might enjoy being a part of the choir rather than spectators. Though the children in the choir appeared a bit bored after singing the same line over and over, by the end of the practice they were asking whether they could also practice on Saturday. Felix declined because he had to work on writing the original compositions. But he gave them a homework assignment: "While you are walking home, cooking dinner, bathing, whatever, you should practice singing your scales." Students giggled when Felix mimicked someone bathing and singing DO-RE-MI. "No one will think you are crazy!" he promised.

Before we ended, Felix introduced a traditional dance from Bunyoro, Runyege. He pointed out the proper Kinyoro way to clap, by moving hands parallel up and down and bringing them together on the upswing and the downswing. We recited a line from the song introduction a few times and then finished. As the choir dispersed to study hall, a young boy approached Felix and said he would like to join the choir. Felix seemed pleased and said he should go ahead and come to practice with his friends. "Many kids are joining on their own initiative this year," Felix told me. He was quite pleased not to have to go to classes to plead and recruit.

The students soon discovered, however, that learning culture in this rigorous forum often felt like more work than most had anticipated; it required dedication and discipline. They had to sacrifice practically all of their free time at school as well as weekend hours in order to keep up, causing them to become somewhat ambivalent toward the activity. Given that children often had relatively full work schedules at home—including homework, chores, assisting in income-generating activities, and going to church—it was a huge sacrifice, and some were prohibited from fully participating by their parents, who needed them more at home. "It's the parents who often make my job difficult," Felix admitted. Parents who see music as an asset in their children's development are rare. "They complain that choir distracts their children from their academic work" he said. Typically, poorer families are more open to letting their children cultivate their musical talents. Felix says that others insist that their children will become doctors and lawyers and decidedly not musicians, so they do not want teachers wasting their child's time with anything that does not help achieve that goal. But Felix asserts, "Music training can liven a dull child so that he starts to do better in other subjects." He and other music supporters also point out that music sometimes unlocks a hidden talent that can lead to a scholarship or other means of income for a child's school fees and other needs. This was certainly Malik's hope, and that of his family when they originally brought him to St. Michael's. Those involved with music feel they must constantly defend its worth as an educational tool, for children and adults. Felix and other music instructors blame the difficulty of educating parents about the value of music in the school curriculum on the exam-oriented culture that the MOE has created. Arts education offers a kind of knowledge that is unavailable in other subjects. So, though education is seen as highly formative of the ideal Ugandan child, some feel that the basic curriculum fails to provide them with the knowledge to maintain cultural continuity. The festival coordinator at the MOE agrees; ironically, she said that they are considering making music an examinable subject in order to curb that problem.

Crucial Contradictions: The Mixed Message of Festival Experience

As the first competition approached, the choir was practicing for up to three hours a day on weekends, and they were often let out of class for the entire day to brush up on one or another of the many categories in the competition. Kizza, a humble but lively fifth-grade boarding student, was chosen as the soloist for "Omulya Nnakka," and Felix spent entire practices grilling him on getting the fast-talking verses right. "The soloist sets the tone for the whole choir! We are all following you," he would rant. He stopped Kizza frequently to work on his speed and style, mimicking how he moves. At one practice, they were at the point near the end of the song when Kizza describes bringing white ants to the *kabaka*, the Buganda king. Felix lost patience with Kizza and brought several children forward to demonstrate the proper movements. But he sent them all back after they tried feebly for a moment, shaking his head hopelessly. The other children laughed. Felix seemed to find shame and embarrassment rather effective learning tools in the choir, but it usually was not too harsh, so the students being teased did not take it too personally, while others had a good laugh over it.

When the admonishments got physical, though, children became more withdrawn. At one point, Felix mocked the drummers coming forward to eat white ants, and he grabbed Kizza by the arm and dragged him roughly throughout the choir to show how he should eat from others' hands. Felix was becoming still more high-strung and critical, but at the same time he kept adding more complicated elements to enhance the song and expected the choir to learn them quickly. Of course, he never made an example of me, but I swiftly fell behind the children, who were practicing at intervals throughout the day while I could not always be there.

As practices progressed, Felix became more particular and temperamental. He was furious with students who arrived late, and he solicited the correct body movements, tempo, and enthusiasm through admonishments and physical threats, balanced by occasional jokes and praises. Halfway through the choir season, children became fearful of Felix. Allan, a fifth-grade boy with a slight stutter and a comically emphatic style of playing the shakers, would cringe when Felix approached, not sure whether he would be clocked on the head or patted on the back by his teacher. Felix had a special affection for Allan, whom he knew had a troubled home life. But whether he handled Allan gently or harshly, Felix saw it as an attempt to help him. He would occasionally justify his actions by carefully pointing out the necessity of beating as an efficient and effective means of discipline.[7] "As long as students skip practices, the stick is required," he would say.

Beating is an appropriate disciplinary measure, even according to children. I once saw a debate between primary school children in which the topic was "Children cannot learn properly unless they are beaten." Many came out strongly in favor of the statement, arguing that children are inherently disorganized and undisciplined, so beatings are necessary to maintain order in the classroom, thus creating an environment

conducive to learning. But did teachers not see the discrepancies between what they taught about children's rights and what they practiced?
I hesitated to ask the teachers outright about this. As a guest in their classrooms, I did not want to appear too critical of their pedagogy. But in discussing it with other Ugandan friends, some of whom were teachers at
other schools, they suggested that it was just a mode of maintaining adult,
pedagogical authority over the children. They also said that, as my experience suggested, teachers see no disjuncture between advocating for
children and beating them. Only "excessive beating" was a violation
of children's rights. The students looked discouraged whenever they
were punished either physically or by ridicule, but whenever I talked to
them about incidents, they denied feeling that admonishments were too
harsh, and even if they were, the students were resilient. "It's alright,"
they would say, "we just have to cope up."

Children's Creative Input: Reflections of Daily Life

Children were indeed accustomed to "coping up," but the festival offered them a gratifying, if indirect, outlet for airing grievances. Whenever I present my research on the festival, however, skeptics ask whether
children themselves have a hand in composing their festival entries.
The appropriate answer is, "Sometimes." Some directors assigned numbers with little input, while others engaged their students in creative
collaboration to create their original numbers, and even some of the
aesthetics of traditional numbers. I myself asked at the initial organizational meeting whether children or teachers write the plays. There was
some discussion, but the general conclusion was that students should
be given general guidelines or a seed idea from the teacher. From there
children fill in the details of the scenario. Then the teacher creates the
written script out of what the students come up with. For example, a
teacher asks students to improvise based on a scenario where a teacher
is abusing a student. The student learns of her rights and challenges the
teacher. The students take that scenario and create a script. That way,
they argued, children will not just be reciting what a teacher has created;
they will be acting.

In festival performances of traditional songs and dances, creativity
and improvisation are discouraged, while following established motifs in
singing and movement is praised. Initially, children in the St. Michael's
choir really wanted to involve themselves in the creative process, to put
new knowledge to use. There was little room to innovate in the tradi-

tional numbers, although judges give marks for "uniqueness" as well as "traditional tone" dress, accompaniment, and dramatization of lyrics. The students had significantly more input on the creation of the play, and they used the opportunity to reflect their seldom-voiced daily realities. One day at practice, Felix said, "I want to know from you people, before we put things into these songs and the play, do we all understand when someone says 'children's rights?'" He asked for explanations, and they answered that it's what the child needs, must get, or must be given.

"Below eighteen you cannot decide much in your life," Felix explained. "So people who live around you, like adults, can guide you. Where do you see children not getting what they need?" Children offered answers such as education, adequate food, freedom of speech, and respect to parents. "What about the parents respecting you!?" he asked. The students only laughed shyly, a little confused by the idea. They got back into the conversation when Felix asked about cases of child abuse or violation of children's rights. He mentioned child sacrifice, rape, and defilement as examples. He also said parents who have the means but do not send children to school are in violation of children's rights. These are the types of things they can put in a play. "I want you to tell me," he said, "when people want to talk about those rights and how they should be kept, what do you want our play to look like? Because these things are many. What do you want our play to have?" He suggested they tell him about problems their own friends might have at home.

Children lit up at the prospect of contributing. One girl offered a scenario of a girl who has to wash clothes when she should be going to school. Felix liked the idea. "But don't forget," he warned, "you as a child as well, at times, you have to do your work." Another suggested street children and mistreatment. All agreed that mistreatment of a child should be in the play.

"Who will mistreat this child?" he asked.

Immediately they chorused, "Stepmother!"

"Why stepmother? They are the ones who mistreat?" he asked.

"Yes!"

"Who has got such an experience? Who can tell us about stepmothers? Maybe I don't know much about them very well," he feigned.

"Eee!" they all moaned skeptically. The "evil stepmother" trope is prevalent in Uganda, mainly predicated on experience and firsthand observation. Ugandan stepmothers are purported to abuse and neglect their stepchildren on a regular basis, allocating precious and scarce resources to their own children and letting their stepchildren go without. People speculate that because of limited resources and jealousy between women, stepmothers vehemently resent having to care for another woman's children when they marry men who already have children. The following essay on the evils of stepmothers was written by a Kampala-area primary school student:

REASONS WHY CHILDREN HATE THEIR STEP MOTHERS

The stepmothers are all cruel and harsh. If you come back home late they just beat and they don't give you food to eat.

Every day you go to the school late, they [first] tell you to wash the utensils and you go to fetch water. In the morning you bath with her children and you carry them to school. When you are late they beat you at school.

Those step mothers are bad and they give their children much food and sometimes they don't give you food. They cane you. . . . If your father gives her money to buy meat and eat, she goes to salon to dye her hair and she comes back home when she has spent the money. She goes to buy for you beans and you eat. She prepares good food at night because she knows the husband is coming. But at day time, she prepares the bad food for the children.

And if her children cry for nothing she comes back and she tells you that why have you beaten my children when even you are not the one. She canes you and tells you to stop those bad manners because I will report you to your father. If you urinate on the bed she beats you and if you steal the food she says who has stolen the food? You say I am not the one who has stolen your food.

The children suggested that in the play, the biological mother dies and then the father gets another wife. Most preferred that scenario to one where the mother was chased away. "Why do you guys want things to do with a mother who died?" Felix asked. A student suggested, "Let the woman be chased away because in the end, maybe the woman will be back and the child will go with her mother."

"I like that!" Felix exclaimed.

I put in my two cents: "I like that idea, too, because in the constitution, it also talks about women's emancipation—that women have a right to be with their children as much as the children have a right to be with the mother. So that's a nice idea because it will talk about women's emancipation *and* children's rights."

"Exactly," Felix said. "So let the mother not be dead, okay?" The students said yes to that. He continued, "And after being chased from the home like Kristen was saying, she has got the right to go and fight for her rights to have her children. Okay."

We moved on to discuss the number of children she would have, and the students noisily disagreed. They wanted the stepmother to come with children she treats nicely, but they could not agree on how many. "Well," Felix asked, "which is abused?"

"Girls!" was the overwhelming answer. Felix wanted to get ideas about abuses a girl would endure. He pointed out that it is best to depict real-life experiences. They suggested a stepmother who does not support her stepchild at all: no school fees, being kept from school, "no eating at all," hard labor, preferential treatment of her natural children. He eagerly wrote the ideas down on a notepad.

"There is something I have asked you which you have not answered," he asked. "Do you get to hear these things by people talking about them, or . . . ?"

"We see them!" several interrupted.

"You experience them!? *You*!?"

They laughed, but none came forward with personal information. "Some of you see them, eh? Others have experienced them. So what else do we experience in our communities?" They related stories of children they knew who were given less food than their siblings, made to do all the housework, or whose hands were burned for allegedly stealing. "Now, let us get some two more that will really cause this child to say, 'I think I can't stay here any more, that will [cause] us to go to the street.'" They suggested physical abuse. He asked, "But do stepmothers really abuse?" and the choir exploded: of course they do! A boy stood, "They say, 'I'm not your mother. I didn't produce you!' and they beat you."

"Do the fathers care?"

"No!" children said. "They don't!" One girl suggested that in the play, the father would let the child go because the stepmother would threaten him to choose between the child and herself. Felix wrote it down.

"Sometimes children we see are suffering right in front of us, but we do nothing," Felix said. Then he told a story about a boy at St. Michael's.

In P5 where I was teaching last term there was a boy who used to come very dirty, like for three days without washing. No combing his hair . . . so badly off. And we used to ask ourselves, "What is wrong with those people? What is wrong with this boy?" Okay, to him he wouldn't talk. You asked him to go home, and he cried.

Now, one day I was with Mr. Museka coming from the market. We saw the boy in school uniform escaping. We got the boy, put him in Mr. Museka's car, and asked him what he was doing. He only said, "I won't answer you."

"Where are you going?"

"I'm going to Mbale."

"To who?"

"My mother!"

"Do you have transport?"

"No. I will walk up to Mbale."

The students reacted with disbelief. Mbale was a hundred miles away.

Now we had to convince him; he refused, he cried. And you know these days people can get ideas that you are kidnapping a child. So we got a police officer; he helped us; we took the boy to the police. He refused to talk. "Let's take him back to school," we said. He refused!

Felix paused in his story and pointed behind us. "That is the boy!" Everyone turned to look, and he continued.

Now they gave us two policemen and we came with them up to here. After we came here, we went to the father's place. Now, reaching there, there was a stepmother who said, "If that boy is to die, let him die! I'm saying yes, I don't care about that boy!"

Now we went to police because the father, the man works at the police station and the father is a very good man. When coming here the guy is always driving; he has got high ranks in the police. When we talked to him, he said, "I know the problem is between my boy and the stepmother. Okay, I may talk to her about this child." And he talked to the mother.

The following the day the boy came and thanked me with all his heart! He dressed smartly, his hair was cut, and since then this boy is a new boy! You ask him, "How is it at home?" and he says, "Yeah! She is now giving me food. She now loves me!" Because maybe after all this had happened, there was a problem that they had to stop. Now, where would that boy be if we had not interfered? A neighbor even knew the boy was being beaten, but they were afraid to interfere. But now he is a very happy boy.

The children sat riveted to Felix's dramatic retelling. When he finished, they seemed satisfied with the story and suggested they incorporate some of it into the play. Felix took his leave, but the rest of us stayed to talk some more. The children were eager to share similar stories with me, so I listened closely. Malik's friend Kizza told me about a stepmother who starved her stepchildren. She left two hundred shillings lying around, so her stepchild took it and bought a pancake. The stepmother found out and burned his fingers so badly they had to be amputated. Sumayiya (chapter 1) told a story about an uncle's neighbor who had a new wife. She left her three-year-old stepchild to bathe herself, which was dangerous.

Neighbors finally told the police, who punished the woman. Was justice done in these cases, I asked? What about the fathers? "Some fathers may be taking care of their kids," they told me, "but the father goes to work and doesn't always know what happens at home between stepmothers and his kids."

In the end, their play was a series of vignettes in which children were subjected to abuses and the more enlightened adults informed others about the benefits of protection of children's rights for the greater advancement of the nation's development goals. It also drives home Turner's theory of social drama because it showed not only that festival dramas reflect everyday realities, but that children are eager to use the plays to highlight issues they have kept private and to push for social change. Many children who experience or witness violence at the hands of adults either keep quiet about it or tell only their closest friends. With his retelling of another child's story, Felix opened up a dialogic space for the students to publicly relate their stories of children's rights violations. After this conversation, Sumayiya often approached me with news of abuses against children that she had either heard around campus or in the media. Putting these issues into dramaturgical language creates a safe space in which to acknowledge injustices and advocate for their abolition because it highlights children's common plight. Despite Sumayiya's preoccupation with child abuse, she told me that children rarely report incidents to the proper authorities, as Police Inspector Nakhanda had urged (see chapter 1). Children feared reprisals from their abusers. Sumayiya claimed that children were much more likely to run away from bad situations, just as she had. Unfortunately, most children do not have the positive options that Sumayiya had; they are increasingly going to the streets instead. The children hoped to highlight such trends through the performance of their play. So while children have varying degrees of creative license and artistic input into festival performances, it is also important to look beyond the question of authorship to understand how children interpret and synthesize what they learn from participating in cultural festivals.

Creating a National Culture

Though opportunities for creative engagement in the traditional pieces were limited, children's festival performances also figured prominently in national representations of a common cultural heritage. Even while adults find essentialized attributes of children conducive to the performance of traditional songs and dances, "tradition" is revitalized and transfigured into "national culture" through the creative reinterpretations of young festival performers. One of the main stated aims of the festival has been to foster national unity. Ali Mazrui has noted, "The slogan of "nation-building" in Africa often tends to be tied to cultural engagement—an involvement in the task of reducing tribal cleavages while trying to create a common national heritage" (Mazrui 1978, 218). According to Othieno, this is in part achieved simply by bringing students from all parts of the country together at the national finals to learn about Uganda's cultural diversity from each other. At the 2000 national festival, the MOE Inspector General remarked proudly to the audience,

The Ministry of Education has got a mission statement which lists the national goals of education, and one of them is forging national unity. If this country will not unify through the education system, then nobody will unify it. So education is the unifying force. These children come here, they meet their friends, they go to new places to share their music, and we are really sure we are producing citizens who will create the national unity. And without unity this country won't move ahead. That's why we have got these national festivals—this is Uganda! We have gathered, and we rejoice together, we strive together, we survive together. That's why we are going to build the national peace.

In addition to observing performances at the national competitions, I spent a lot of time observing and interacting with children off stage and in preparation for performances. Generally, children reported that they enjoyed being in the city and meeting other children at the festival, though language differences imposed communication barriers. If these original songs are meant to educate, their audience is limited—especially within the Kampala area. The St. Michael's choir typically did a folk song in Luganda because though only about 30 percent of the students are Bagandan, Felix claimed that most children are familiar with the language as a result of living in the city. I talked to one of the girls who was chosen to solo in the original composition during a rehearsal, and she shared the written words with me so I could copy them down. I asked her if she could explain what the song meant, and she said, "I don't know. My family is Kenyan, and though I've lived in Kampala most of my life, I don't know Luganda very well. I can just sing the words." I found that a lot of other students at St. Michael's did not understand what they were singing, either, so they certainly would not understand the songs sung by other school choirs at competitions.

This problem persists to the national level, where the goal may be to bring children together to learn about the theme and Uganda's diversity, but not being unable to understand each other obviously makes it difficult for them to share ideas. Still, some national festival performers claimed they had met friends from all over Uganda, often by communicating in English. Others reported having made friends only with children from regions with ethnic and linguistic similarities. Though children were not exactly forging national networks of friends—nor typically staying in touch after festival—they still felt united with all the children they met, at least for the duration of the festival. According to Othieno, teachers have reported to MOE that when students see others performing dances they had previously only heard about, they return home from the festivals having learned traditional dances from other areas quite well.

"A national culture is definitely being created through the festivals," mused the senior Luweero choir director, George, as he fiddled with a thumb piano. Although the cultures of Uganda are diverse, he pointed out, they are still more closely related to each other than any of them is to Western culture. "Children are creating the folk songs of tomorrow," he declared.

"You think so!?" I asked.

"Yes! People may no longer sing the old songs in the village, but the children today who are singing songs about the constitution in the traditional African style will hopefully teach those to their children and so forth."

"Aren't they a bit different because of the political content?"

"Many of the old songs also served political purposes," he pointed out, "for kings and witchdoctors, for example."

Traditional Dances: Illustrations of National Culture

Children are reinventing tradition not only by creating new songs but by repopularizing indigenous traditional dances. Audiences seem to enjoy traditional dances the most, and, indeed, they are the most lively, vigorous, loud, and jubilant of all the categories. They are always the last category of the day—a sort of noisy, exciting, grand finale—and they get people to stick around until the end. Ugandan traditional dances tend to be communal affairs, involving a large group of dancers and quite a number of choir members singing and clapping. The drums are heavily emphasized and are sometimes the only instruments. Certain elements of dress also contribute to the music: Karimojong women wear leather

17 A primary school choir performs the *amagunju* dance. Photo by the author ca. 2001.

loincloths with bead and cowrie shell trim that jingles when they jump up and down, swinging the cloth from side to side; Banyoro men wear shakers of dried seeds around their calves that create a rhythm as they step. A large choir sometimes backs up the dancers, who usually wear brightly colored clothing or articles that accentuate movement, like the goatskins and grass skirts that Baganda women who wear to highlight the hips.

St. Michael's gave a wonderful traditional dance performance. They settled on a Kiganda dance called *amagunju* (fig. 17), a lively celebratory dance that originally only the Obutiko (mushroom) clan could perform in order to entertain the *kabaka* at galas. The St. Michael's choir squeezed onstage in their *gomesi* and *kanzu* costumes. They chanted the title slowly but loudly and swayed back and forth, their voices gradually rising. They added clapping high to one side and then the other, and at the crescendo, the drums kicked in with a swift, festive rhythm. A line of four girls shuffled onto the stage from one corner, criss-crossing with a line of four boys from the other corner who were bent at the waist, swinging their legs out wide to the side as they entered. After the two lines circled around and met at the back of the stage to the cheering and jubilant singing and clapping of the choir, the girls danced forward, all hips.

Their rhythmic, Kiganda-style hip shaking was accentuated by goat-skins and grass skirts tied at their waists. They kneeled in greeting before the audience, and the drums signaled a change to a slower beat. They paired with the boys and moved into a square pattern. The boys, already sweating from the effort, vigorously stomped and kicked out to the sides as the girls did more spirited hip and foot work in front of them. Another change, and all the dancers moved to center stage, the girls bending in a planting motion, while the boys swept their arms low as if slashing grain. The girls then slowly twisted their way into a circle while the boys, now a bit drunk from the local brew that used to flow at the *kabaka*'s parties, staggered into the middle of the circle and sat down with their legs spread apart in front of them. They emphatically slapped the ground and clapped to the beat to encourage the dancing girls, whose pace impossibly quickened. The choir clapped and ululated as they sang praises. The energy was incredible, and the crowd clapped too as the drums picked up the pace. The dancers got into a line, alternating boys and girls, and danced euphorically in a large arch around the stage. The boys hung back, still quick-stepping and swinging their arms and legs from side to side. The girls took small, quick *bakisimba* steps to the front of the stage as the choir and dancers all triumphantly punched the air, shouting "YAY-YAY!" The girls held their positions, dancing furiously to the audience. At fever pitch, the drummers suddenly gave the drums one hard slap to end the song, and the audience exploded into ecstatic applause. The hall was alive with appreciation, and the students were proud to the point of bursting.

Due to the influence of Western missionary education, many of the parents of children I worked with were not taught traditional dances when they were young. "People began neglecting ethnic traditions because of an educational bias," the Mpigi director at the national festival pointed out to me. Schools sometimes inculcated a Western cultural bias, if not outright disdain for African cultural ways. He said that when these children's parents and grandparents were young, they were taught that those dances and songs were only for uneducated people, and it became unfashionable for educated people to practice them as part of social or family gatherings. The children in his choir did not know the *bakisimba* dance before he started to teach them "because they don't know them at home." For most students, the school choir was their only opportunity to learn some traditional Ugandan songs and dances. Sumayiya and some of her friends said they were already familiar with the choir selections because they had seen them on local television shows that occasionally feature performances. Others were performed at family functions, such as a wedding. But few could say that they learned them in the village or in the context for which they were originally written, because folk songs are now generally performed only for entertainment rather than to celebrate the activities described, such as hunting white ants.

Popular conceptions of emergent national culture were increasingly constructed in opposition to Western culture yet in line with Christian tenets. "The introduction of Western culture has really squeezed local cultures," George explained. "The problem is that when people adopted Christianity, they also embraced Western culture, and they have never separated the two." This was why Ugandans had turned their backs on traditional culture. George's sentiments echoed those of a Uganda cultural icon who was partly responsible for the National Theater itself: poet Okot p'Bitek, who also decried colonial and missionary policies discouraging African dance for their long-term effects on culture. For him, "the ultimate test of the educational revolution is the re-acceptance of the African dance of passion into the fold of legitimate aesthetics" (Mazrui 1978, 215). In 2000, MOE officials, choir directors, and performers were dealing with precisely that problem. Many thought that this generation's main challenge was to separate religion from Western culture—and adopt the good of both—so that Ugandans could be good Christians but still maintain indigenous cultural practices. For example, the Tororo choir director explained his choir's traditional dance to me and pointed out that the girls used to perform topless. Now, however, audiences would find this distasteful, so the girls wore matching halter tops instead. He said that festivals gave them the opportunity to revive traditional dances, but in newly acceptable ways. "We are trying to modify it in certain areas," he said. "Some parts are too immoral. We are trying to educate the community that such things cannot exist in the community now. You find the mother of your wife dancing with you almost naked, which is very shameful. So we revise it and give them a modern way of dancing. The kids are keeping it alive and modifying it to fit their society." Othieno remembered that when she first started teaching, the Karimojong would perform the *lelo* dance bare-breasted, and the boys were supposed to fondle the girls' breasts. Now they wear bras, shorts, and wrappers, and they do not make such explicit movements. People now welcome those changes that discourage "immorality" because of their religious convictions as well as their concerns about AIDS, promiscuity, and other related social problems typically described (in a strange twist) as "modern."

"Authenticity": (Re)defining the Traditional

In this context, it is important to note how contemporary performance is transforming traditional dances. For traditional categories, the judges' emphasis is on "appropriate" forms and "authenticity." These are loaded terms that require more explication. Judging from the criteria, the goal of the festival seemed to be to keep old forms of dance alive, in their purest forms. But directors pointed out how dances were being modified to suit contemporary sensibilities. Othieno told me that "authenticity" referred to the tone with which people sang, their basic movements, the costuming, and appropriate pronunciation. "Those aspects of traditional song are not meant to change," she claimed. Her reply was quite transparent, indicating that she had not really weighed the concept of authenticity against her assertion that culture is not static.

Part of the confusion regarding authenticity may arise from the need of Ugandans to legitimate their own cultural forms for the sake of creating national culture, and for cultural legitimacy as a nation. Folklorist Regina Bendix says that "nationalism builds on the essentialist notions inherent in authenticity, and folklore in the guise of native cultural discovery and rediscovery has continually served nationalist movements since the Romantic era" (Bendix 1997, 7). If this is the case in the Ugandan context, what does the festival's replication of traditional dance and song indicate about national belonging? One answer is that it raises the role of children to purveyors of national cultural traditions. Though traditional dances are increasingly performed in public venues like weddings, hotels, and tourist locations, these are not judged and scrutinized in the same high-stakes fashion as they are at school festivals. The festival also diversifies concepts of national culture for the sake of inclusion; the dances were seemingly being co-opted through the festival to comprise an emergent "national" culture, yet they retained their ethnic affiliations throughout, being absorbed instead into a diverse national cultural repertoire. Being "authentically" rooted in the precolonial past, then, is one way to reconfigure the traditional songs and dances of different indigenous groups as appropriately national. After all, a common history is constitutive of national identity. Bendix writes that efforts to democratize monarchies gave rise to European nationalism, "yet the notion of national uniqueness harbors a conservative ethos of the past. Because of the insistence on national purity or authenticity inherent in the idea of a unique nation, the notion of authenticity ultimately undermines the liberating and humanitarian tendencies from which it grew"

(Bendix 1997, 8). Despite this shift, the MOE and teachers like Felix consider it important to retain "authentic style" in traditional categories, yet they often fail to take full account of all the performative dynamics in which the festivals and performers operate (Chernoff 2002). For example, students from many schools wore school uniforms, T-shirts, or shorts with school insignia as part of their dance costumes, which indicated the realignment of traditional culture with the educated, and this was an acceptable adaptation, whereas judges criticized other costuming choices for various reasons, revealing some telling disparities. At one performance, a soloist for a traditional song wore a bark-cloth tunic, tied around one shoulder, with his blue gym shorts and polished black school shoes. He had drawn a mustache and goatee on with ash and carried a turquoise broomstick fashioned into a spear. In the end, judges did not question the authenticity of his dress; instead, they questioned the safety of wearing school shoes and watches while performing certain dances.

Because today's children are performing very different versions of traditional dances, we cannot assume their cultural performances to be juvenile versions of adult culture. Lawrence Hirschfeld argues that "in making their own cultural traditions, children deploy singular conceptual skills that significantly constrain and mold not only their own cultural productions but also those of adults" (Hirschfeld 2002, 612). More than an isolated environment in which children receive the social messages intended for them, the music festival performances are "secreted from the social drama and in turn surround it and feed their performed meanings back to it" (Turner 1986, 90). But as Cati Coe points out in her ethnography of Ghanaian cultural festivals, governmental efforts to create a national culture through schools inevitably cause tradition to be transformed through the politics of representation (Coe 2005). In Uganda's current program to create a national culture, the government— purposefully or inadvertently—leaves the interpretive field open for children to reinterpret tradition and employ dramatic devices to reconcile development and rights discourse with cultural traditions, thus reversing the assumed educational process in which adults always guide children in the social reproduction of cultural tradition. These performances become political moments in which children reconcile traditional performance practices with both contemporary sensitivities and progressive social policies. The performance of tradition thus transforms the cultural landscape and makes children its stewards. In the end, the crucial question must not be so much whether "authenticity" has been maintained (and I have tried to show the spurious nature of the concept) but whether Uganda can achieve, through cultural production, a sense of unity across the diverse traditions of her people.

The Ideal Society: Developing a "Culture of Constitutionalism"

Aside from building national culture, festival organizers strive to promote national development and create a "culture of constitutionalism" through mass education about the constitution's contents. One of the first things that Museveni's National Resistance Movement did upon taking power in 1986 was to establish a constitutional commission that would write a new constitution (the last version having been abrogated by Obote in 1966) based on widespread popular political participation. Meetings were held throughout the country to explain the purpose and potential content of a new constitution, and all Ugandans were encouraged to submit memoranda. Then a Constitutional Assembly was elected to debate the submitted memoranda and draft a constitution. They collected almost twenty-six thousand submissions, 23 percent of which were from children and students (Waliggo 1994, 28). As mentioned in chapter 1, the resulting document, promulgated in 1995, incorporates democratic values that signify a break with Uganda's violent history. The preamble references this history as its starting point, and affirms its renewed commitment to democracy in the face of struggles against tyranny as its resolve:

PREAMBLE TO THE UGANDAN CONSTITUTION (UGANDA 1995)

We the People of Uganda:

RECALLING our history which has been characterized by political and constitutional instability;

RECOGNISING our struggles against forces of tyranny, oppression and exploitation;

COMMITTED to building a better future by establishing a socio-economic and political order through a popular and durable national Constitution based on the principles of unity, peace, equality, democracy, freedom, social justice and progress;

EXERCISING our sovereign and inalienable right to determine the form of governance for our country, and having fully participated in the Constitution-making process . . .

DO HEREBY, in and through this Constituent Assembly solemnly adopt, enact and give to ourselves and our posterity, this Constitution of the Republic of Uganda, this 22nd day of September, in the year 1995. (Uganda 1995)

The next steps in the process were to translate and distribute the new constitution in local vernacular languages, prepare for general elections, enact new laws as detailed in the constitution, "and finally," Waliggo writes, to build up "a strong and permanent culture of constitutionalism" (Waliggo 1994, 28). The designation of the constitutional theme for the national music festival is a direct contribution to this effort.

Throughout the two seasons I observed, the festival became a microcosm of the ideal Ugandan constitutional society that aims to redress social and legal discrimination against historically marginalized groups. For example, one school put on a play that dealt with women's rights by depicting a widow and her daughter who were pushed off their land by her dead husband's brother and were headed for a life of poverty until someone informed them that their rights were being violated, and that they could take legal recourse to get the land back. By doing that, the woman could also ensure her daughter's rights by providing a home and sending her to school. Audience members were impressed; many did not know this.

Sometimes the plays would appeal as much to social attitudes as to constitutional legalities. Another play addressed women's rights, but it was unusual in that it explored the reservations men have about relinquishing their powers to women. The play was about a jobless man who drank a lot and beat his wife. They got into a heated debate when she was given an opportunity to work to help feed the children. Her husband objected because she needed to look after the children and the home. He refused to do domestic work himself because, he told his wife, "It would make me the wife and you the husband!" She knew it was her constitutional right, however, so she pushed the issue until they came to blows. A neighbor, who was "an emancipated woman," came to the rescue, and when she refused to vacate the man's property, he attacked her also. Men and women came from all around and took sides in the debate about whether he had a right to beat other people (aside from his wife) on his property. Then most started to come around to understanding how the woman could benefit the family by taking work. The husband said insecurely, "But will people think I'm not a man?" They convinced him he was not compromising his masculinity by letting his wife put the entire family back on its feet. Still, the tax collectors had to come and arrest him for default before he was finally persuaded. He pleaded for more time since his wife was about to start work, and they gave it to him. The women cheered, and the men looked doubtful, but the woman went to work and helped the family until the man also got a job. They had everything they needed, and their relationship with each other improved through mutual respect. Usually, such conflicts were too easily resolved in the other plays; this was more realistic in that it highlighted one of the biggest obstacles to women's empowerment: men. The play showed how patriarchal attitudes created insecurities about relinquishing social power over others. This conflict was resolved without the interference of law enforcement.

In addition to gender issues, festivals highlight other types of difference positively. Disability is one of them. The 1995 Constitution specifically prohibits discrimination against people with disabilities, but the inclusion of disabled children in the festival publicly signaled progressive social advances. The MOE's goal is to mainstream disabled children as much as possible, but at this stage, it sometimes involves grouping them in such a way that draws attention to their disabilities. Yet the children themselves were adept at proving their own abilities and claiming their rights. Dressed immaculately in a white tailored gown and matching head wrap, a fourth-grade girl with shriveled legs came out on crutches, sat in a chair, and delivered a speech as a representative of the Department of the Ministry for People with Disabilities and the Elderly. She spoke eloquently, saying,

Ladies and gentlemen, before the 1995 constitution, people with disabilities were treated as people of no class, or nothing, in the societies where they lived. With the Uganda constitution in place, people with disabilities have the right [to be respected with human dignity].

"The state shall take appropriate measures to ensure that they realize their full mental and physical potential." This will help us to get full potential and therefore develop ourselves, families, and the nation.

Ladies and gentlemen, who is not aware that we recently held our parliamentary elections peacefully without any forged document, bribing, corruption, going to court, recounting of votes—unlike our counterparts, the able people? [audience cheers] Who is not aware that we disabled people also labor for nine months to produce children to this world like able women . . . ? Do we have good disabled people who are effective at work? All these are indicators of disabled people in development.

The structure of her speech subtly illustrates the gap between law and praxis: while the constitution instantly conferred certain rights on disabled people, the girl still went on to show how disabled people actually deserve rights and dignity from their fellow countrymen, "the able people." Her point seemed well taken; when she had finished to enthusiastic applause, the emcee came out and told her, "Thank you, Madam. In fact, you have presented the speech better than able people! They thought that you could not."

After a school with two blind drummers performed at the national festival, the same emcee brought them back onto the stage and reminded the audience, "Disability is not inability." He even asked the audience to repeat the adage: "Disability is not *what*?"

"Inability!"

"Thank you," he said, satisfied.

Race was indexed very differently, with much more attention to "outsiders" than to various Ugandan ethnic groups. White people in plays indexed an international development presence. In one play, two white characters—portrayed by actors who wore masks made of pink construction paper and twine rope for their blond hair—were present at the opening of a development project. Their presence confirmed for locals the rising cosmopolitanism of the small village in which the project was completed, even though those characters spoke their few lines in the vernacular.

St. Kizito's play was about Uganda's past "life president"—in this play, the name is Opio, though the actor spoke exactly as Amin had in his regime—who had kicked out the Indians. (The school had one Indian boy in their choir—and the only one in the national festival.) It showed how Amin impounded Indians' property in an effort to create a "black economy." Ugandan people then suffered for lack of knowledge about how to run industries that Indians had dominated. Then it showed how the new constitution and the return of Indians were beneficial to all— the Indian boy returned and supplied important goods to the others. After the play was over, the emcee brought out the little Indian boy and asked the audience to praise the "wonderful performer." The audience clapped, and the emcee told him, "Please come again," as though he were still a guest in the country.

Noticeably absent, though, are references to Ugandan ethnic differences and the social problems that have historically arisen as a result. African original compositions and creative dances often dealt with issues of past tyranny, but they characterized it as the fault of autocratic, incompetent leaders rather than ethnic strife. The African original composition that Felix wrote followed what I discovered was a fairly common formula: It summarized the political systems of Uganda's precolonial past, and showed how colonialism changed that, and how the constitutions that Uganda promulgated after independence were abused. Lastly, it portrays how the current government restored order and how the new

Constitution will facilitate development. Many creative dances and original African compositions tended to take this form, in which pre-NRM Uganda is characterized as undergoing suffering that was relieved when Museveni took power. Rarely are names or sectarian politics mentioned; the songs instead refer vaguely to dictators limiting people's freedoms and food being scarce. In a typical creative dance, dancers were knocked down to illustrate the tyranny of Uganda's past. Then they were slowly picked up as one child wearing a long gown in the colors of the national flag swept over everyone. Children in uniforms marched to school, others wore doctor's coats, and one dance step seemed to imply that they were driving along in the NRM bus, the national government's symbol and metaphor for progress. Many young performers at the national level contrasted that period with their own, in which stability allows them to go to school uninterrupted.

Off the stage, though, performers explored ethnic differences explicitly. Non-Nilotic children commented with fascination on northern traditional dances and costumes, such as those of the Karimojong. The Karimojong are nomadic warrior/hunters who live in the far northeast corner of the country, the location of Colin Turnbull's famous ethnography about Karimojong cousins, the Ik, *The Mountain People* (Turnbull 1972). The Karimojong were in the media at the time of my fieldwork because of a government initiative to disarm them of weapons that they used in cattle raids on neighboring communities. Southern Ugandans saw them as one of the only Ugandan ethnic groups still clinging to traditional ways. They were therefore a bit of a cultural curiosity to others, from whom their traditions differ significantly. Even their costuming is different—a visual marker of cultural difference between ethnic groups. In addition, most students from northern and extremely rural schools were older than the others, reflecting the delay in education among poverty- and war-affected children. But song and dance became a method of communication that broke down many cultural presumptions and tensions between students.

During the festival, children's choirs took up a number of constitutional issues, but children's rights were the most popular, for obvious reasons. Through their performances, participants embraced their identities as children and displayed a sense of solidarity around the issue of children's rights. Children I worked with regularly cited the words of the youth anthem to reiterate their central role in the nation, and they decried the ways that adults treated them. Students in festival performances drew on the discourse of constitutionalism to reinforce positive children's rights messages, but also to launch bold critiques of adult behavior toward them that does not follow the tenets of constitutional children's rights. In one 2001 play, a mother wanted to marry off her young daughter, but the girl wanted to go to school instead. The father intervened, asking, "Are we educating this child for public opinion or for her own future?" He mentioned the rights of children to education that are in the constitution, and the mother retorted, "Did the constitution produce my children!?"

"The constitution has given these children power," the father replied. The mother continued to insist that a woman can only succeed by making a wise choice about who she marries. But eventually the father prevailed, the girl was educated, and she grew up to become a doctor who opened a dispensary and dug boreholes in her community.

Rhetorical questions like "Did the constitution produce my children?" or statements challenging the authority of the government over parents' child-rearing were common jokes in children's songs and dramas, but they likely reflected attitudes that children commonly overheard from adults in their communities, as many plays were based on children's experiences. UNICEF representative Mads Oyen (see chapter 1) once told me, "Most Ugandans have no idea what's in the constitution, and if they did, they'd be furious!" He claimed that they, like the characters in the play, would likely refuse to accept that the constitution, which overturns traditional, patriarchal values, has any jurisdiction over them, especially in their own domestic spheres. Social and economic objectives listed in the constitution include respect for the rights of children, such as a right to education and health care (Republic of Uganda 1995), and, though the goals are admirable, neither the state nor individual families always have the means to actualize them. The constitution remains especially insignificant in rural areas, where children's festival dramas are often set. Village patriarchs are thus cast by children as antagonists. With their rickety gaits, cotton beards, and their irascibility, they usually act as comic relief in the plays, and their attitudes are overturned by the young, representing the triumph of progressive constitutional rights over antidevelopment patriarchy and traditional male/elder privilege. For those groups whom the new constitution protects, though, the children's plays create scenarios in which villagers welcome the changes, and the dramas reinforce the idea that people should use constitutional protections and entitlements to uplift themselves, especially historically disadvantaged groups like women, children, and the disabled. "We capitalize on the women and children," Othieno said, "because those are people whom we think have really been ignored."

Thus, the constitution *is* producing Ugandan children; as discussed in chapter 1, the explicit reference to children's rights in the new consti tution is meant to produce a new concept of the child subject through international rights discourses who is both more empowered in her community and more beholden to the state than the ideal children of more traditional, indigenous conceptions.

Children themselves used festival categories such as plays and speeches to further a children's rights discourse in which the welfare of children figures prominently in national development and therefore deserves protection. Many performers took the opportunity to show how children's rights are being reformulated in relation to the nation and to contribute their voices to that reformulation. Still more made a crucial link between the freedom from oppression by adults guaranteed in the new constitution and their development into fully productive citizens: a "pillar of tomorrow's Uganda" cannot effectively support the nation if it is broken. Children's attention to their national and international identities as children was rather impressive and at times politically savvy; they were very aware of how their status as children was metaphorically tied to the nation's growth and development, and they used that link to argue for adult recognition of their own rights. One child even employed a developmental metaphor for the (re)birth of the nation, referring to Uganda as "a nation still in the womb," and the 1995 constitution as a "democratically developed child" that would help lead the nation to total independence. "You have to cut the umbilical cord and let those parts die," he suggested, "so the baby can live."

Performative interpretations of new Ugandan laws and the UN Convention on the Rights of the Child show students' approval of the special protections and entitlements for children. Not only in the national festivals, but also in smaller performance venues, children would take certain liberties under the collectivism of the performance to air complaints to their teachers and parents in the audience regarding issues such as child abuse and poor health care. At an end-of-the-year variety show put on by a primary school attended by my friends' children, a class recited a poem wherein they stomped their feet and pointed their fingers, shouting in unison, "Parents, STOP ABUSING CHILDREN!" None of them would be likely to talk to a parent in such a manner individually, but the performance context allowed them to use children's rights discourse to hold parents accountable for their obligations to protect and uphold children's rights. Children can therefore use performance as a site of collective

empowerment, thereby expressing their conscientious political and social views.

Students at the national festival told me they had learned a bit about
children's rights from the festival, but they loudly disagreed on whether
their parents knew or understood their rights. The Mpigi director claimed
that his choir's African original composition had already established some
efficacy: "The parents who listened to the song even cried," he said,
"because the children hadn't spoken to them about such things before."
The choir had already been invited to perform some of their numbers at
other community functions.

Negotiating the Space of Childhood Identity

Children must negotiate their identities in areas where they experience
tensions between the disparate identity constructions of ideal children
and the actual experience of childhood. As mentioned elsewhere in this
book, they often found themselves caught between the contradictory
notions of the ideal child subject, their actual experiences as children,
and the kinds of claims that people were making on them. As children's
rights discourses were rapidly propagated through the Ugandan school
system by government and NGO awareness campaigns, children were
still targets of crime (e.g., defilement, abuse, and neglect), and suffered
from poverty and lack of security on a daily basis. These campaigns only
heightened their awareness of their own perilous position in society. The
festival was no different, but it was one of the few areas in which they
could safely express their concerns and frustrations about these issues.
First, they had to successfully navigate the same issues in the festival
itself.

As practice wore on, it became more difficult for the students of St.
Michael's choir to actually enjoy what they were doing. Despite the
heavy responsibilities placed on them, including three practices per day
that took up practically all of their allotted leisure time at school, Felix
wanted to see carefree, happy childhoods reflected in their performances
and their stage personae, through dance gestures and facial expressions
as well as their tones of voice. Felix suggested that if the children were not
actually happy, they should either force it or fake it; after all, they were
children, and it was their right and obligation to enjoy their childhoods.
"Be happy!" Mr. Kisakye pleaded. "Have a smile on your face! I mean,
love what you are doing. It is part of your children's rights! People were
clapping and dancing without enthusiasm. You are *children*! And our

theme is children's rights. Do you show that in the dance? No," he said, crestfallen, "You were kind of dull." The choir sat somewhat listless when they heard this, feeling adult authority and the pressure of competition encroaching on their ability to truly enjoy what they were doing—and to be the "happy" children they were expected to be—while the teachers remained oblivious to the irony of their own words. They were regularly caned and hit by the same people who told them of their rights: their teachers and parents. This left children both highly anxious about their own safety and frustrated at their inability to change their own situations of poverty and powerlessness.

Borrowing Adult Authority to Make Children's Rights Arguments

Often it seemed that students did (and could do) nothing about it, but through performative devices such as satire in plays and identity negotiation in speeches, children utilized the festival stage to launch social critiques based on the very ideals it was intended to emulate. In fact, festival performers often negotiated their powerless child identities by posing as adults—especially elected officials—emulating the model citizens they are expected to become. When fourth-grader Isaiah was led onto the stage at the national music festival finals, he sauntered out confidently with his hands relaxed and at his sides. He wore a double-breasted suit and tie to match his solemn expression, causing him to look much older than his ten-or-so years. Isaiah introduced himself as "the RDC of Iganga," at which the audience laughed: Iganga is a region in southeastern Uganda, and the resident district commissioner is a mid-level position in the current National Resistance Movement government—an office that could obviously never be occupied by a child. Isaiah addressed colleagues and peers of the RDC at length before beginning:

I would like to greet you and thank you, and I am telling you that even if it gets to sunset and dark, we have enough houses in this village for you to spend the night.

Ladies and gentlemen, allow me to talk about the issue of education, and more so, the education of a girl child.

It is really sad, my fellow Basoga friends, that we have this sorry state of neglecting the girl child. We have decided to take only boys to school and leave the girls to languish at home. You have given out your daughters to go and work as house girls at a tender age, denying them the right to education. . . . An entire female generation is remaining behind just because of your selfishness.

Today, I want you to go when you have seen the light [laughs]. We elected people to go and make the constitution. It was made, promulgated, and now it is in full force.

The 1995 Uganda constitution gives all citizens a right to education. Chapters 4 and 4.30 states that all Ugandans have a right to education, and furthermore, it encourages affirmative action in favor of a marginalized group of people.

Here, a girl child can say, The girl child is marginalized in society [Audience agrees]. It is the girl child who cooks and it is the girl child who goes for water [Audience agrees]. It is the girl child who takes the goats out to graze as well as the associated domestic work [Audience agrees]. And you cannot give the girl child the opportunity to go to school!? [In disgust] Ah! [Audience erupts in laughter] . . .

Fellow tribesmen, I want to remind you that a country's development depends on the education of its people. If you educate a boy, the culture will be one-sided, and you have educated an individual. But if you educate a girl, you have educated the *whole* nation [Applause].

Fellow tribesmen, I want to remind you that it is the girls who are the mothers of the nation and the mothers of the world.

Ladies and Gentlemen, the ball is in your hands. I wish you a safe journey back home. Thank you very much for listening.

As he spoke, Isaiah strode confidently back and forth across the stage, used dramatic pauses, employed hand gestures, and furrowed his brow in a manner more typical of an old man than a nine-year-old. In essence, his presentation strategy was to adopt the identity and behavior of an adult—through posture, attire, and the appearance of independence and experience—in order to speak authoritatively about the rights of certain children. Further, Isaiah chose to imitate a representative of the state, a resident district commissioner. In this manner, his status as a nine-year-old subverted the ultimate authority of the state through mimicry and satire. It was an ironic but extremely effective strategy: other children who chose to speak from the subject position of a child received less audience attention and respect. Whereas audience members spoke to each other or fidgeted during other performances, Isaiah held the audience's attention throughout his speech, and his ability to unsettle generational authoritative hierarchy by mocking state agents was met with emphatic audience approval.[8]

While performances like Isaiah's employed some important devices that illustrate how competing or disparate identities are reconciled in festival context, they also indicated some dilemmas that children face when trying to claim authority and control over self-representation and rights. Though it was obvious that Isaiah had been heavily coached by his trainers, he demonstrates how, to claim their rights, children must usurp the proclaimed power of a child's subject position and identify as adults in order to be heard. This strategy necessarily falls back on a fundamental distinction between children's rights and other human rights: children's rights are actually *protections* rather than rights that directly empower children themselves. Thus, the power to enact and defend these rights rests with others; adults must be the stewards of these rights by acting "in the best interest" of children (Franklin 1986; Ennew and Milne 1990). Isaiah draws on the power of adult authority to bolster his argument, yet part of that power still has to do with the audience's recognition that the speaker is actually a child. That acknowledgment also lends power to his words by highlighting the child's ability to adopt and deliver an adult authoritative voice—a voice that some denied. One judge at a district-level festival criticized speeches where children posed as adults, saying, "Kids can't speak as if they are political leaders like presidents or residential district commissioners." He also said they should not be argumentative or overexcited in their tones, and that teachers should not give them "big, complicated English words when there are surely simpler ones to use." Yet Isaiah had done all of these things and had proven effective; he won that year's national speech competition.

Children might also strategically use their identities as children to elicit sympathy and establish common ground with the audience. A third-grade, private-school student spoke passionately about "the suffering of the child," asking for abuses to stop and using phrases like "we are the backbone of this nation; the foundation on which it stands." She also pleaded with parents not to hurt children, pointing out that "you were once like us." Thus, the child subject position works simultaneously—and seemingly contradictorily—on a number of levels both to free children of their burdens and to convince adults of their productive possibilities.

Establishing Educational Authority

Throughout the festivals I attended, the announcers would ask the audience, "Have you heard what this child has said? Have you gotten the message?" in order to reiterate the festival's educational purpose. It might seem difficult for children to express their points of view *as children* in a society that still strongly links age to status, but one way they manage to do so is through tactics similar to the Ugandan radio songs discussed by Helen Mugambi (Mugambi 1997). Popular music artists of the early independence period adopted the authoritative styles of traditional oral narratives to convey a message of national unity, which was spread effectively through broadcast technology: "Artists use structured openings [to radio songs] as a means of reassembling, re-creating, or reconfiguring

Uganda as a multiethnic nation" (Mugambi 1997, 212). Like radio songs, children's festival songs may begin by employing traditional narrative phrasing such as, "Relatives, friends, here is my story" (Mugambi 1997, 208). Many African original compositions, for example, take the form of a village meeting with an interested and attentive audience. This was the winning school's format in 2001:

Soloist: All of you residents are welcome, please.
Choir: Ah, we got here a long time ago and sat.
Soloist: Oh friends
    [Choir repeats each of the soloists' lines]
    All of you residents are welcome, please.
    Oh friends, all of you women and men are welcome.
    You've given me encouragement, friends.
    I invited you because of what is going on in our village. (× 2)
    Resident Kabunga, I'm glad to see you [shakes hands with him].
    Madam Nalubowa [the drunkard],
    come on, come on [while signaling her to get closer to the group].
    Settle down and I'll tell you the reason for the invitation.
    The reason for this invitation regards our constitution.
    You have to know about the constitution.
    Oh friends, that is why you've been invited.
    Now settle down and know what the constitution says.

According to its organizers, the festival encourages a reversal of educational authority in this way. As Othieno pointed out, children participating in the festivals are often informing their elders about important social issues, which in the past have included AIDS and immunization. After a speech at the 2000 national festival by a boy who quoted heavily from specific articles of the constitution, the charismatic emcee said, "See? The children know the constitution better than us! . . . This knowledge is only found here in the MDD festival." The MOE seems to have aptly recognized that children, given their special aptitude for cultural learning, should be targeted for such a task. As Hirschfeld points out, "The child brings to bear specialized cognitive skills and domain-specific programs that make development possible (Hirschfeld and Gelman 1994). In a sense, the novice is the expert: an expert at learning. . . . Culture cannot be understood *except* in terms of the cognitive architecture of children and the specialized learning mechanisms that the architecture affords" (Hirschfeld 2002, 616). Further, I would argue that children are suited to formulate reconfigurations of cultural constructs because of their ability for *interpretive* learning. As their performances in the festival show, they are sharp cultural observers, able to discern the positive and negative aspects of both tradition and cultural change.

The performances help bring disparate elements together to be constantly renegotiated—through rescriptings of the cultural past and interpretations of the present state of national identity. Many critics (e.g., Bhabha 1986) have likened this to the palimpsest, a writing surface used one or more times after earlier writing has been erased. But reinscribing the slate does not mean that the former text has been completely obliterated. It may still be legible, and its meanings may actually have been built upon in its reinscriptions. Writing about this concept in particular relation to postcolonial Africa, Werbner and Ranger state, "The cultural politics of identity plays dynamically upon that palimpsestual tension . . . to negate, renegotiate, or *playfully* compromise present authority. In turn, it also reaffirms authority, or its possibility, by counteracting the traces of colonial and precolonial sociality within the post-colonial" (Werbner and Ranger 1996, 4; my emphasis).

Children creatively employ this mechanism in the festivals, through the play of form and meaning, reaffirming their own authority over cultural meaning. For example, in the 1996 final competition, whose theme was about the importance of freedom and the integrity of the new constitution (which was almost finished being drafted at that time), many skits involved parodies of notorious characters in Uganda's history, from white colonists to guerrilla soldiers and dictator Idi Amin. Through their mimetic gestures, performers criticized the legitimacy of former rulers. But when children began to dance ballots into boxes and march triumphantly to the front of the stage with constitution in hand, they showed respect for the accomplishments of their current government and democratic principles.

Getting the Message? Comments on the Festival's Effectiveness

Despite these observations, directors sometimes doubted whether children were learning the lessons of the festival. George repeated what Felix had claimed: at this stage especially, the emphasis is so much on competition that children were not absorbing messages about the theme. They do not typically have time to reflect until after the competition. "And it doesn't reach all the students. My school has a thousand pupils, and only fifty are in the choir." Ultimately, he thinks that the adult audience actually learns more from the performances than the children do because the students get so caught up in memorizing lyrics and movements. This was a common opinion among adults, but I did see that, especially where children were able to participate in composing and creating festival pieces, they had developed at least a basic understanding of the issues.

Of course, choirs often had prejudices against judges. Felix knew many of them, leading him to have some doubts about their qualifications; he knew they were not always deployed in their areas of expertise. In addition, their lack of attention to the theme was reflected both in the guidelines for the judges and in their spoken and written commentaries. Of the ten categories, only six are required to meet the theme at all. The festival itself therefore places more importance on the transmission of culture than of civic and political education.

If the festival has fallen short in some of its goals, it has still somehow succeeded in engendering children's respect and even admiration for the constitution. At the national festival, children from all over the country told me they had learned a lot about the constitution. They tended to interpret it rather broadly, but they could typically articulate its provisions and principles as well as any adult. Though they usually did not know why the MOE had asked them to sing about it, and they sometimes had trouble verbalizing particular articles or concepts, they understood that it enforces the peace and security that they now enjoy, and this made it immensely valuable. In addition, as they learned more about children's rights, the festival opened up dialogue on something that they had been silent about and had never questioned. Maybe, they hoped, understandings of children's needs would gradually improve—if not for them, at least for their children.

Meanwhile, many directors attributed the festival's success to the musical and performative elements traditionally involved in the dissemination of information—through drumming and dancing, for instance—in the premodern African past. They believed that these modes of sharing information were culturally more effective than certain forms of the mass media. Many simply inferred the festival's success from gradual changes that they saw around them rather than from direct feedback from the community. (Parents would rarely credit their children with teaching them, but they congratulated the choir trainers for creating good performances around development themes.) Stories of the past told through songs, by their elders, and in social studies classes have given Ugandan children a sharp sense of their own national historical context—especially compared to their parents' and grandparents' generations. Again, national development—made possible by peace and stability—is a central marker that distinguishes growing up in today's Uganda from growing up in the past. One sixth-grade boy participating in the festival told me, "I've learned that Uganda is now changing; it has a vision to become a bright country because now we have very many buildings. Now transport is not difficult; it is simple. I like to be a Ugandan because I am now seeing the changes which are coming."

Resolving Tensions: St. Michael's Season Ends on a Positive Note

St. Michael's choir made a great showing at the zone and division festivals, but they came in third, missing the district festival cutoff by a few points. We took the choir members to see the district competition before wrapping up the season. After returning to the school, Felix told the students to go to the auditorium so he could talk to them for a minute. "Please, students, let it not be the end." He suggested that they start a choir club "so that you love it in your hearts," and to prevent having to learn all their festival pieces in a rush next year. "We can learn songs and dances and go to perform them in different venues such as disabled persons' homes and other schools. Perhaps we can even be on television. We can include from first to seventh grades, elect leaders, and so on."

The students clapped, excited by the prospect of learning both traditional dances and lip-syncing to popular songs. Felix continued, "I would like to thank you from the bottom of my heart for showing enthusiasm and dedication." Some of them had never been to the choir, and though the experience was difficult, they stuck with it. He also asked forgiveness for sometimes losing his temper and hitting or caning them. He explained that the stress of the competitions led him to do it, but it did not mean that he hated them.[9] "It doesn't mean that I think you are bad people. No! Indeed," he said, "I love you so much." So if he annoyed anyone, he hoped they would forgive him so they could continue with the choir together and make it better. By making this admission and asking forgiveness, Felix both put himself at the children's level and reinforced his authority as an adult and a teacher. "Eee," the children nodded in acceptance. He said he would even miss them because he had spent every free minute of his time either with the choir or thinking of what to do next with the choir. "So let this not be the end," he said.

Conclusion: The Socially Productive Space of Performance

Children who participated in the festival had been remarkably skillful at negotiating the paths laid out for them by adult festival organizers and at pointing out the shortfalls of guiding ideologies. Through reformulations of cultural heritage in traditional dances and the artistic illustration of a nation's hope in songs and creative dances, children were retransmitting learned messages of unity, democracy, and respect for the constitution to their audiences. Their performances showed that children value the importance of cultural connection, generational continuity, progressive political ideology, and justice. Through performative devices such as satire in plays and identity negotiation in speeches, they also launched critiques of cultural ideals by showing audiences what daily obstacles they faced in reaching development goals. Through it all, children were reinterpreting cultural traditions and progressive social policies to fit their own social worlds, in which they are perfecting the art of citizenry—not for use in their future adult lives, but now, as child citizens, thus forging new paths for themselves and their nation's development. Parents' improved understanding of constitutional rights as a result of their children's performances proved this, confirming Hirschfeld's theory that "the novice is the expert." Indeed, given the centrality of children in forging Uganda's new constitutional culture, children's "cognitive architecture" is essential to its interpretation.

Drawing on Bourdieu's metatheory of practice, in which the agency circulating in social relations is expressed symbolically and discursively through structures that comprise a *habitus* (Bourdieu 1990), Holland et al. point out that "the improvisations that are characteristic of all social behavior make a difference to the habitus of the *next generation*. That is, the forms of novel activity created by a senior generation provide the experiential context in which their children develop the habitus of the group" (Holland et al. 1998, 45). If we agree with Bourdieu and Holland, then adults have, literally and figuratively, "set the stage" for children exploring issues of national identity through the figured world of the music festivals. But it is equally possible that these improvisations effect change immediately, such as through child-child and child-adult socialization.

The festival design allows children to utilize the stage as a forum for experimenting with their social realities and relating the ideal social structure laid down in the law to the current structures of daily life that prevent them, as children, from attaining full citizenship rights. Though festival activities can be highly structured by adult directors and festival organizers, children tend to negotiate the boundaries laid out for them quite skillfully and productively. Providing that space for children may facilitate their socialization into dominant discourses on the character of national identity, but we must not assume that children are simply indoctrinated without critically engaging the ideas imposed upon them. By seeing such events as sites where adults and children, government and populace engage in mutually constitutive imaginings of contemporary Uganda, we may start to understand how children actively shape the ideologies of the societies in which they live. The festivals become crucial sites where children can affect social change and create alternative discourses, cooperatively interpreting nationalism and citizenship from their own viewpoints as well as fashioning their own places within them, thus transforming the very ideals of national belonging from which their identities derive.

Cultural performance can therefore serve as a mechanism for the negotiation and improvisation of national identity by allowing children to locate themselves within and across public space that makes certain claims on children but from which they are typically excluded, and in which their voices are regularly silenced. When the audience is listening, they are thus invited by child citizens to rethink their own ideas about citizenship, community, and national identity, and to redraw conceptual boundaries that limit children's capacity for social action. Through critical engagement and improvisational play, children can and do make important contributions to the process of building a culture of constitutionalism, but adults are still ultimately the gatekeepers of that process. Its effectiveness as an exploratory space for such negotiations will depend on positive and engaged participation by all involved. Let's hope the audience is listening.

Epilogue

Since I completed fieldwork in December 2001, events in Uganda have underscored the importance of the issues raised in this book. It seems now more than ever that children's attempts to take a central role in building their society are endangered. They are facing even more setbacks in their rights and threats to their very survival. I had hoped to be able to report happy news, but the children I introduced in this manuscript are still struggling with their daily realities of poverty, insecurity, and powerlessness. This epilogue provides an update on their situations.

I have tried several times to get in touch with World Vision staff and to get news of Lord's Resistance Army escapees Richard and Chancy, but my attempts have been unsuccessful. The World Vision main office in Kampala assured me that everyone in Gulu is fine, but I longed for more specific information. I did hear that in 2004, Violet's daughter escaped from the LRA and is now back with her mother after eight years in rebel captivity.

The situation in northern Uganda, despite having gotten much worse, may soon be getting better. The Sudan Comprehensive Peace Agreement signed on January 9, 2005, gave the Sudanese People's Liberation Army (SPLA) political rule over southern Sudan. This made it possible for the SPLA to host the Ugandan government and the LRA in peace talks in Juba. Reinforcing the notion put forward in chapter 7 that performance is a productive space for political negotiation, children at the World Vision center have cut an album with songs urging Kony to stop fighting.

This is not the message Kony has received from the international community, however. After the terrorist attacks of September 11, 2001, the Bush Administration added the LRA to their growing list of terrorist organizations. Labeling the LRA as international terrorists only cemented Museveni's alliance with the United States who, according to U.S. State Department official Eunice Reddick, continue to provide the Ugandan army with "non-lethal" assistance in their military campaign against the LRA.[1] Unfortunately, the United States is not yet so forthcoming with their support and assistance for the Juba peace talks. Foreign diplomats and relief workers have often advocated for peaceful resolutions to the conflict, but as a UN official pointed out, "This insurgency is unique, because they [the LRA] don't seem to want anything negotiable. Kony consults the spirits on a daily basis to dictate the battle. How do you negotiate with spirits?" (Integrated Regional Information Network 2004a).

To further complicate matters, Museveni asked the International Criminal Court (ICC) in the Hague to indict Kony and other top LRA leaders for crimes against humanity in October 2005. This has become a major sticking point in peace negotiations in Juba because the LRA leadership will not come to the table unless the charges against them are dropped. Further, these are the first major indictments issued by the newly formed ICC, so they have much at stake. International law trumps Ugandan national law and their offer of amnesty, so the ICC refuses to agree to the Ugandan government's requests to drop the charges for the sake of peace.

The Juba peace talks continue, with great caution and hope, as I write this epilogue. Night commuting by children has abated, but conditions in the IDP camps remain absolutely abysmal; their population soared to nearly two million in 2006, and more than one thousand people die in the camps every week from unsanitary conditions, disease, or violence. The Acholi can wait no longer for a positive transformation of this dire situation.

With the possibility of a peaceful resolution perhaps nearer than it has ever been, people in Acholiland are starting to look toward the future. Major questions remain about how best to reintegrate ex-LRA rebels into society. Many communities have utilized traditional ceremonial procedures for the reconciliation of ex-LRA soldiers and compensation of victims. Traditional mechanisms have been somewhat successful, but they were never designed to deal with conflict on so massive a scale, and many debate the degree to which they should be used in place of, or in concert with, juridical measures. Many activists, scholars, and aid organizations are also engaging in discussions about land resettlement and economic recovery. The consensus, however, is that the Acholi want peace now, and justice later.

In 2005, Museveni also pushed through a constitutional amendment that rescinded term limits so that he could run for president in the 2006 elections. He won the elections and began his twentieth year in power. But thanks in part to growing international awareness of the situation in northern Uganda, led in part by a vital North American youth movement in support of northern Uganda, Museveni's star status in development circles is beginning to tarnish.

Even children from Kampala have felt the effects of war in northern Uganda. Jill Obonyo finally got her wish to go to the village, but her trip was cut short by LRA attacks. In a 2003 letter, she wrote,

I have been in the village in Lira, but I was forced to come back because of the insecurity which is there. Kony had raided the whole village so we slept in town. Lucky enough our property was not destroyed but a lot of people were killed and many displaced. I was working in the garden with my relatives but the climate was not all that good but at least I managed to weed the garden, dug the bushes around and swept the compound.

Michael and Jill both sat for the national Primary School Leaving Examinations (PLE) in 2001 and 2002 respectively, and they entered boarding secondary schools. Their parents are continually struggling to pay their fees. Jill's mother wrote a letter explaining, "I tried to take the children and register them under the needy in Lira, but Kony intensified; we had to run back. . . . The children often come home without reports because the fees have not been paid. Now I am renting three rooms to raise everything." Her parents' struggle puts more stress on Jill to excel while making it difficult for her to concentrate on her learning. "School is not all that fine because of the situation at home but at least I am in secondary school now and I will make sure I work hard to become what I want." With sponsorship, she and her brother have excelled.

I never heard from talkative Asir again. Jill said that he was in her P7 class in 2002 and also sat for his PLE, but she has not seen him since she left Kubili Primary School. He and his family have not written, so I am not certain whether his father Mr. Owora was able to raise the funds to enroll Asir in secondary school. He may have gone to join his brothers and sisters in the village in Tororo. I hope that, wherever he is, he is fulfilling his goal of helping his family and community.

The St. Michael's music club had barely gotten off the ground when teacher Mr. Kisakye left St. Michael's for other pursuits. Most of the members have completed primary school. Malik is still playing drums with the choir at his Kampala secondary school. Music is consistently his best subject. His uncles and grandmother are still struggling to raise him and keep him in school. With them, he has found a more stable home than at any of his previous six households.

Of all the children I met in Uganda during my fieldwork, I am in the most regular contact with Sumayiya, who ran away from her mother to attend school. She became fond of me for my sympathetic ear, and she still writes regularly to seek guidance and assistance. I send her occasional school supplies, books, and journals to help her record her feelings. In 2003, Sumayiya heard that her mother had passed away, which brought up feelings of regret at having left her.

Sumayiya passed her PLE in November 2003. She was one of two students in all of St. Michael's to earn a distinction, thus securing a place in secondary school. Her cousin Jackie, who did not do as well on the same district exam despite her private schooling, became enraged that Sumayiya had bested her, and she ripped up Sumayiya's certificate. Then some of Sumayiya's male cousins staying in the household tried to rape her. Feeling unsafe, she left her aunt and uncle's home and went to live with her older brother. She also moved to a less expensive secondary school and picked up a job cleaning floors. I am helping her with her fees at a boarding school so that she does not have to drop out. She hopes that once she graduates, she can help support some of her younger siblings.

UNAIDS, the Joint United Nations Programme on HIV/AIDS, reports that "double orphans"—children who have lost both parents, like Sumayiya and Malik—are on the rise in Africa. They estimate that the number of AIDs orphans in Africa will continue to rise from 13 million in 2001 to more than 25 million in 2010 (UNAIDS 2002, 3). These developments illustrate how national political problems continue to reduce children's abilities to advance the ideals set forth in citizenship discourses. Children's rights rest on an international discourse whose promulgation from the top down is based on distilled statistical realities—infant mortality, abuse, and neglect—but fails to encompass the qualitative reality of children's everyday lives. Children lack support: familial, structural, and otherwise. The contradictions children face when trying to claim the full citizenship rights proclaimed in the discourses of children's rights and national development hold up an unflattering mirror. Yet these children are not giving up. Like many children throughout Africa, and indeed the world, their hardships have bred in them resilience and determination. They are still striving to effect social change and make positive differences for themselves and their families.

Despite their father's death, quiet James and his brother Alex also completed their PLEs and entered St. Michael's Secondary School. Keeping them in school takes the whole family's effort. James's older brother Stephen occasionally sends me e-mail greetings. Stephen is trying to contribute to his brothers' education by selling handmade ceramics, but he is hindered by lack of materials. James is still in the egg business. Stephen recently wrote, "I am happy to inform you that James and Alex have already started their first term of S2.... I really want to see my brothers continue with their education. I am impressed of their hard work both at school and at home because they take up odd jobs and at the end of the day are able to raise half of the fees. That keeps me determined with my future goals." Fortunately, James was offered a merit scholarship, but they all still pitch in for Alex.

When children find themselves in situations like those of Sumayiya and James and his siblings, they often must enter the informal economy in order to generate some income for themselves and for the entire family. In this way, they take on adult social roles that often, as Nyambedha and Aagaard-Hansen point out, are "in disharmony with the ascribed role and steep age hierarchies of former times" (Nyambedha and Aagaard-Hansen 2003, 175). It is becoming apparent that as young people make their way toward development goals, they are reconfiguring children's and adults' "proper places" in society (Olwig and Gulløv 2003, 13). Most children are able to meet the challenge of taking on "adult" responsibilities, yet doing so does not further their rights and privileges in the emerging nation. Children are supposed to be protected under the CRC, but many are instead looking out for themselves and their families, with little or no support from the state. The work they do is seldom acknowledged or adequately compensated. The result, as Olga Nieuwenhuys has argued, is that "current child labor policies...fail to address the exclusion of children from the production of value, [and thus] reinforce paradoxically children's vulnerability to exploitation" (Nieuwenhuys 1996, 237).

Many dedicated individuals, community groups, and national and international organizations remain committed to raising the status of children. As stated in the CRC, children must have peace, security, and support. Responses to children's voices must move beyond rhetoric, however. I hope that this book has been a step in that direction. I have argued here that Ugandan children's political consciousnesses arise from their interpretations of their historical context as well as Uganda's present historical moment, seen as a crucial juncture in its transition to a full democracy. It would be interesting to follow these children as they grow, and to see how this consciousness influences their values and opinions as adults. Did Jill's village experience, for example, engender more sympathy for northern children, or create in her a more salient sense of national or child identity? In any case, difficult circumstances have led to the failure of axioms of childhood protection, both local and international. By default, the responsibility falls to this generation of young Ugandans to slow the cycle of violence and lighten the burden of poverty, lest they perish under its weight.

Notes

1. In Uganda, adjectives describing ethnic affiliation such as—*ganda* receive prefixes to denote different noun-class usages: for example, *Ki-* for things, *Lu-* for language, *Mu-* for a singular person, *Bu-* for a place, and *Ba-* for a group of people.

2. Many have written about this phenomenon in Rwanda and its consequences (see Malkki 1995; Gourevitch 1998), some of which have had long-term effects on Ugandan ethnic identity and national politics. Ugandan scholar Mahmood Mamdani suggests that the appellations Hutu and Tutsi are political identities rather than cultural or ethnic, and that the 1959 revolution in Rwanda failed because it furthered the colonial legacy regarding the political importance of origins. According to Mamdani, " the preoccupation with origins . . . is the mark that colonialism has left on us all" (Mamdani 2002, 499).

3. Approaches to political analysis based on Weberian notions of state formation assume that the emergence of the modern nation-state means the end of patrimonialism, yet this approach assumes that individuals gradually become bound to the state as citizens, an alliance that eclipses other social ties. This has not typically been the case in Africa. Instead, African politicians have adopted what Patrick Chabal and Jean-Pascal Daloz (1999) term a neo-patrimonial approach.

4. A grievous exception to this was made in northern Uganda, where NRA troops committed numerous atrocities against civilians in response to Acholi soldiers' participation in southern massacres under Amin and Obote (see chapter 6).

5. In 1907, Winston Churchill toured Africa. In his memoir, *My African Journey*, he wrote, "Uganda is truly the pearl of Africa" (Churchill 1908), coining the phrase that now serves as one of the key nationalist slogans.

6. Anthonia Adindu and Norma Romm posit that "development basically requires building up and nurturing processes for meaningful involvement of people in defining possibilities for action in both personal and collective levels. It is about affording people the opportunity to make considered and responsible choices while they simultaneously take into account their involvement in the social fabric" (2001, 53). This model proved successful in the early period of NRM rule.

7. Many speculate that Museveni's sudden change of heart and vigorous campaign for repealing the ban on political parties were efforts to appease international donors, who were disappointed with the slow pace of political change. Others opposed to the Movement System but in favor of the repeal urged the populace to boycott the referendum, arguing that a fundamental democratic right of political affiliation should not have to be put to a vote at all. Both sides claimed the referendum as a victory (Integrated Regional Information Network 2005b).

8. Tripp (1998) effectively highlights the participation of women in political activity, which usually falls outside the purview of gendered approaches to examining civil society and democratization. This leads to some engaging questions about the possibilities and potentials for children's direct participation in civil society activities.

9. Postman's basic argument is that the printing press "created literacy as a new criterion for fully social adulthood" (Wallace 1995, 289). This mode of separation of child and adult worlds also meant that adults, by virtue of print media, could restrict "pre-literate" children's access to adult social knowledge. Thus, sensitive topics (e.g., sex and violence) were encoded in print. This endures in what one might call "spelling speech," through which parents discuss taboo topics in the presence of their children by spelling out words rather than simply pronouncing them.

10. Under disastrous, neoliberal, structural adjustment programs, children in developing countries are often pushed by poverty into the informal cash economy. Throughout Africa, the AIDS pandemic, which has claimed the lives of many of their parents, makes it even more imperative for children to work to support their families.

11. Pamela Reynolds has done extensive fieldwork with children in southern Africa, exploring issues of self and cognition in relation to urbanity (Reynolds 1989), labor (Reynolds 1991), and cultural/traditional apprenticeship (Reynolds 1996). Steven Parish has examined conceptualizations of children among the Newar as they relate to moral understandings of self in Hindu society (Parish 1994). Jean Briggs's *Inuit Morality Play* (1998) is an ethnography of a three-year-old Inuit girl, chronicling how she learned to become an effective actor in Inuit culture by building on cues from adults

that gave her a sense of the potentials and dangers around her. Briggs calls these exchanges "morality play" for the way they engage children in moral conundrums that sharpen their situational decision-making skills.

12. A possible exception is Rwebangira and Liljeström's edited volume, *Haraka Haraka . . . Look Before You Leap: Youth at the Crossroad of Custom and Modernity* (1998), which chronicles the results of the University of Dar Es Salaam's Reproductive Health Study. Focusing on the social institutions that control certain rites of passage into adulthood related to reproductive health, such as marriage and parental obligation, the study examines social change and erosions of moral order in Tanzania.

13. Only two UN member countries to date have not signed the CRC: Somalia and the United States—Somalia because it has effectively had no government in the past two decades. The United States has not signed the CRC

because of the particular human rights tradition in the U.S., which treats rights as the legally enforceable obligations of a state towards its citizens. . . . Children do not have rights because as legal minors, they cannot go to court to enforce those rights. . . . Social and economic rights (to education, health care, etc.) should not be regarded as rights because they cannot be enforced in the same way. This critique rests on a distinction between basic civil rights and political rights that can be respected chiefly by restraining government action, and social and economic rights that require more substantial resources and public action to be realized. (de Waal and Argenti 2002, 3–4)

To child rights advocates, this explanation is feeble at best, but it stays true to the U.S. trend against ratification of most international conventions.

14. The "ABC" approach to HIV prevention—"abstinence, be faithful, and use condoms"—has been the major prevention program, but it has repeatedly come under fire from numerous religious leaders and government officials, who argue that it sends mixed signals about sexual behavior. At the 2004 Bangkok International AIDS conference, President Museveni even rejected condoms as institutionalizing relational mistrust and therefore inappropriate for Ugandan society (Integrated Regional Information Network 2005a). Public debate of ABC's efficacy remains active.

15. U.S. Department of Health and Human Service's Centers for Disease Control and Prevention (November 2005), *Global AIDS Program: The Emergency Plan in Uganda*. Retrieved 27 January 2006, from http://www.cdc.gov/nchstp/od/gap/countries/uganda.htm.

16. Dr. Edward Kirumira has conducted research that shows how schools fail to address issues of girls' sexual maturation, affecting their attrition rate. For more information, see the Web site of the Femshuleni Basic Learning Competencies and Sexual Maturation and Practices Project: http://www.femshuleni.org/country/uganda.htm (2006).

17. This may change if Museveni follows through on his promise to institute universal secondary education by 2007.
18. According to customary law, children belong to their father's families and are therefore their responsibility in the event of his death.
19. Studies by Geissler et al. with Kenyan and Ugandan primary schoolchildren find that "children aged between 10 and 18 years have a broad knowledge of herbal and biomedical remedies and that they use them frequently, often without adults' involvement" (362).

CHAPTER ONE

1. Sumayiya's case never reached the courts. Though the 1996 Children's Statute established some children's and family courts to handle such custody cases, they are underutilized. People usually still prefer traditional means for settling domestic disputes involving child custody (Republic of Uganda 1996).
2. UNICEF, *About UNICEF: Who We Are—UNICEF's Mission statement*, available online at http://www.unicef.org/about/who/index_mission.html?q=printme. Accessed October 18, 2006.
3. The use of the word *youth* is both highly persistent and problematic in Africa. The term is often deployed politically, especially in situations of armed conflict. In these discourses, youth are both the instigators and the victims of political violence. Further, the term is usually construed as masculine, marginalizing young females from public debate, often to their detriment when it comes to youth-assistance programs (de Waal and Argenti 2002).
4. I have never heard of this happening, however.
5. Article 32 of the CRC states that children have the right "to be protected from economic exploitation and from performing any work that is likely to be hazardous or to interfere with the child's education, or to be harmful to the child's health, or physical, mental, spiritual, moral or social development." See the UNICEF website at the page entitled The Convention on the Rights of the Child. Accessed October 18, 2006.
6. See chapter 7 for more on the demonization of stepparents, particularly stepmothers.
7. This is a reference to a recent spate of abandoned babies left in refuse locations that was eliciting a public outcry.

CHAPTER TWO

1. Children rarely talked to me about leaving Uganda. Sumayiya spoke of being a flight attendant and Asir said he wanted to be a pilot, but they were generally much more likely to talk about fulfilling their family/national

duties locally rather than emigrating. For more on this topic, see "The African 'Brain Drain' to the North: Pitfalls and Possibilities," special issue, *African Issues* 30, no. 1 (2002).

2. See chapter 4 for an ethnographic example of this.

3. Vittore's name is evidence of Italian Catholic missionaries' lasting influence in his home region in northern Uganda.

4. Statistically, age four is still quite young for Ugandan children to start school. Though it may be average for urban areas with available preschools, people in rural areas reported that children did not typically start school until they were seven years old. However, these children usually skipped preschool and enrolled directly in Primary 1.

5. Newspapers and radio are the most accessible forms of media for children in the city.

CHAPTER THREE

1. There is much tension between African Ugandans and Indians, who formed a substantial merchant class during the colonial period, which engendered mistrust between Ugandans and Indians upon independence. In the 1962 constitutional debates, the status of Indians in Uganda was a particularly contentious issue. Most assembly members (who were African) opposed granting Indians full citizenship because they feared the power of their potential voting privileges, as well as their potential ability to own land (Barya 2000, 11). Prewitt's 1971 case study revealed that African Ugandans mistrusted Indians more than any other ethnic group, including whites (Prewitt 1971, 224). Indians became the scapegoats for other Ugandans' slow economic progress and were ousted by President Idi Amin in 1972. They were invited back by Museveni's government to reclaim their properties, but social tensions still remain.

2. The kingship was restored in July 1993, during my first visit to Uganda, and most residents of Kampala—Baganda and otherwise—were caught up in the festivities. My housemate, a Ugandan woman with grown children, was invited to the coronation ceremony and came home elated. She carried a glossy photo of the young King Ronald Mutebi sitting on his throne dressed in monarch's regalia, including generous amounts of gold, velvet, and leopard skin. "You should have seen it!" she beamed. "It was a glorious celebration! There were so many people there! There was not a cloud in the sky, and then, just as the official coronation was completed, it started to rain just a little bit." This indicated that his reign would be prosperous.

CHAPTER FOUR

1. Even though it has provided a relative sense of political security, the government has been accused by international human rights bodies of repressing

275

political opponents and the media (Human Rights Watch/Africa 1999), most recently in the 2006 presidential elections.

2. Coincidentally, the *New Vision* newspaper reported several incidents of underage voters being arrested, most of which involved children using the names of deceased adults to try to vote.

CHAPTER FIVE

1. Mahmood Mamdani has made the pertinent point that many African nations continue to define citizenship on the basis of indigenousness, as it was defined by colonial powers that demarcated tribal and national boundaries. These conceptions of citizenship have contributed to some of the conflicts in the African Great Lakes region because of long-standing problems of refugees (Mamdani 2002).

2. The migration pattern is very unidirectional: people who live in the village do not talk of taking their holidays in the city, though they might have relatives there. People who go to the city from the village intend to find employment and join the ranks of other migrant laborers who send money to home villages and return only for certain holidays (Ferguson 1999).

3. Though the civil wars are thought to have ended in 1986, the northern region, particularly Acholiland, has experienced continued insurgencies from the Lord's Resistance Army, a radical, religious, rebel group that wants to overthrow the government to run the country according to the Ten Commandments. They have abducted thousands of Acholi children over the past fifteen years to be used as soldiers, porters, and sex slaves. Many in Acholiland feel that their suffering has been ignored—and even perpetuated—by the government (Cheney 2004).

4. The mass exodus of rural children from northern Uganda to city centers to avoid abductions by the rebel Lord's Resistance Army, dubbed the "night commuter" phenomenon, is creating new categories of "homeless" children in Uganda. See chapter 6 for a detailed account.

5. Olga Nieuwenhuys has argued that because they devalue children's work, adults unwittingly make children particularly vulnerable to labor markets by excluding them from compensation for their labor (Nieuwenhuys 1996). Some adults educated in children's rights see child labor as exploitative—which it is—but they aim to eliminate children from the labor force rather than recognizing value in children's work. Opinions like Jill's avoid this trap by acknowledging that children's contributions to their communities are valuable and should be recognized as such.

CHAPTER SIX

1. This includes people under the age of eighteen, according to the United Nations Convention on the Rights of the Child.

2. This was an unfounded rumor.

3. Muslim influences are likely to have derived from contact with the northern Sudanese government, which has been supporting the LRA for many years. Sudan's government is currently controlled by Arabs who practice shariah law. Until 2005, they were engaged in their own decades-long civil war with the southern Sudanese, particularly the Sudanese Peoples' Liberation Army (SPLA), composed largely of Nilotic Christians.

4. The donation of the facility represents the extent of the government's involvement, outside of rescue and debriefing by the army. The center was attacked once in August 1996, but the LRA did not succeed in overrunning it because they attacked it from the wrong end, behind the wall opposite the gate. For a while, World Vision staff closed down and moved south to Masindi District (Kiryandongo). They came back when they thought the LRA was through because of inactivity in 1998 and 1999, but then the LRA resurfaced in December 1999, attacking some of the IDP camps on the outskirts of town. World Vision has stayed put since then, and has not been seriously threatened.

5. Proceeds from the sale of de Temmerman's book go toward LRA abductee rehabilitation programs, particularly school fees.

6. Amnesty International points out that "the degree of ownership over child members of the "family" is such that their condition is consistent with the international definition of slavery" (Amnesty International 1997, 16).

7. Three thousand shillings was about US$1.75 at the time.

8. Lucy's education level was actually above average for the area. While men in northern Uganda complete an average of six years of primary school, women complete only two (Paardekooper, de Jong, and Hermanns 1999, 530).

9. Interestingly, Ugandan parents from other regions made exactly the opposite statement to explain the main difference between the their experiences and those of their children's generation: "Since 1986, our children have only known peace." The fact that Acholi soldiers perpetrated the violence that characterized the lives of today's young parents when they were growing up in between 1962 and 1986 may explain their apathy toward the current Acholi situation.

10. When the numbers of internally displaced people increased around the world, the UNHCR expanded its mandate to include them, thus allowing the UNHCR to operate humanitarian missions inside IDP camps.

11. I do not mean to suggest that Western constructions of childhood are completely monolithic. There has been profound ambivalence surrounding children and violence in the West as well, where many are dealing with the issue by pushing for children to be tried as adults for violent crimes. For more, see Jenks 1996.

12. For example, a World Vision counselor related a story in which a man who was carjacked on the road to Kitgum overheard a child begging

his commander to let him kill the man because he had not killed anybody yet.

13. Personal communication with a representative of the Uganda Child Rights NGO Network.

14. Susan Shepler examines comparable strategies used by repatriated Sierra Leonean child soldiers (Shepler 2002a).

15. All of the following quotations were taken from written testimonies submitted to Human Rights Watch by Aboke Secondary School girls who were abducted in the 1996 raid on their school.

CHAPTER SEVEN

1. The National Theatre is the capital's major theatrical venue, hosting regular plays and musical performances put on by Uganda's many performing arts groups. It is a dilapidated old theatre that holds several hundred people, but it is still heavily utilized, with several performances every week. The building also hosts a European cultural and linguistic training center, but international acts tend to book at hotels and other more upscale venues.

2. The Ministry recently introduced a "Western music" category as well. The rules are similar to those of other categories: the "standard" conventions of that type of music must be followed. They do not elaborate on what this means.

3. Uganda was one of the first sub-Saharan African countries hit hard by the AIDS virus in the 1980s, and the subsequent success of Uganda in containing the spread of the disease has often been attributed to the National Resistance Movement government's rapid action, which included openness about AIDS to facilitate prevention and calls for assistance from the international community.

4. The Uganda National Music, Dance, and Drama Festival Syllabus for 2000 and 2001 states, "Each dance has its prescribed costumes that must be used, without which the beauty and identity of that dance is destroyed" (Uganda Ministry of Education and Sports 2000, 4).

5. Concerning authenticity, the syllabus asks, "Is the dance as authentic or original as it should be in its own ethnic area?" This question, of course, is not as transparent as it is designed to be. There are many different interpretations and uses of authenticity (see Bendix 1997).

6. While children are considered "natural" dancers, and stereotypes of Africans as having an inherent propensity for rhythm abound, my observations during choir practices were that children worked very hard to master the dance moves they were being taught. Felix told me that dance is often the hardest art to teach children. In fact, the children rarely have any prior association with the instruments and the dance steps. "They have never seen or handled a drum or a thumb piano in their homes," he said, "especially if they have

grown up in the city." He often calls on the experienced children to teach others, and if they are enjoying themselves, they catch on quickly.

7. To determine the roots of this attitude would require research beyond the scope of this study, but some psychologists have criticized essentialized notions among African and African-American communities that their children are different from nonblack children in that they "require" more physical disciplinary measures such as whipping in order to teach their children manners (Wright 1998). The same psychologists who describe this stereotype also ardently refute its truth.

8. Linguistic code-switching, where speakers would switch between English and one or more indigenous languages, was another common strategy in the speeches. One lower-primary girl dressed in a *gomesi* spoke about children's rights, too, saying that children who work for money are victims of child labor, which is bad because it interferes with their education. She also stated that early marriages of young girls amounts to sexual abuse. She spoke mainly in English but switched to Luganda at key points, mostly when seeking affirmation of her argument. She appealed to the audience with words like *Banange* (friends), used to seek the sympathy of the listener through common identification. Such strategies were common and elicited a positive reaction from the audience. This code-switching is significant in that the structuring of different identities links locality and ethnic background to national identity through the use of language.

9. There is actually a Luganda proverb that states, "To beat a child is not to hate it" (Kilbride and Kilbride 1990, 36).

EPILOGUE

1. Reddick made these statements at the Peace Within Reach in Northern Uganda Symposium and Lobby Day in Washington, D.C., on October 9, 2006.

References

Ackroyd, J., and A. Pilkington. 1999. "Childhood and the Construction of Ethnic Identities in a Global Age: A Dramatic Encounter." *Childhood* 6:443–54.

Adindu, A., and N. Romm. 2001. "Cultural Incongruity in Changing Africa" In *Social Problems in Africa: New Visions*, ed. A. Rwomire, 53–70. Westport, CT: Praeger.

Aitken, S. C. 2000. "Play, Rights and Borders: Gender-Bound Parents and the Social Construction of Children." In *Children's Geographies, Critical Geographies*, ed. S. Holloway and G. Valentine, 119–38. New York: Routledge.

Alanen, L. 2001. "Explorations in Generational Analysis." In *Conceptualizing Child-Adult Relations, Future of Childhood Series*, ed. L. Alanen and B. Mayall, 11–22. New York: Routledge/Falmer.

Allio, E. 2002. "Kony Attacks From Sudan." *New Vision*, 25 February.

Amnesty International. 1997. *"Breaking God's Commands:" The Destruction of Childhood by the Lord's Resistance Army."* Report no. AFR, 59/01/97. New York: Amnesty International.

Anderson, B. 1991. *Imagined Communities: Reflections on the Origin and Spread of Nationalism*. New York: Verso.

Anderson, S. S. 1989. "Teaching National Identity: Ethnicity in Peruvian Books for Children." MA thesis, University of California–Berkeley.

Arce, A. 2000. "Creating or Regulating Development: Representing Modernities through Language and Discourse." in *Anthropology, Development, and Modernities*, ed. N. Long and A. Arce 32–51. New York: Routledge.

Archard, D. 1993. *Children: Rights and Childhood. Ideas*. New York: Routledge.

Aries, P. 1962. *Centuries of Childhood*. London: Cape and Penguin Books.

Askew, K. 2002. *Performing the Nation: Swahili Music and Cultural Politics in Tanzania.* Chicago Studies in Ethnomusicology. Chicago: University of Chicago Press.

———. 2004. "Aesthetics and Poetics in Post-Socialist Tanzania." Anthropology Department Colloquium, University of California–Santa Cruz, 2004.

Barkan, J. D., M. L. McMulty, and M. A. O. Ayeni. 1991. *"Hometown" Voluntary Associations, Local Development and the Emergence of Civil Society in Western Nigeria.* Report no. 478. Nairobi: Institute for Development Studies, University of Nairobi.

Barton, T., A. Mutiti, and the Assessment Team for Psycho-Social Programmes in Northern Uganda. 1998. *Northern Uganda Psycho-Social Needs Assessment Report.* Kisubi, Uganda: UNICEF.

Barya, J.-J. 2000. "Reconstituting Ugandan Citizenship Under the 1995 Constitution: A Conflict of Nationalism, Chauvinism, and Ethnicity." Working Paper no. 55. Kampala, Uganda: Centre for Basic Research.

Bateson, G. 1972. *Steps to an Ecology of the Mind.* New York: Ballantine.

Bayart, J.-F. 1993. *The State in Africa: The Politics of the Belly.* New York: Longman.

Behrend, H. 1999. *Alice Lakwena and the Holy Spirits: War in Northern Uganda, 1986–1997.* East African Studies. Athens: Ohio University Press.

Bendix, R. 1997. *In Search of Authenticity: The Formation of Folklore Studies.* Madison: University of Wisconsin Press.

Bennett, T. W. 1998. *Using Children in Armed Conflict: A Legitimate African Tradition?* Cape Town: Institute for Security Studies.

Berentzen, S. 1989. *Ethnographic Approaches to Children's Worlds and Peer Cultures.* Report no. 15. Trondheim, Norway: Norwegian Center for Child Research.

Bhabha, H. 1986. "Remembering Fanon: Self, Psyche, and the Colonial Condition: Foreword to Frantz Fanon." In *Black Skin, White Masks.* London: Pluto Press.

Billig, M. 1995. *Banal Nationalism.* Thousand Oaks, CA: Sage.

Black, M. 1996. *Children First: The Story of UNICEF, Past and Present.* New York: Oxford University Press.

Bornstein, E. 2001. "Child Sponsorship, Evangelism, and Belonging in the Work of World Vision Zimbabwe." *American Ethnologist* 28:595–622.

Bourdieu, P. 1990. *The Logic of Practice.* Stanford, CA: Stanford University Press.

———. 1993. *The Field of Cultural Production: Essays on Literature and Art.* Cambridge: Polity Press.

Boyden, J. 1997. "Childhood and the Policy Makers: A Comparative Perspective on the Globalization of Childhood." In *Constructing and Reconstructing Childhood: Contemporary Issues in the Sociological Study of Childhood,* ed. A. James and A. Prout, 190–229. Washington, DC: Falmer Press.

Boyle, P. M. 1999. *Class Formation and Civil Society: the Politics of Education in Africa.* Brookfield, VT: Ashgate.

Brandes, S. 1979. "Ethnographic Autobiographies in American Anthropology." *Central Issues in Anthropology* 1:1–17.

Briggs, J. L. 1998. *Inuit Morality Play: The Emotional Education of a Three-Year-Old.* New Haven, CT: Yale University Press.

Byron, R., ed. 1995. *Music, Culture and Experience: Selected Papers of John Blacking*. Chicago: University of Chicago Press.

Callaway, A. 1974. *Educating Africa's Youth for Rural Development*. The Hague, Holland: Bernard van Leer Foundation.

Candia, S. 2002. "Domestic Violence Rife in City Police Barracks." *New Vision*, 22 May.

Carneiro da Cunha, M. 1995. "Children, Politics, and Culture: The Case of Brazilian Indians." In *Children and the Politics of Culture*, ed. S. Stephens, 282–91. Princeton, NJ: Princeton University Press.

Chabal, P., and J.-P. Daloz. 1999. *Africa Works: Disorder as Political Instrument*. Bloomington: Indiana University Press.

Cheney, K. E. 2004. "'Our Children Have Only Known War:' Children's Experiences and the Uses of Childhood in Northern Uganda." *Children's Geographies* 3:23–45.

Chernoff, J. 2002. "Ideas of Culture and the Challenge of Music." In *Exotic No More: Anthropology on the Front Lines*, ed. J. MacClancy, 377–98. Chicago: University of Chicago Press.

Christensen, P., and A. James. 2000. *Research with Children*. New York: Falmer Press.

Christensen, P., A. James, and C. Jenks. 2000. "Home and Movement: Children Constructing 'Family Time.'" In *Children's Geographies, Critical Geographies*, ed. S. Holloway and G. Valentine, 139–55. New York: Routledge.

Churchill, W. 1908. *My African Journey*. London: Hodder and Stoughton.

Coalition to Stop the Use of Child Soldiers. 2001. "The Impact of Soldiering on Children: A Global Problem." Vol. 2001. London: The Coalition to Stop the Use of Child Soldiers.

Cocks, T. 2003. "Northern Tragedy Shocks UN Boss." *New Vision*, 10 November.

Coe, C. 2005. *Dilemmas of Culture in African Schools: Youth, Nationalism, and the Transformation of Knowledge*. Chicago: University of Chicago Press.

Cohen, A. P. 1994. *Self-Consciousness: An Alternative Anthropology of Identity*. London: Routledge.

Coleman, J. S. 1994. "Nationalism in Tropical Africa." In *Nationalism and Development in Africa: Selected Essays*, ed. R. L. Sklar, 20–47. Berkeley and Los Angeles: University of California Press.

Coles, R. 1986. *The Political Life of Children*. Boston: Atlantic Monthly Press.

Comaroff, J., and J. Comaroff. 1987. "Sui Genderis: Feminism, Kinship, Theory, and Structural 'Domains.'" In *Gender and Kinship: Essays Towards a Unified Theory*, ed. J. Collier and S. Yanagisako, 53–85. Stanford, CA: Stanford University Press.

———. 1999. *Civil Society and the Political Imagination in Africa: Critical Perspectives*. Chicago: University of Chicago Press.

Cooper, F. 1997. "Modernizing Bureaucrats, Backward Africans, and the Development Concept." In *International Development and the Social Sciences: Essays on the History and Politics of Knowledge*, ed. F. Cooper and R. Packard. Berkeley and Los Angeles: University of California Press.

Corsaro, W. A., and L. Molinari. 2000. "Entering and Observing in Children's Worlds: A Reflection on a Longitudinal Ethnography of Early Education in Italy." In *Research with Children*, ed. P. Christensen and A. James, 179–200. New York: Falmer Press.

de Berry, J. 2001. "Child Soldiers and the Convention on the Rights of the Child." *Annals of the American Academy of Political and Social Science* 575:92–105.

De Coninck, J. 1992. *Evaluating the Impact of NGOs in Rural Poverty Alleviation: Uganda Country Study*. Report no. 51. London: Overseas Development Institute.

de Temmerman, E. 2001. *Aboke Girls: Children Abducted in Northern Uganda*. Kampala: Fountain.

de Waal, A., and N. Argenti, eds. 2002. *Young Africa: Realizing the Rights of Children and Youth*. Trenton, NJ: Africa World Press.

Denzer, L., and N. Mbanefoh. 1998. "Women's Participation in Hometown Associations." In *Hometown Associations : Indigenous Knowledge and Development in Nigeria*, ed. R. Honey and S. I. Okafor, 123–34. Intermediate Technology Studies in Indigenous Knowledge and Development. London: Intermediate Technology Publications.

Dodge, C. P., and M. Raundalen. 1991. *Reaching Children in War*. Bergen, Norway: Sigma Forlag.

Doornbos, M. 1988. "The Uganda crisis and the National Question." In *Uganda Now*, ed. H. B. Hansen and M. Twaddle, 254–66. Eastern African Studies. Athens: Ohio University Press.

Durham, D. 2000. "Youth and the Social Imagination in Africa: Introduction to Parts 1 and 2." *Anthropological Quarterly* 73:113–20.

Ebron, P. A. 2002. *Performing Africa*. Princeton, NJ: Princeton University Press.

Edwards, C. P., and B. B. Whiting, eds. 2004. *Ngecha: A Kenyan Village in a Time of Rapid Social Change*. Lincoln: University of Nebraska Press.

Ehrenreich, R. 1998. "The Stories We Must Tell: Ugandan Children and the Atrocities of the Lord's Resistance Army." *Africa Today* 45:79–102.

Ennew, J. 2002. "Future Generations and Global Standards: Children's Rights at the Start of the Millennium." In *Exotic No More: Anthropology on the Front Lines*, ed. J. McClancy, 338–50. Chicago: University of Chicago Press.

Ennew, J., and B. Milne. 1990. *The Next Generation: The Lives of Third World Children*. Philadelphia, PA: New Society.

Epstein, A. L. 1978. *Ethos and Identity: Three Studies in Ethnicity*. Chicago: Aldine.

Eremu, J. 2002. "NGOs Fuel Child-Headed Families." *New Vision*, 7 November.

Eriksen, T. H. 1993. *Ethnicity and Nationalism: Anthropological Perspectives*. London: Pluto Press.

———. 1997. "The Nation as Human Being—A Metaphor in a Midlife Crisis? Notes on the Imminent Collapse of Norwegian National Identity." In *Siting Culture: The Shifting Anthropological Object*, ed. K. F. Olwig and K. Hastrup. New York: Routledge.

Evans, D. R. 1971. "Secondary Schools as Agents of Socialization for National

Goals." In *Education and Political Values: An East African Case Study*, ed.
K. Prewitt. East African Publishing House Studies, no. 12. Nairobi: East
African Publishing House.

Evans, R, ed. 2001. *Ten Years After: Celebrating Uganda's Success in Implementing Children's Rights*. Andover, UK: UNICEF; printed by Thruxton Press.

Eyoh, D. 1998. "African Perspectives on Democracy and the Dilemmas of Postcolonial Intellectuals." *Africa Today* 45, nos. 3–4: 281–306.

Fabian, J. 1983. *Time and the Other: How Anthropology Makes Its Object*. New York: Columbia University Press.

Fairhead, J. 2000. "Development Discourse and Its Subversion: Decivilisation, Depoliticisation, and Dispossession in West Africa." In *Anthropology, Development, and Modernities*, ed. N. Long and A. Arce, 100–111. New York: Routledge.

Ferguson, J. 1994. *The Anti-Politics Machine: "Development," Depoliticization, and Bureaucratic Power in Lesotho*. Minneapolis: University of Minnesota Press.

———. 1999. *Expectations of Modernity: Myths and Meanings of Urban Life on the Zambian Copperbelt*. Perspectives on Southern Africa, no. 57. Berkeley and Los Angeles: University of California Press.

Finnstrom, S. 2001. "In and Out of Culture: Fieldwork in War-Torn Uganda." *Critique of Anthropology* 21:247–58.

Fischer, M. M. J. 1991. "The Uses of Life Histories." *Anthropology and Humanism Quarterly* 12:24–27.

Franklin, B, ed. 1986. *The Rights of Children*. Oxford: Basil Blackwell.

Furley, O. W., and T. Watson. 1978. *A History of Education in East Africa*. New York: NOK Publishers International.

Geertz, C. 1973. *The Interpretation of Cultures*. New York: Basic Books.

———. 1983. "From the Native's Point of View: On the Nature of Anthropological Understanding." In *Local Knowledge*, ed. C. Geertz. New York: Basic Books.

Geissler, P. W., L. Meinert, R. Prince, C. Nokes, J. Aagaard-Hansen, J. Jitta, and J. H. Ouma. 2001. "Self-Treatment by Kenyan and Ugandan Schoolchildren and the Need for School-Based Education. *Health Policy and Planning* 16: 362–71.

Geschiere, P., and J. Gugler. 1998. "The Urban-Rural Connection: Changing Issues of Belonging and Identification." *Africa* 68:309–19.

Giddens, A. 1991. *Modernity and Self-Identity: Self and Society in the Late Modern Age*. Stanford, CA: Stanford University Press.

Gottlieb, A. 2004. *The Afterlife Is Where We Come From: The Culture of Infancy in West Africa*. Chicago: University of Chicago Press.

Gourevitch, P. 1998. *We Wish to Inform You That Tomorrow We Will Be Killed with Our Families: Stories from Rwanda*. New York: Farrar, Strauss, and Giroux.

Gugler, J. 2002. "The Son of the Hawk Does Not Remain Abroad: The Urban-Rural Connection in Africa." *African Studies Review* 45:21–41.

Hansen, H. B., and M. Twaddle, eds. 1998. *Developing Uganda*. Eastern African Studies. Athens: Ohio University Press.

Harris, G. G. 1978. *Casting Out Anger: Religion among the Taita of Kenya*. New York: Cambridge University Press.

———. 1989. "Concepts of Individual, Self, and Person in Description and Analysis." *American Anthropologist* 91:599–612.

Hirschfeld, L. 2002. "Why Don't Anthropologists Like Children?" *American Anthropologist* 104:611–27.

Hirschfeld, L., and S. Gelman. 1994. *Mapping the Mind: Domain Specificity in Cognition and Culture*. New York: Cambridge University Press.

Hogle, J. A. 2002. *What Happened in Uganda? Declining HIV Prevalence, Behavior Change, and the National Response*. Washington, DC: U.S. Agency for International Development.

Holland, D., J. William Lachotte, D. Skinner, and C. Cairn. 1998. *Identity and Agency in Cultural Worlds*. Cambridge, MA: Harvard University Press.

Holloway, S., and G. Valentine, eds. 2000. *Children's Geographies. Critical Geographies*. New York: Routledge.

Honey, R., and S. I. Okafor, eds. 1998. *Hometown Associations: Indigenous Knowledge and Development in Nigeria*. Intermediate Technology Studies in Indigenous Knowledge and Development. London: Intermediate Technology Publications.

Human Rights Watch/Africa. 1999. *Hostile to Democracy: The Movement System and Political Repression in Uganda*. New York: Human Rights Watch.

Human Rights Watch/Africa, and Human Rights Watch Children's Rights Project. 1997. *The Scars of Death: Children Abducted by the Lord's Resistance Army*. New York: Human Rights Watch.

Ibingira, G. S. K. 1973. *The Forging of an African Nation: The Political and Constitutional Evolution of Uganda from Colonial Rule to Independence, 1894–1962*. New York: Viking Press.

Integrated Regional Information Network. 2002a. "UNICEF Repeats Call for Release of LRA Abductees." Electronic newsletter of the United Nations Office for the Coordination of Humanitarian Affairs, 6 March. Archived online at www.irinnews.org.

———. 2002b. "Uganda/Sudan: UNICEF Alarm over Safety of LRA Abductees." Electronic newsletter of the United Nations Office for the Coordination of Humanitarian Affairs, 2 April. Archived online at www.irinnews.org.

———. 2002c. "Uganda/Sudan: Focus on Missing Child Abductees." Electronic newsletter of the United Nations Office for the Coordination of Humanitarian Affairs, 5 April. Archived online at www.irinnews.org.

———. 2002d. "Uganda: Special Report on Concerns at Anti-LRA Campaign." Electronic newsletter of the United Nations Office for the Coordination of Humanitarian Affairs, 18 April. Archived online at www.irinnews.org.

———. 2002e. "Uganda: Renewed LRA Attacks Raise Fresh Humanitarian Concerns." Electronic newsletter of the United Nations Office for the Coordination of Humanitarian Affairs, 26 June. Archived online at www.irinnews.org.

———. 2004a. "Uganda: UNICEF Executive Director to Visit Northern Uganda."

Electronic newsletter of the United Nations Office for the Coordination of Humanitarian Affairs, 13 May. Archived online at www.irinnews.org.

———. 2004h "Uganda: EC Approves Package Targeting IDPs in the North." Electronic newsletter of the United Nations Office for the Coordination of Humanitarian Affairs, 16 June. Archived online at www.irinnews.org.

———. 2005a. "Uganda: Rights Group Criticises Emphasis on Abstinence." Electronic newsletter of the United Nations Office for the Coordination of Humanitarian Affairs, 30 March. Archived online at www.irinnews.org.

———. 2005b. "Uganda: Referendum Ends 20-year Ban on Political Parties." Electronic newsletter of the United Nations Office for the Coordination of Humanitarian Affairs, 1 August. Archived online at www.irinnews.org.

Iskander, M. 1987. *UNICEF in Africa, South of the Sahara: A Historical Perspective.* UNICEF Monograph 6. New York: UNICEF.

Jacobson, D. 1973. *Itinerant Townsmen: Friendship and Social Order in Urban Uganda.* The Kiste and Ogan Social Change Series in Anthropology. Menlo Park, CA: Cummings.

James, A. 1993. *Childhood Identities: Self and Social Relationships in the Experience of Childhood.* Edinburgh: Edinburgh University Press.

———. 1998. "Imaging Children 'At Home,' 'In the Family,' and 'At School': Movement between the Spatial and Temporal Markers of Childhood Identity in Britain." In *Migrants of Identity: Perceptions of Home in a World of Movement.* ed. N. Rapport and A. Dawson, 139–60. Ethnicity, and Identity Series. New York: Berg.

James, A., C. Jenks, and A. Prout, eds. 1998. *Theorizing Childhood.* Oxford: Polity Press.

James, A., and A. Prout, eds. 1997. *Constructing and Reconstructing Childhood: Contemporary Issues in the Sociological Study of Childhood.* Washington DC: Falmer Press.

Jenkins, H. 1998. "Introduction: Childhood Innocence and Other Modern Myths." In *The Children's Culture Reader*, ed. H. Jenkins. New York: New York University Press.

Jenks, C., ed. 1982. *Sociology of Childhood: Essential Readings.* London: Batsford Academic and Educational.

———. 1996. *Childhood: Key Ideas.* New York: Routledge.

Kabadaki, K. K. 2001. "The Feminization of Poverty in Rural Sub-Saharan Africa." In *Social Problems in Africa: New Visions*, ed. A. Rwomire, 93–110. Westport, CT: Praeger.

Kajubi, W. S. 1991. "Educational Reform During Socio-Economic crisis." In *Changing Uganda*, ed. H. B. Hansen and M. Twaddle, 322–33. Eastern African Studies Series. Athens: Ohio University Press.

Karlstrom, M. 1999. "Civil Society and Its Presuppositions: Lessons from Uganda." In *Civil Society and the Political Imagination in Africa: Critical Perspectives*, ed. J. L. Comaroff and J. Comaroff, 104–23. Chicago: University of Chicago Press.

Kasfir, N., ed. 1998. *Civil Society and Democratisation in Africa: Critical Perspectives*. Portland, OR: Frank Cass.

Kasozi, A. B. K. 1994. *The Social Origins of Violence, 1964–1985*. Kampala: Fountain Publishers.

Katz, C. 1991. Sow What You Know: The Struggle for Social Reproduction in Rural Sudan. *Annals of the Association of American Geographers* 81:488–514.

———. 2001a. "Growing Girls/Closing Circles: Limits on the Spaces of Knowing in Rural Sudan and United States Cities." In *Gendered Modernities: Ethnographic Perspectives*, ed. D. L. Hodgson, 173–202. New York: Palgrave.

———. 2001b. On the Grounds of Globalization: A Topography for Feminist Political Engagement. *Signs: Journal of Women in Culture and Society* 26: 1213–34.

———. 2003. "The State Goes Home: Children, Social Reproduction, and the Terrors of 'Hypervigilance.'" Paper presented at the session entitled "Insecurity: The Body, Social Reproduction, and the State," at the annual meeting of the American Anthropological Association Chicago, IL.

Kilbride, P. L. 2000. *Street Children in Kenya: Voices of Children in Search of a Childhood*. Westport, CT: Bergin and Garvey.

Kilbride, P. L., and J. C. Kilbride. 1990. *Changing Family Life in East Africa: Women and Children at Risk*. University Park: Pennsylvania State University Press.

Kiros, T., ed. 2001. *Explorations in African Political Thought: Identity, Community, and Ethics*. New York: Routledge.

Kneller, G. F. 1965. *Educational Anthropology: An Introduction*. New York: John Wiley & Sons.

Krog, A. 2000. *Country of My Skull: Guilt, Sorrow, and the Limits of Forgiveness in the New South Africa*. Vol. 1. New York: Three Rivers Press.

Kuper, A. 1997. *Anthropology and Anthropologists: The Modern British School*. London: Routledge.

Laerke, A. 1998. "By Means of Re-membering: Notes on a Fieldwork with English Children." *Anthropology Today* 14:3–7.

LaFontaine, J. 1986. "An Anthropological Perspective on Children in Social Worlds." In *Children of Social Worlds: Development of a Social Context*, ed. M. Richards and P. Light, 10–30. Cambridge, MA: Harvard University Press.

Langness, L. L., and F. Geyla. 1981. *Lives: An Anthropological Approach to Biography*. Novato, CA: Chandler and Sharp.

Lansdown, G. 1994. "Children's Rights." In Mayall 1994, 33–44.

Levinson, B. A., D. E. Foley, and D. C. Holland, eds. 1996. *The Cultural Production of the Educated Person: Ethnographies of Schooling and Local Practice*. Albany: State University of New York Press.

Levinson, B. A., and D. C. Holland. 1996. "The Cultural Production of the Educated Person: An Introduction." In Levinson, Foley, and Holland 1996, 1–56.

Long, N., and A. Arce. 2000. "Reconfiguring Modernity and Development from an Anthropological Perspective." In *Anthropology, Development, and Modernities*, ed. N. Long and A. Arce, 1–31. New York: Routledge.

Lusk, D., and C. O'Gara. 2002. "The Two Who Survive: The Impact of HIV/AIDS on Young Children, Their Families and Communities." *HIV/AIDS and Early Childhood Coordinators' Notebook: An International Resource for Early Childhood Development HIV/AIDS and Early Childhood* 26: 3–21.

Malkki, L. 1995. *Purity and Exile: Violence, Memory, and National Cosmology among Hutu Refugees in Tanzania*. Chicago: University of Chicago Press.

Mamdani, M. 1996. *Citizen and Subject: Contemporary Africa and the Legacy of Late Colonialism*. Princeton Studies in Culture/Power/History. Princeton, NJ: Princeton University Press.

_____. 2002. "African States, Citizenship, and War: A Case Study." *International Affairs* 78:493–506.

Martin Shaw, C. 1995. *Colonial Inscriptions: Race, Sex, and Class in Colonial Kenya*. Minneapolis: University of Minnesota Press.

Mayall, B. 1994. "Children in Action at Home and School." In *Children's Childhoods: Observed and Experienced*, ed. B. Mayall, 114–27. Washington DC: Falmer Press.

_____, ed. 1994. *Children's Childhoods: Observed and Experienced*. Washington DC: Falmer Press.

_____. 1999. "Children and Childhood." In *Critical Issues in Social Research: Power and Prejudice*, ed. S. Hood, B. Mayall, and S. Oliver, 10–24. Vol. 1. Philadelphia, PA: Open University Press.

_____. 2000. "Conversations with Children." In *Research with Children*, ed. P. Christensen and A. James, 120–35. New York: Falmer Press.

Mazrui, A. A. 1978. *Political Values and the Educated Class in Africa*. Berkeley and Los Angeles: University of California Press.

_____. 2001. "Ideology and African Political Culture." In *Explorations in African Political Thought: Identity, Community, and Ethics*, ed. T. Kiros, 97–131. New York: Routledge.

Mead, M., and M. Wolfenstein. 1954. *Childhood in Contemporary Cultures*. Chicago: Chicago University Press.

Meinert, L. 2003. "Sweet and Bitter Places: The Politics of Schoolchildren's Orientation in Rural Uganda." In *Children's Places: Cross-Cultural Perspectives*, ed. K. F. Olwig and L. Gulløv, 179–96. New York: Routledge.

Mitchell, J. C. 1956. *The Kalela Dance: Aspects of Social Relationships among Urban Africans in Northern Rhodesia*. Vol. 27 of *Rhodes-Livingstone Papers*. Manchester: Manchester University Press.

Monga, C. 1996. *The Anthropology of Anger: Civil Society and Democracy in Africa*. Boulder: Lynne Reiner.

Moro, J. 2004. "Depopulate Acholiland, Orders Kony." *New Vision*, 28 February.

Morris, B. 1994. *Anthropology of the Self: The Individual in Cultural Perspective*. Anthropology, Culture and Society. Boulder, CO: Pluto Press.

Mugambi, H. N. 1997. "From Story to Song: Gender, Nationhood, and the Migratory Text." In *Gendered Encounters: Challenging Cultural Boundaries and Social Hierarchies in Africa*, ed. O. H. Kokole, 205–22. New York: Routledge.

Muhereza, F. E., and P. O. Otim. 1998. "Neutralizing Ethnicity in Uganda." In *Ethnicity and the State in Eastern Africa*, ed. M. A. M. Salih and J. Markakis, 190–203. Uppsala: Nordiska Afrikainstitutet.

Museveni, Y. 1997. *Sowing the Mustard Seed: The Struggle for Freedom and Democracy in Uganda*. London: Macmillan.

Mushanga, T. M. 2001. "Social and Political Aspects of Violence in Africa." In *Social Problems in Africa: New Visions*, ed. A. Rwomire, 157–72. Westport, CT: Praeger.

Ndebele, N. 1995. "Recovering Childhood: Children in South African National Reconstruction." In *Children and the Politics of Culture*, ed. S. Stephens, 321–34. Princeton, NJ: Princeton University Press.

Ness, S. A. 1998. "Choreographing the Cultural: Festival, Tourism, and Dance in the Philippines." Paper presented at an Anthropology Colloquium held at the University of California at Santa Cruz, 1998.

New Vision. 2002a. "A Young Nation [editorial]." *New Vision*, 9 October.

———. 2002b. "Defilement Leads Crime." *New Vision*, 30 October.

———. 2003. "UPE Milestone [editorial]." *New Vision*, 27 January.

Nganda, C. N. 1996. "Primary Education and Social Integration: A Study of Ethnic Stereotypes in the Ugandan Basic Textbooks for Primary School English and Social Studies." African Studies Series no. 38. Bayreuth, Germany: E. Breitinger.

Nieuwenhuys, O. 1996. "The Paradox of Child Labor and Anthropology." *Annual Review of Anthropology* 25:237–51.

Nsamenang, A. B. 2002. "Adolescence in Sub-Saharan Africa: An Image Constructed from Africa's Triple Inheritance." In *The World's Youth: Adolescence in Eight Regions of the Globe*, ed. B. B. Brown, R. W. Larson, and T. S. Saraswathi, 61–104. New York: Cambridge University Press.

Ntabadde, C. 2002. "50% of Children Sexually Abused." *New Vision*, 10 June.

Nyambedha, E. O., and J. Aagaard-Hansen. 2003. "Changing Place, Changing Position: Orphans' Movements in a Community with High HIV/AIDS Prevalence in Western Kenya." In *Children's Places: Cross-Cultural Perspectives*, ed. K. F. Olwig and E. Gulløv, 162–76. New York: Routledge.

Ocwich, D. 2004. "World Court Probes Kony." *New Vision*, 12 January.

Ofcansky, T. P. 1996. *Uganda: Tarnished Pearl of Africa*. Boulder, CO: Westview Press.

Ojwee, D. 2002. "Ex-Rebels Want Otti, Kony Dead." *New Vision*, 25 June.

Okumu, D. F. W. 1997. "The Participation and Use of Children in African Civil Conflicts." *Center for International Security and Strategic Studies: Mississippi State University* 1:1–36.

Oloya, O. 2002. "Are the Acholi Mum for Fear of Rocking the Boat? [editorial]" *New Vision*. 19 February.

Olwig, K. F., and E. Gulløv, eds. 2003. *Children's Places: Cross-Cultural Perspectives*. New York: Routledge.

Paardekooper, B., J. T. V. M. de Jong, and J. M. A. Hermanns. 1999. "The Psychological Impact of War and the Refugee Situation on South Sudanese Children in Refugee Camps in Northern Uganda: An Exploratory Study." *Journal of Child Psychology and Psychiatry* 40:529–36.

Paige, J. R. 2000. *Preserving Order Amid Chaos: The Survival of Schools in Uganda, 1971–1986*. New York: Berghahn Books.

Parikh, S. 2004. "Sugar Daddies and Sexual Citizenship in Uganda: Rethinking Third Wave Feminism." *Black Renaissance* 6:82–107.

Parish, S. M. 1994. *Moral Knowing in a Hindu Sacred City: An Exploration of Mind, Emotion and Self*. New York: Columbia University Press.

Parkin, D., ed. 1975. *Town and Country in Central and Eastern Africa*. Studies Presented and Discussed at the Twelfth International African Institute. New York: Oxford University Press.

Pigg, S. L. 1992. "Inventing Social Categories Through Place: Social Representations and Development in Nepal." *Comparative Studies in Science and History* 34:491–513.

Plotnicov, L. 1967. *Strangers to the City: Urban Man in Jos, Nigeria*. Pittsburgh, PA: University of Pittsburgh Press.

Postman, N. 1982. *The Disappearance of Childhood*. New York: Delacotte Press.

Powdermaker, H. 1966. *Stranger and Friend: The Way of an Anthropologist*. New York: W. W. Norton.

Prewitt, K, ed. 1971. *Education and Political Values: An East African Case Study*. East African Publishing House Studies, no. 12. Nairobi: East African Publishing House.

Qvortrup, J. 1997. "A Voice for Children in Statistical and Social Accounting: A Plea for Children's Right to be Heard." In *Constructing and Reconstructing Childhood: Contemporary Issues in the Sociological Study of Childhood*, ed. A. James and A. Prout, 85–106. Washington DC: Falmer Press.

Republic of Uganda. 1992. *Government White Paper on the Education Policy Review Commission Report*. Kampala: Republic of Uganda.

———. 1995. *Constitution of the Republic of Uganda*. Republic of Uganda: Uganda Printing and Publishing Corp.

———. 1996. *The Children Statute*. The Republic of Uganda.

Reynolds, P. 1989. *Children in Crossroads: Cognition and Society in South Africa*. Grand Rapids, MI: William B. Eerdmans.

———. 1991. *Dance Civet Cat: Child Labour in the Zambezi Valley*. East African Studies. Athens: Ohio University Press.

———. 1995. "Youth and the Politics of Culture in South Africa." In *Children and the Politics of Culture*, ed. S. Stephens, 218–40. Princeton, NJ: Princeton University Press.

———. 1996. *Traditional Healers and Childhood in Zimbabwe*. Athens: Ohio University Press.

Reynolds, S., and M. A. Whyte. 1998. "The Values of Development: Conceiving Growth and Progress in Bunyole." In *Developing Uganda*, ed. H. B. Hansen and M. Twaddle, 227–44. Athens: Ohio University Press.

Robson, E., and N. Ansell. 2000. "Young Carers in Southern Africa: Exploring Stories from Zimbabwean Secondary School Students." In *Children's Geographies. Critical Geographies,* ed. S. Holloway and G. Valentine, 174–93. New York: Routledge.

Rose, N. 1989. *Governing the Soul.* London: Routledge.

Rosen, D. M. 2005. *Armies of the Young: Child Soldiers in War and Terrorism.* The Rutgers Series in Childhood Studies. New Brunswick, NJ: Rutgers University Press.

Rubin, E. 1998. "Our Children Are Killing Us." *New Yorker,* March 23, 56–64.

Runyan, W. M. 1986. "Life Histories in Anthropology: Another View." *American Anthropologist* 88:181–83.

Rwebangira, M. K., and R. Liljeström, eds. 1998. *Haraka Haraka . . . Look Before You Leap: Youth at the Crossroad of Custom and Modernity.* Uppsala, Sweden: The Nordic Africa Institute.

Rwezaura, B. 1998. "Competing 'Images' of Childhood in the Social and Legal Systems of Contemporary Sub-Saharan Africa." *International Journal of Law, Policy and the Family* 12, no. 26:253–78.

Sangarasivam, Y. 2003. "Militarizing the Feminine Body: Women's Participation in the Tamil Nationalist Struggle." In *Violence and the Body: Race, Gender, and the State,* ed. A. J. Aldama, 59–76. Bloomington: Indiana University Press.

Sargent, C., and N. Scheper-Hughes, eds. 1998. *Small Wars: The Cultural Politics of Childhood.* Berkeley and Los Angeles: University of California Press.

Schumaker, L. 2001. *Africanizing Anthropology: Fieldwork, Networks, and the Making of Cultural Knowledge in Central Africa.* Durham, NC: Duke University Press.

Schwartzman, H. B. 1978. *Transformations: The Anthropology of Children's Play.* New York: Plenum Press.

———, ed. 2001. *Children and Anthropology: Perspectives for the Twenty-first Century.* Westport, CT: Bergin and Garvey.

Sen, A. K. 1999. *Development as Freedom.* Oxford: Oxford University Press.

Serpell, R. 1993. *The Significance of Schooling: Life Journeys in an African Society.* Cambridge: Cambridge University Press.

Shepler, S. 2002a. "Globalizing Child Soldiers." Paper presented at the Berkeley-Stanford Joint Center for African Studies Annual Spring Conference entitled "Rethinking Globalization from an African Perspective," at the University of California–Berkeley.

———. 2002b. "Les Filles-Soldats: Trajectoires d'apresguerre en Sierra Leone." *Politique Africaine* 88:49–62.

Skinner, D., and D. C. Holland. 1996. "Schools and the Cultural Production of the Educated Person in a Nepalese Hill Community." In *The Cultural Production of the Educated Person: Ethnographies of Schooling and Local Practice,* ed. B. A. Levinson, D. E. Foley, and D. C. Holland, 273–99. Albany: State University of New York Press.

Southall, A. 1975. "Forms of Ethnic Linkage between Town and Country." In *Town and Country in Central and Eastern Africa,* ed. D. Parkin, 265–75. New York: Oxford University Press.

Southall, A., and P. Gutkind. 1957. *Townsmen in the Making*. Kampala: East African Institute of Social Research.

Spigel, L. 1998. "Seducing the Innocent: Childhood and Television in Postwar America." In *The Children's Culture Reader*, ed. H. Jenkins, 110–35. New York: New York University Press.

Ssekamwa, J. C. 1997. *History and Development of Education in Uganda*. Kampala: Fountain Publishers.

Stambach, A. 2000. *Lessons from Mount Kilimanjaro: Schooling, Community, and Gender in East Africa*. New York: Routledge.

Stephens, S. 1995. *Children and the Politics of Culture*. Princeton Studies in Culture/Power/History. Princeton, NJ: Princeton University Press.

Thorne, B. 1997. *Gender Play: Girls and Boys in School*. New Brunswick, NJ: Rutgers University Press.

Trager, L. 1998. "Home-town Linkages and Local Development in South-western Nigeria: Whose Agenda? Whose Impact?" *Africa* 68:360–82.

Tripp, A. M. 1998. "Expanding 'Civil Society': Women and Political Space in Contemporary Uganda." In *Civil Society and Democratisation in Africa: Critical Perspectives*, ed. N. Kasfir, 84–107. Portland, OR: Frank Cass.

Turnbull, C. 1972. *The Mountain People*. New York: Simon & Schuster.

Turner, V. 1986. *The Anthropology of Performance*. New York: PAJ Publications.

Turyahikayo-Rugyema, B. 1982. "The Development of Mass Nationalism, 1952–1962." In *Uganda: The Dilemma of Nationhood, Studies in East African Society and History*, ed. G. N. Uziogwe., 217–55. New York: NOK Publishers International.

Uganda Child Rights NGO Network. 1997. *Response to the Government of Uganda Country Report on the Implementation of the United Nations Convention on the Rights of the Child*. Kampala: Uganda Child Rights Network.

Uganda Ministry of Education and Sports. 1998. *Proposal for Funding of Uganda Schools and Primary Teachers College's Music Festivals, 1998*. Kampala, Uganda: Ministry of Education and Sports.

———. 2000. *Uganda National Music, Dance and Drama Festival Syllabus for 2000 and 2001*. Kampala, Uganda: Ministry of Education and Sports.

Uganda Ministry of Education National Curriculum Development Centre. 1999. *Uganda Primary School Curriculum*. Vol. 1. Kampala: National Curriculum Development Centre.

UNAIDS. 2002. *Children on the Brink 2002: A Joint Report on Orphan Estimates and Program Strategies*. Washington, DC: U.S. Agency for International Development.

UNICEF. 2001. *The State of the World's Children 2001: Early Childhood*. New York: United Nations.

USAID, and the World Bank. 1999. "Education for All: The Ugandan Experience." Washington DC: USAID.

Waliggo, J. M. 1994. "Constitution-Making and the Politics of Democratisation in Uganda." In *From Chaos to Order: The Politics of Constitution-Making in*

Uganda, ed. Holger Bernt Hansen and M. Twaddle, 19–40. London: James Curry.

Wallace, J.-A. 1995. Technologies of 'The Child': Towards a Theory of the Child-Subject. *Textual Practice* 9:285–302.

Wasike, A. 2002. "UPDF to Rescue Abducted Children." *New Vision*, 22 March.

Werbner, R. P. 1984. "The Manchester School in South-Central Africa." *Annual Review of Anthropology* 13:157–85.

Werbner, R., and T. Ranger. 1996. *Postcolonial Identities in Africa*. Postcolonial Encounters. Atlantic Highlands, NJ: Zed Books.

Whiting, B., and C. P. Edwards. 1988. *Children of Different Worlds: The Formation of Social Behavior*. Cambridge, MA: Harvard University Press.

Whiting, J., and B. Whiting. 1975. *Children of Six Cultures: A Psycho-Cultural Analysis*. Cambridge, MA: Harvard University Press.

Willis, P. 1981. *Learning to Labor: How Working-Class Kids Get Working-Class Jobs*. New York: Columbia University Press.

Wingo, A. H. 2001. "Good Government Is Accountability." In Kiros 2001, 151–70.

Witter, S., and J. Bukokhe. 2004. "Children's Perceptions of Poverty, Participation, and Local Governance in Uganda." *Development in Practice* 14:645–59.

Women's Commission on Refugee Women and Children. 2001. *Against All Odds: Surviving the War on Adolescents. Promoting the Protection and Capacity of Ugandan and Sudanese Adolescents in Northern Uganda*. New York: Women's Commission on Refugee Women and Children.

———. 2004. *No Safe Place to Call Home: Children and Adolescent Night commuters in Northern Uganda*. New York: Women's Commission on Refugee Women and Children.

Wright, M. A. 1998. *I'm Chocolate, You're Vanilla: Raising Healthy Black and Biracial Children in a Race-Conscious World—A Guide for Parents and Teachers*. San Francisco: Jossey-Bass.

Zeleza, P. T., and C. R. Veney, eds. 2002. "The African 'Brain Drain' to the North: Pitfalls and Possibilities." Special issue, *African Issues* 30, no. 1. New Brunswick, NJ: African Studies Association Press.

Index